CAPITAL CONSEQUENCES

Library of Congress Cataloging-in-Publication Data

King, Rachel, 1963–

Capital consequences : families of the condemned tell their stories /
Rachel King.

   p. cm.

Includes bibliographical references.

ISBN 0-8135-3504-2 (hardcover : alk. paper)

1. Death row inmates—United States—Biography. 2. Prisoners' families—
United States—Case studies. 3. Capital punishment—United States—
Case studies. I. Title.

HV8699.U5K56 2005

364.66—dc22   2004008241

A British Cataloging-in-Publication record for this book is available from the British Library.

Manufactured in the United States of America

This book is dedicated to Kim Ancona, Ray Krone, Leah Schendel, Manny Babbitt, Troy Hodges, Abdullah Hameen, Linda Gilreath, Gerrit Van Leeuwen, Fred Gilreath, Baerbel Poore, Kevin Stanford, Ricky Bryant, Georgia Reed, Scott Reed, Earline Baker, Bruce Gardner, Larry Robison, Jennifer Burns, Sally Fogle, Clay Griffin, Dave Herman, Julie Kerry, Robin Kerry, Reggie Clemons, Marlin Gray, Antonio Richardson, Leicester Sherrill, Kay Sherrill, John Eastlack, and all the families and loved ones of murder victims and death row family members. May we find a way to live without violence.

CONTENTS

FOREWORD

Rachel King makes clear that there are capital consequences to the family members of capital defendants. Her book tells the story of the pain, isolation, fear, frustration, and loss experienced by capital defendants' family members. It tells of the permanent separation, due to execution, between mother and son, wife and husband, brother and brother, cousin and cousin, and a host of other family relationships, as well as, most poignantly, between father and child. In the coming pages a father explains that from behind the bars of death row he still tries to be a positive influence in his daughter's life, ending every letter with a math or grammar problem for her to solve. A daughter makes clear that her father has always been a part of her life and became even more important to her as she aged.

In a recent study, a team of researchers and I sought to understand the effects of a capital charge on family members and the sources of those effects.[1] In interviews with nineteen family members we found that over half of the family members who were the primary support person to a capital defendant experienced depression and symptoms associated with post-traumatic stress disorder (PTSD).[2] Both depression and PTSD stem from pain and terror and carry chronic and debilitating consequences. For some of the people interviewed in our study, their depression and PTSD symptoms resulted in psychiatric hospitalization, job loss, abandonment of years of sobriety, or death.

All of the family members interviewed in our study indicated that on the day of the arrest their life was turned upside down, never to return to what was previously normal. They said that since the arrest, there are days that are bearable but there are not days that are good. Family members described lives filled with chronic pain and guilt. Some mothers said that they spent their days "praying and crying, and crying and praying." One mother thought she was coming out of her four-year depression until she realized that she still did not have it in her to open the blinds to her house. Several family members said that they were afraid to go outside. They explained that the newspaper made their loved one appear so horrific that retaliatory violence both felt like and was a real possibility. Other family members abandoned years of volunteer work both because they were afraid to leave the house and because they no longer felt worthy.

Family members were steeped in guilt. They felt responsible for not being able to secure mental health treatment, for not giving their loved one money—perhaps thwarting him from stealing—for not prohibiting him from seeing his new friends whom they believed to be bad influences, for his issues with anger, and for having raised him in a family riddled with domestic violence. One mother explained that she felt guilty for even giving birth to her son, for if she had not, she explained, he would not be living out his life on death row.

At the center of the family members' experience was their terror of execution, and many family members questioned how they would bear it when the time came. Yet it is not only the threat of death and its actuality that places a burden on the family members. For some family members, their experience with pain began prior to the commission of a crime.

What we found in our study, and what King illustrates in her book, are the numerous stories of family members' desperate search for adequate mental health care for a loved one lost in hallucinations. This was especially true in the case of Lois Robison ("A Mother's Love"), who sought help for years for her mentally ill son. While adequate and sustained treatment was unattainable, Lois Robison and family members like her never stopped looking for it and worrying, as they knew that without competent mental health treatment tragedy might result.

As we did in our research, King found that the larger community is another source of pain and fear. Family members talked about the intimidating juxtaposition of notoriety and isolation following a capital crime and the fears associated with retaliatory violence and its threats. Uniformly, the family members discussed their loss of belief in a fair criminal justice system and the accompanying sense of helplessness and betrayal. Whether starting as someone who was dubious of the system to begin with, or as one who held an intrinsic belief in the values and systems found in the United States, all family members' views of the criminal justice system were shattered. Actions of defense attorneys, prosecutors, police, and judges underpinned the families' loss of faith in the justice system.

Disillusionment with the criminal justice system extends beyond the trial and into the process of visitations. Defendants' family members can have visitation, something murder victims' family members will never have again. Yet the process of death row visitation carries burdens that seemed to family members designed to humiliate and cause stress as well as physical pain. In our study, elderly family members talked about severe back pain caused by having to crouch down to talk to their loved one through a waist-high hole in the Plexiglas.

The macabre stories of execution permeate King's book. The rituals associated with execution, such as a last meal designed to bring pleasure and comfort as part of the ritual of the ultimate punishment, appear bizarre. In some cases the last meal and execution occur without a contact visit, as was the case with Esther Herman ("It Could Happen to Anyone") who had to wait until the body of her son was brought to the funeral parlor to hug him goodbye. In our study a sister talks of her mother's pain in not being able to even touch the hand of her son from the moment of his conviction through his execution.

Katherine Norgard has given the unique pain that family members of the condemned experience a name, "chronic grief." Family members grieve the maturation of their loved one—in our study a mother explained that she could no longer go to weddings or graduations as those were mile markers that her son would not reach; they grieve the loss of a relationship outside of the prison walls; and they grieve for others in their family who are also feeling this unique pain and for the children growing up in the shadow of an execution. Their grief is not only for themselves and their loved ones, it is also for the person who lost his or her life in a murder, and for his or her family members.

King also tells of the need that many family members of defendants have to make contact with the victims' family members. In that instant in which a life is taken, the two families, who often had no prior inkling of one another, become intimately, inextricably, and permanently enmeshed. Defendants' family members often talk of their desire and need to apologize, offer their condolences, or explain that their loved one had become lost to them as a result of the mental illness that occupied his mind. Yet, sitting on opposite sides of the courtroom, defendants' family members have no idea how to make their feelings known, and the criminal justice system actively discourages any contact.

However, there is a recent movement afoot in the field of criminal justice that actually seeks to encourage interaction between offenders and victims. In its largest sense, restorative justice seeks to transform conflict that emanates from the commission of a crime, and thereby support the healing of the victims, communities, and offenders. Restorative justice purports that offenders need to be held accountable for their actions and the needs of victims, and the community and the offender must be acknowledged in order for all involved to begin healing. Restorative justice also argues that the healing of family members of defendants and victims can be linked. Research has shown that for some victims' family members it is only the offender who can answer the questions that plague them: why their loved one was killed and what those last moments were like for him or her.

The need for restorative justice with capital offenders and their family members is examined in a recent study by Eschholz, Reed, Beck, and Leonard[3] and in a forthcoming book by Beck, Eschholz, and Andrews. These data mirror King's findings that family members of capital defendants are desperate to make contact, and that the criminal process discourages any sort of engagement, including an offer of condolence.

Yet King makes clear that it is not only families that experience collateral damages from the death penalty. The argument could be made from reading King's book that the capital process also hurts the judicial system. King's book is filled with stories of compromised systems and interactions found within the criminal justice system.

Turning a loved one in to the police can often be painful, and yet that pain can be assuaged with the assurance of a nondeath charge. Such was the case for the Unabomber's brother David Kaczynski. This, however, was not the case for Bill Babbitt. This story of deception, told in "A Hero's Life," describes the pain experienced by Babbitt when he realized that information he gave the police would not be used to support psychiatric care, as he had been led to believe, but would rather be used by the prosecutor to seek a death charge. Kaczynski himself believes that Babbitt was treated very differently than he was, as Babbitt's race and social status placed him in a class in which he lacked the resources that Kaczynski had access to.

Shadowing King's book is the reminder that we do indeed live in a society in which class and race make a difference in the treatment that one receives from the criminal justice system. In addition to racial bias in charging and sentencing, King also raises issues of overt racism on the part of the people, including public defenders, whose job it is to uphold fairness and impartiality. In fact, it might even be argued that the largest capital consequence to the children of capital offenders, be they white or of color, is that they, like their ancestors before them, are growing up in a world in which prejudice, bigotry, and class continue to pervade the criminal justice system.

Thus, perhaps King's book is most important for its indictment of the capital system. Through the perspective of offenders' family members, she offers readers an insider's view of the problems found in capital trials. While race and class are important subtexts found throughout King's book, they are not the only problems raised in the capital process. In the chapters ahead King offers a vivid portrait of the ways in which the criminal justice system that is supposed to redress wrongs often creates more pain and conflict for victims, offenders, and their families.

—ELIZABETH BECK

tion whose primary mission is to end the death penalty. Photos documented the unfathomable pain and grief of those who had lost loved ones to murder.

I asked Rachel to help me with a project dealing with the other side of the issue—the impact of a death sentence on the family members of the condemned. My adopted son, John, had been sentenced to death in 1991. From my own experience, I knew how difficult it is for families of the condemned to assimilate the death penalty into their own lives. Living under a constant cloud of grief, I sought to interview other families, desperately hoping to understand and heal my family's and my own unrelenting pain and to contribute some understanding and compassion for others suffering the same plight.

John's death sentence was the most devastating loss in my life. Young and still alive, he had no future. He would never again celebrate birthdays or holidays with me. He could not be an ordinary part of my life. I was even prohibited from touching him.

The *Florida State University Law Review* published our article in the summer of 1999. Interviewing other family members of the condemned, I discovered a kinship with them that cut across any differences between us. All of the families of the condemned experienced stigmatization, social isolation, depression, and chronic grief. Our personal and family identities had been swallowed up by the horrific crime of our loved one. We were often seen as, and certainly felt, guilty by association.

We had all unwillingly joined a new category of spiritual, emotional, and psychological distress. We were isolated from one another, and there were no support groups for us to join. We found one another only by chance while visiting our loved ones on death row, where interaction was discouraged by the correctional system.

Over and over, other family members used the words "devastation" and "despair" to describe their pain. As a group, we had universally lost our belief in practically everything. At the time, I speculated whether our injuries were beyond repair. We seemed to be experiencing "chronic grief."

Grief is a natural part of life. Some professionals think of grief as a process of letting go, moving on, recovering, and returning to a normal state. In her book *On Death and Dying,* Elisabeth Kubler-Ross advanced the theory that grief has a series of stages.

Chronic grief is a psychic wound that will not easily heal. It is encased in shame, hopelessness, and isolation from community support. Family members of the condemned are marginalized when their government decrees that the family's loved one is dispensable and the machinery of the death penalty begins its slow grind toward the goal of execution. The ongoing loving bond between the family members and the condemned becomes invisible to others outside death row.

Family members of the condemned experience repeated nightmares, sleepless nights, difficulty concentrating, impaired short-term memory, hypervigilance, a constant aching grief, and episodes of uncontrollable crying. We try to avoid thinking about the death penalty so we might go on with our lives, but intrusive thoughts plague our every hour. It is as though we have a huge *D* on our forehead marking us as members of a caste suffering from indelible despair.

People experiencing grief have support groups available to help them. We have none. There are books and articles to read to help people process the grief and understand their experience. Nothing was available in 1991 to help families of the condemned. Poetry abounds about grief. There is no poetry about the condemned.

The grieving can find solace from their faith community or comfort in a memorial service or some other ritual designed to help them cope. Although most major religions have national policies opposing the death penalty, members of these religions reflect society at large in supporting executions. How can a family member of someone condemned to death find solace in a congregation that supports and cries out for more blood—an execution? As for rituals, there are none for the family members of the condemned.

For me, John's death sentence was the end of the world I had known. I struggled to find ground to stand on. My entire family narrative had been broken and swept away. I knew no one else in my situation. I became a member of a select minority. Only 2,481 people were on America's death row when John was sentenced to death in 1991. Families who happen to be a racial or other minority, as many are, are propelled into still another category to separate them from the whole—family of the condemned.

Victor Frankel understood despair. He was a survivor of another type of death sentence—a World War II German concentration camp. *Man's Search for Meaning* is his account of his struggle to make meaning in his life after his release from the camp and all the horror, loss, and despair he suffered there. His book reached some small sane corner of my mind after John's death sentence.

Some of the people highlighted in Rachel's book *Capital Consequences* became alcoholics in response to a death sentence in the family. Many experienced severe weight loss, depression, heart problems, diabetes, anxiety, sleep disorders, chronic fatigue, and other forms of psychiatric illnesses. Each one was just trying to cope, usually in isolation, with unrelenting pain and sorrow.

Having a loved one sentenced to death is a spiritual assault. It affects and changes every aspect of the family member's life.

Prior to John's death sentence, I had been a joyous person. My joy evaporated when John was sentenced to death. Physically, my gut wrenched. I had been gregarious and social. There was no bridge across the shame, alienation, and stigma I lived with after his sentence. I felt adrift from my family and my friends. A constant pain gripped my soul.

Many of us, stumbling along, discovered that we had to find a reason to continue living after our loved one was condemned to die. Meaning had to be restored to our existence. Nothing in our personal histories any longer made sense or served as a guide to what we were facing.

Lois Robison, one of the women in this book, became a crusader to save her son's life and ask for compassion for the mental illness that had overtaken him. Becoming active in Citizens United for the Rehabilitation of Errants (CURE) and working for abolition of the death penalty became organizing forces in her life.

I created an organization in Arizona to end the death penalty. I became involved at a national level, serving on the board of the National Coalition to Abolish the Death Penalty, participating in the Journey of Hope alongside murder victim family members who were advocating for abolition, and speaking around the country. Saving John's life and ending the death penalty at first were an obsession, which eventually grew into a calling. I am convinced my love for my family and activism ultimately saved my life.

Families of the condemned struggle as they try and move in two directions at once. We long to return to that part of our lives that is still viable while trying to transform ourselves into some new reality of who we are after a death sentence. Some of us try to break the attachment to our loved one who has been sentenced to death, believing it will lessen our suffering. It is a connection not easily severed.

We cannot run away from the love we feel in our hearts. And we know, beyond a shadow of a doubt, that it is unjust for our loved one to be judged by a single action, no matter how evil.

Introduction

Capital Consequences is a sequel, of sorts, to my first book, *Don't Kill in Our Names: Families of Murder Victims Speak Out Against the Death Penalty*, published by Rutgers in 2003. Both books are the end result of a project that began in 1996, when I first started photographing and interviewing family members of murder victims and family members of people on death row. I had been living in Alaska and working on a campaign opposing legislation to reinstate capital punishment. Alaska had not had a death penalty since it became a state in 1949, but in 1994 the powerful Senate majority leader introduced a bill to bring it back, and he had the votes to pass it.

As part of our opposition campaign, we invited a woman named Marietta Jaeger to tour Alaska sharing her experience as a family member of a murder victim. Marietta's seven-year-old daughter, Susie, had been kidnapped, sexually abused, tortured, and murdered by a serial killer in Montana, yet in spite of, or perhaps because of, this tragedy, Marietta had come to oppose the death penalty. Marietta shared her personal story with many Alaskans, including legislators, who later told us that hearing her story convinced them to oppose the measure.

Marietta was a member of Murder Victims' Families for Reconciliation (MVFR), an organization of people who have had family members murdered or family members killed by state execution and oppose the death penalty. It was from Marietta that we realized the power of murder victims' family members as advocates against state killing. Barbara Hood, a friend and colleague actively involved in the opposition campaign, suggested that we put together a publication of photographs and quotes of MVFR members, and in 1996 I began photographing and interviewing them. Over the next several years I interviewed nearly one hundred families.

One of the people I met in my travels was a woman named Katherine Norgard whose son, John, was on death row in Arizona. She asked me if I would be interested in writing an article with her about death row family members, and together we wrote "What About Our Families? Using the Impact on Death Row Family Members as a Mitigating Factor in Death Penalty Sentencing Hearings," published in the summer 1999 issue of the *Florida State University Law Review*.[1]

After several years of collecting stories of murder victims' family members and death row family members, I felt compelled to share the information with a larger audience and embarked on the idea of writing a book advocating against capital punishment using the stories and experiences of people most intimately affected by it. When I first submitted a book proposal to Rutgers, it included publishing the stories of both the murder victims and death row family members together. Although Rutgers was interested in the proposal, the editor suggested that it would be better to publish the stories of the two groups separately. He wanted to start with the stories of murder victims, believing people who supported the death penalty would be more open to reading about the death penalty from the perspective of those one would expect to support it.

One would think that the experience of writing the two books would be comparable; they were similar in length, style, and content. If anything, the second book should have been easier to write, since I had already developed a formula of combining narrative and first-person voice and conducted most of the interviews. As it turned out, though, the second book has been fraught with frustrations that I did not experience with the first one.

With less than two weeks before the book was due at the publisher, three of my ten families had not given me final authorizations to publish their stories and were considering dropping out of the project. Another participant had already threatened to pull out but changed her mind. These four chapters accounted for 40 percent of the book.

Ultimately, only one family pulled out of the project; however, that was still extremely upsetting. I had spent dozens of hours interviewing family members and the defense attorney and dozens more researching the story by reading trial transcripts, newspaper articles, personal letters, journal entries, and mental health histories, just to name a few. The chapter of the family that decided to pull out of the project was the best written and most powerful of the book. I am disappointed that I spent so much time on something that will not be published and that readers will not learn of this family's experiences.

On the other hand, one man who initially was not willing to be in the book changed his mind, he told me, because of the fact that I was willing to spend hours working with him, listening to his concerns and rewriting until he felt comfortable. His participation has been a gift.

This reluctance to participate was in sharp contrast to the experience of writing *Don't Kill in Our Names,* where no one pulled out or threatened to pull out of the project. I was not making last-minute phone calls pestering people to send me their authorizations, nor did I stay up nights worrying that someone would change his or her mind.

When I am able to step back and look at the situation from the death row family's perspective, I understand why they were so distrustful. Society spent years preparing to kill their loved one. Part of preparing for the execution is a ritual process of dehumanization. The story of the crime is repeatedly told—either in court or in the media—from the perspective of the murdered person and is rarely evenhanded. The murderer is painted as a killer worthy of death. Other aspects of his life, the times when he was kind, generous, and loving, are overlooked. The participants worried that I would paint a similar picture of their loved one's life, and even though I assured them that they would be able to review anything before it went to publication, it was hard for them to trust me.

In implementing the death penalty, society not only overlooks the positive aspects of the condemned person's life, we disregard the impact that the execution will have on the people that love him. We ignore the fact that he has a mother, father, sister, brother, daughter, son, and others who will be permanently harmed by the execution. When I think of all these families have been through, I understand their wariness and am grateful they were willing to participate in this project.

With both books, the most difficult decision was choosing the stories to include. Everyone I interviewed had a compelling story, each worthy of its own book. With *Don't Kill in Our Names,* I chose stories that made the best case against the death penalty. Focusing on the strongest arguments against the death penalty—racial and economic bias, incompetent counsel, wrongful convictions, prosecutorial misconduct, and the issue of executing juveniles and mentally retarded people—I chose stories that illustrated these problems. Before each section, I wrote a brief introduction on the subject explaining how the stories illustrated the problem. Thus I used the emotional stories of victims' family members to make a rational argument against the death penalty.

Capital Consequences, however, did not lend itself so easily to this format. My first criterion was to pick stories told from the perspective of different family members. In most families, one person became the primary spokesperson for the family. Sometimes that person was the defendant's wife, sometimes his mother, sometimes a sibling, sometimes a child, and in two cases a cousin. I didn't want each story to be told by the wife of a defendant or the parent of a defendant, because I wanted the reader to see how the death penalty affects the entire family.

The next consideration was selecting stories that were at different stages in the legal process and had different outcomes. Not everyone who is sentenced to death is actually executed. Sometimes the sentence is reversed or commuted, and sometimes the person is exonerated. Last, I wanted stories from different regions lest the reader get the mistaken impression that the problems illustrated in these chapters only occur in some parts of the country.

Although not chosen for this reason, the stories in *Capital Consequences* point out many of the flaws in the justice system. Innocent people were wrongfully convicted and sentenced to death; race and class were factors; defense attorneys made mistakes; prosecutors withheld evidence from defendants and brought charges against innocent people; people who were mentally ill at the time of the crime were executed despite the fact that they had no understanding of their crime; juveniles, who otherwise had no legal rights, were sentenced to death.

Indeed, it would be hard to read this book and conclude that we have a fair criminal justice system. As noted capital litigator Steven Bright has written, capital punishment is not for the worst crime but for those who have the worst lawyer.[2] Death rows in the United States are not populated by wealthy and powerful people. They are filled with the most vulnerable—poor people, people of color, the mentally retarded, the mentally ill, and youth. And, more often than most people realize, the system gets the wrong person. As of August 2004, 114 innocent people have been released from death rows during the previous three decades.[3] No one is sure how many innocent people have been executed.

Yet the fact that our justice system is not perfect or fair is not the primary message of this book, nor is it the reason why I believe the death penalty must be ended. *Capital Consequences* challenges us as a society to question the morality of a punishment that devastates the lives of innocent people. Every time we execute a person, we create new victims—innocent children, spouses and parents who do not deserve to have their loved one killed. Each execution ripples out through the generations, shredding families and destroying lives.

I hope this book causes people, especially people who support capital punishment, to pause and ask themselves some important questions such as these:

- What is the long-term effect of an execution on the family members, especially the children, of the condemned?
- How fair is a system that gives prosecutors, who have their own biases, prejudices, and values, the power to decide which people are charged with death-penalty-eligible crimes and which are not?
- How can we justify a system where in cases of multiple defendants some go free and some are executed and juries, prosecutors, and judges sometimes pick the wrong people?
- How do we justify executions as a form of punishment when wealthy people have access to a different type of justice than poor people?
- If the family members of the victims do not want the killer executed, should the state take that into consideration when deciding the appropriate punishment?
- Should we execute people who are mentally ill? What if the family members sought help for their mentally ill relative and none was forthcoming? Does the state share any responsibility for that person's crime?
- What responsibility does the state bear to provide services to people who have been physically or sexually abused, or have mental illnesses or other problems, to ensure that these people do not pose a danger to others?
- If family members assist authorities in solving a crime by turning in a mentally ill family member on the guarantee that their loved one will receive help, should the state be allowed to violate that promise and execute the mentally ill person?
- If new evidence casting doubt on the validity of a conviction and death sentence is revealed after the appeal is concluded, should the state be allowed to proceed with the execution?
- If a person has made extraordinary efforts to rehabilitate himself and has succeeded at doing so, should he be executed even if he no longer poses a danger to others and is making a positive contribution to society?

When all is said and done, I believe that this book is even more powerful and important than the first. The pain of the murder victims' families was tremendous, but the pain of the death row families is in some ways more desperate. With murder a person or group of people makes the horrible choice to kill another. Often it is done in the heat of passion, under the influence of drugs or alcohol or when the killer is not in his right mind. The surviving family members have to come to terms with the crime and find a way to go on with their lives.

In the case of the death penalty, the entire society makes a calculated decision, planned out over many years, to kill a person. Family members of people on death row are not betrayed by a single person or small group of people; they are betrayed by the entire society, and they have to figure out a way to come to terms with that betrayal and continue to live within that society.

Death row family members shared many common experiences with each other and with murder victims' family members. Dealing with a homicide or a possible execution took all of the family's financial and emotional resources. When families looked to the government for help, it was usually not there. Victims' services are woefully inadequate in most jurisdictions, and any assistance that might be available for counseling, medical expenses, or funeral expenses is not available to death row family members, who are not legally considered victims.

Many families did not have the capital to hire private counsel or pay for the associated expenses of defending a capital case, such as paying for expert witnesses and investigators. Those who had resources spent nearly all they had on paying for the defense. Several families mortgaged their homes, sometimes repeatedly, and depleted their retirement accounts.

Worse than losing their life savings was losing the support and love of relatives and friends. Some people could not cope with the stigma of having a family member charged with a capital crime, so they withdrew their support, leaving the burden to fall more heavily on others. Neighbors, friends, and even church associates neglected the families in their greatest hour of need.

Family members have to endure being under public scrutiny, subjected to harassment and poor treatment by the media. Coverage of the crime is at best one-sided and at worst completely inaccurate.

Families have to accept the inhumane conditions their loved one endures on death row. Most death row prisoners are locked in their cells all the time, let out only for a shower or exercise a few hours a week. Prison authorities make it difficult for families to visit death row, using strict and arbitrary rules to interfere with visits or prevent them altogether. Some prisoners are abused while in custody, and their families have no recourse to protect them. If not physically abusive, prison guards mistreat prisoners by withholding food or keeping the cells uninhabitable—too hot, too cold, or too filthy. Letters and phone conversations are monitored and restricted. Some jurisdictions forbid contact visits, refusing a mother the last opportunity before his execution to hug or kiss her child good-bye.

We will end the death penalty in this country, eventually, because it is the right thing to do. I hope that exposing the harm that we do to the families of the condemned will hasten its demise. Even those who support the death penalty, I believe, will conclude that any "benefit" that accrues from executing a tiny fraction of murderers is not worth the harm that is done to thousands more people whose pain and grief will ripple through future generations.

CHAPTER 1

It Could Happen to Anyone

On December 30, 1991, Amy Wilkinson called her older brother, Ray Krone, at his home in Phoenix, Arizona, to wish him a happy new year. Amy lived in York, Pennsylvania, in the southeastern part of the state, near Harrisburg, where the family had lived for several generations. She and Ray had both graduated from Dover Area High School, the same school that their parents and grandparents had attended. Both Amy and her younger brother, Dale Jr., still lived in their hometown, near their parents, Carolyn and Dale, who were getting divorced but still lived near each other. Like her mother, Amy worked in the medical profession, overseeing billing for a doctor's office. She was a single parent, raising a two-year-old son named Ben.

Although Ray loved his family and hometown, he had wanted to move west. He particularly loved the Arizona desert, with its wide-open spaces and rugged mountains. After high school, Ray joined the Air Force and was stationed in Maine near the Canadian border. After a couple of years he requested an assignment out west and jumped at the opportunity to move to Arizona.

After serving in the Air Force for six years, he received an honorable discharge and took a job as a mail carrier in Phoenix. Ray enjoyed his bachelor life. He owned his own home, along with a truck, a Corvette, and a motorcycle. He was an extrovert who liked to be with other people. He played softball, usually on the team of a local bar, and was an accomplished dart player who won most of the local competitions. One of the places where he regularly played darts was the CBS Lounge at Seventeenth Avenue and Camelback in Phoenix.

Although the two siblings lived at opposite ends of the country, they were close. In 1987, Amy and her boyfriend had visited Ray while vacationing in Arizona. When they returned home, her boyfriend committed suicide. It was very hard for Amy to continue living in York with the constant reminders of the tragedy, so when Ray invited her and Ben to live with him in Phoenix, she took him up on the offer. Amy was relieved to have a safe place to live away from the stress of her life in Pennsylvania and grateful that her brother made her feel so welcome. Amy lived in Arizona about two years before returning to Pennsylvania.

Ray's roommate, Steve, an Air Force buddy, answered the phone and told Amy that the police had come by asking questions about a murder, and Ray had agreed to go to the station with them. Steve promised to have Ray call Amy as soon as he returned home.

The murdered woman's name was Kim Ancona. Her killer had bitten her left breast, and the police were looking for matching bite marks. At the station, homicide detective Charles Gregory asked Ray to bite into a Styrofoam cast, which he agreed to do. Dr. John Piakis, the Maricopa County forensic odontologist, took photographs and made a dental cast of Ray's bite mark. Blood, saliva, and hair samples were also taken from him. Detective Gregory interrogated Ray for hours, but Ray continued to maintain his innocence, saying that he was not Kim's boyfriend and knew nothing of her murder. After several hours he was released. Later that afternoon, Ray called Amy.

AMY: Ray told me that Kim Ancona, a bartender at the CBS Lounge, had been murdered in the men's restroom while she was closing down the restaurant. Ray knew her a little, but the police were claiming that they found his phone number in her address book and that someone had told them that Kim had said that a man named Ray was going to help her close the bar that night. They assumed that Ray was her boyfriend. Ray said he was not seeing Kim and had no idea about the murder. He hadn't even left his home the night of the murder. He told me not to worry. He said that the whole thing was a big mistake and he was confident the police would figure it out. He told me not to tell our parents because there was no point in worrying them about nothing.

There was never any doubt in my mind that Ray was innocent. If he had killed someone, he would have told me. I trusted him completely. Ray was a rock in our family. Totally reliable.

While Ray was reassuring his sister, Detective Gregory was making his case against Ray. Dr. Piakis examined Ray's bite mark, along with those of several other suspects, and rendered his opinion that it was "highly probable" that Ray had bitten Kim Ancona. The mark was somewhat unusual because it was caused by someone who had one front tooth that jutted out more than the others, as did Ray. Dr. Piakas contacted Dr. Ray Rawson, a forensic odontologist from Las Vegas, Nevada, and he concurred with Dr. Piakas that the bite mark was a very good match.

Phoenix Police Department criminalist Scott Piette examined the blood, hair, and saliva. None of the blood at the scene could be attributed to Ray, nor could the pubic hairs found on the victim's body. However, swabs taken from the breast near the bite mark tested positive for salivary amylase with an H antigen. This could have been made by a person with type O blood who is a secretor—someone who secretes antigens into his saliva—which Ray was, but so were nearly half the population. However, based on this information, the police returned to Ray's home and on New Year's Eve 1991 arrested him for the kidnapping and murder of Kim Ancona.

Ray called Amy from jail and continued to reassure her that everything would get worked out. "How can they prove I did something that I didn't do?" he asked. He asked Amy again not to mention anything to anyone. Amy kept her word but wondered if she shouldn't be doing something to help her brother. Three weeks later, a Maricopa County grand jury indicted Ray for first-degree murder, kidnapping, and rape. Ray called Amy and told her that she had better tell the family what was going on.

AMY: Those three weeks were hell because I couldn't tell anybody and I didn't know what to do. I thought maybe I should tell people even though Ray had told me not to. The first person I told was our mom. I went down to my mom's place and she was having dinner with Jim Leming [at the time, Jim and Carolyn were dating, and they would later marry]. I told them that Ray had been arrested. Mom said, "For what?" And I told her murder. My mom pretty much lost it. I don't remember what happened after that. I then went to my dad's house, and he didn't say anything. He didn't know how to react.

CAROLYN: When Amy told us that Ray had been arrested for murder I said, "You've got to be kidding. Is this some kind of a joke?" Amy told us that Ray said that he hadn't done it and told us not to worry. Of course, I was very worried, but I believed Ray. He had never been in trouble with the law. If he said he hadn't done it, than I knew he was innocent.

Amy Wilkinson (left), Ray Krone, and Carolyn Leming.
Provided with permission of the family.

Some of Ray's friends looked into hiring him a lawyer, but most wanted between $30,000 and $40,000 up front as a retainer. Carolyn worked as the manager of a billing department at the local hospital. She would have liked to help Ray, but she was going through a divorce and all her assets were tied up in the legal battle. Ray didn't see any point in draining the family's finances to defend himself for a crime he hadn't committed. The court appointed Geoffrey Jones to represent Ray.

Though the state had indicted Ray, it had very little evidence against him. Its case was based on the bite mark and the innuendos that Ray and Kim were dating and had made plans to meet that night. It was relatively unusual for the state to base its entire case on bite mark evidence without other forensic evidence; however, Detective Gregory was convinced that Ray was the killer.

Geoffrey did not have extensive experience representing clients in serious felony cases. He was also hamstrung by the fact that the court, as was common in Arizona, limited the funds he could use for hiring expert witnesses and an investigator. When Geoffrey requested funds to hire a bite mark expert, the court ordered a mere $1,500, a fraction of the $10,000 the state had already paid its expert.

Instead of consulting with a forensic expert, Geoffrey asked his friend Dr. Bruce Etkin, an area dentist, to look at the bite mark evidence and help him understand it. After looking at the photographs and dental cast, Dr. Etkin told Geoffrey that it appeared to him that the mark could have been made by Ray. However, he admitted that he was not a forensic odontologist and had never before examined bite mark evidence. Geoffrey did not contact any other forensic bite mark experts.

In March, Carolyn and Jim were able to arrange time to make the cross-country trip to Arizona to visit Ray. The couple met with Geoffrey Jones, who told them that he "lived, slept, and breathed" Ray's case and said he would do everything he could to help Ray. He told Carolyn and Jim that he was limited by the court's refusal to allocate more money for experts. On the spot, Jim wrote out a check for $2,000 to help pay for expenses.

During their visit, prosecutor Noel Levy offered Ray a plea agreement to plead to a less serious form of homicide and avoid the death penalty. Geoffrey told Ray about this offer, and Ray was furious. "I'm innocent. I'm not going to plead to any murder." Ray questioned whether Geoffrey was prepared for trial, but continued to be confident that he would win.

Carolyn and Jim spent most of their time in Phoenix visiting with Ray at the infamous Maricopa County Jail run by Sheriff Joe Arpio, who called himself "the toughest sheriff in America." He bragged that he kept his costs low and could feed the inmates on forty-five cents a day. He had been known to serve bologna sandwiches green with mold. He also dyed the jail clothes pink; they became something of a novelty and were selling for significant amounts of money on eBay. When the sheriff learned of the moneymaking opportunities, he sold the uniforms himself on eBay and used the money that he made to buy a huge neon vacancy sign, which he hung outside the jail. His motto was that there was always room for more criminals, even though most people housed in county jail had not yet been convicted and were presumed innocent.

CAROLYN: I had never been in a jail. I've got to tell you the authorities don't make it easy on people. They are used to the criminals having families and friends that are somewhat of the same breed as they are. It is a rough bunch of people, and they get to know the system. We had no idea what to do.

It was difficult to even find Maricopa County Jail. The entrance was a small room, about ten by ten feet, with one window and a few chairs.

Nobody was around. Finally someone came. We said that we were there to visit Ray, and they were very rude. They told us to "Sit down!" We had to give identification and all that kind of thing. We had to leave our things in a locker, get a number, and wait in line.

They would call a certain number of people for one-hour visits unless you were from out of state. Then you were allowed two hours if you got it approved ahead of time. There were times you would go and sit there and your number never got called. There was also one time our number got called and after one hour we were told our time was up. I said we were approved for two hours, and the guard yelled, "I'm telling you your time is up." You can't argue with them. The guy upstairs refused to accept what they approved downstairs. I cannot explain to you the feeling that you are as guilty of something as the prisoners. They just make you feel terrible. They really didn't care that we had just arrived from out of state.

It was one large room where all the prisoners were, and we talked to Ray through wire. There was no contact allowed. Other people were around talking and kids were running around and it was dirty. Some of the young people are right in with the hardened criminals. There is no segregation—they are all thrown together. There are a lot of people in jail. You can have a boy that is in there for smoking marijuana and someone else who is in there for killing someone. It is a traumatizing experience for anybody.

Ray and Jim had never met before, but Jim made it very clear that he would do whatever he could to help Ray. Ray knew it was a financial hardship for his family to go to Phoenix for the trial, so he urged them not to attend. In the meantime, Ray's local friends tried to keep things going for him. The post office had suspended Ray as soon as he was indicted, but Ray had savings, and between that and money from renters he was able to continue to pay his mortgage and managed to hold his life together, barely.

• • • •

The trial was scheduled to begin on July 29, 1992, before Superior Court Judge Jeffrey A. Hotham. Six months between indictment and trial was record speed for a serious homicide case. Prosecutor Levy's theory of the case was that Kim and Ray had been dating and had made arrangements for Ray to meet her at the bar on the night of her murder to help her close. That theory, along with the bite mark evidence, was the sum total of the state's case against Ray. In fact, the bite mark was so much at issue that the case was nicknamed the "Snaggletooth Case."

Because of lack of resources or, perhaps, initiative, Geoffrey Jones had not adequately prepared to challenge the state's bite mark evidence. Things got much worse for the defense when, the Friday before the trial was scheduled to begin, prosecutor Levy gave Geoffrey a video prepared by his bite mark expert, Dr. Ray Rawson, which he intended to use at trial. The video was professionally produced with rotating graphics that overlaid the Styrofoam impression made by Ray on the bite mark on Kim's breast. The video explained in layperson's terms how Dr. Rawson had come to the conclusion that Ray was the biter. Ray was shown the video on Sunday, the day before his trial was scheduled to begin.

Arizona discovery rules require the prosecution to turn over evidence well in advance of trial so that the defense can adequately prepare for trial. Geoffrey Jones moved to prevent the state from using the video on the grounds that he could not prepare to impeach the evidence. He asked for the trial to be continued or the evidence excluded. Judge Hotham denied both requests. Geoffrey Jones sent the video to Dr. Homer Campbell, a forensic odontologist from San Antonio, but Dr. Campbell did not have enough time to examine the tape.

The trial began on schedule. The state called nineteen witnesses, the primary ones being criminalist Scott Piette, Detective Gregory, and Dr. Rawson. One weakness in the state's case was the fact that no one had seen Ray at the bar the night of the murder. Instead, the state called Kate Koester, a friend of Kim Ancona's, who testified that Kim had told her that a man named Ray would be closing the bar with her on the night that she was murdered. Geoffrey objected to this statement on the grounds that it was hearsay—a statement made by a person who does not have firsthand knowledge of a fact but was merely told something by someone else. Hearsay is usually not admissible because it is impossible for a defendant to "cross-examine" a statement of a witness who is not in court. There are some exceptions to the hearsay rule, one of which applies if the statement is offered to show the state of mind of a person, instead of to prove a fact. The state argued that Kate's statement demonstrated Kim's state of mind on the night of the murder. The defense argued that the statement was offered to prove that Ray had plans to go to the bar on the night of the murder. Judge Hotham allowed the statement.

But the state's star witness was, without a doubt, Dr. Ray Rawson. Although he had impressive paper credentials, he was not an experienced forensic witness. What Dr. Rawson lacked in experience, however, he made up with charisma. Along with his high-tech video, Dr. Rawson made a compelling case that Ray's teeth marks matched the biter's.

Geoffrey Jones called five witnesses, including Ray, and no expert witnesses. Ray himself was not in any shape to testify. Because of all the noise at the jail and the fact that he had to get up at 4:30 A.M. on trial days, he asked for something to help him sleep. The jailers gave him Thorazine, a powerful antipsychotic medicine that usually puts people into a catatonic state. Although physically present at his trial, Ray was not mentally sharp. After a short trial—five days—the jury deliberated for two hours and returned its verdict on August 7, 1992: guilty.

CAROLYN: We were at home when Geoffrey Jones called and said it was over and Ray had been convicted. Geoffrey broke down crying. He was very upset. He could hardly talk, he felt so bad about it. It was a couple of days before Ray could even call. I'm not one who gets hysterical or goes into a fit or anything. I was just numb. I was hearing the words but the words weren't really sinking in. I remember just lying on the bed and crying. I don't think you can explain the disbelief and the horror and the helpless feeling that you get. We couldn't believe this had happened and we didn't know what to do.

After Ray was convicted, the post office sent him a letter terminating his employment. His savings were starting to dwindle, and he feared that he would soon lose his house. Things got worse on November 20, 1992, when Judge Hotham sentenced Ray to death.

CAROLYN: Looking back, I see that we were very ignorant and naïve. We knew Ray was innocent, and we really thought that everything would work out okay. Ray has always been the kind of person who says, "I can handle this. It is my problem. Don't let it change your life." He kept telling us that there was no way they could find him guilty. Ray was adamant that I should not come out to Phoenix for the trial. He thought it was enough of a worry for us just going through it.

I was glad that Jim and I had gone out there to see him. His attorney said they had nothing on him, and we were told that it was going to be a very brief trial and there wasn't anything much we could do. I trusted that the system would work. The one thing we learned is not to have blind faith in the system. From then on we never took anything for granted. We never left any stone unturned or let any possible lead go unearthed.

After he was sentenced to death, Ray was transferred to the Arizona Department of Corrections facility in Florence, about an hour and a half south of Phoenix. Steve had married and moved out, and Ray couldn't pay the mortgage. The bank foreclosed on his house.

RAY: When I was first arrested, I was sure that I'd be going home once they realized that everything I had told them was the truth. The first few days and weeks I was annoyed. It was really a matter of thinking about the inconveniences to my life like making sure the dog got fed, or missing my softball games. But then my attorney told me that my bite mark matched the one on the victim. I was outraged. Then things moved quickly. I was in trial within six months. In less than a year I was on death row.

At first I managed to pay all my bills, but then my savings ran out. After the bank foreclosed on my mortgage, the VA (Veterans Administration) sent me a letter telling me that I owed $28,000. I wrote back and said there was no way that I could pay because I was on death row. I said that I had always paid my bills and even paid my mortgage from prison but I couldn't keep doing it. They wrote back a letter and said that under the circumstances I qualified for a waiver, so it didn't end up hurting my credit.

I ended up losing all my stuff. I had a Corvette, a four-wheel-drive truck, and a Volkswagen camper bus, and I raced stock cars. I wasn't stuck on any one type of activity. I played softball and golf and snow-skied and water-skied. But a guy who was living in the place after Steve left pretty much cleaned me out—he had taken guns, stereo equipment, skis, a lot of that stuff was gone. A friend got my Corvette and some clothes and photo albums to hold on to for me. Anything else that was left I gave to friends or got taken away by whoever took the property.

I was glad to have the photo albums. I certainly couldn't replace photos from growing up. But I was in prison, and all the stuff in the outside world didn't mean anything to me. What kept me going was my friends and family. They were rooting for me, and I didn't want to let anyone down. I had always played sports. I was a team player. I didn't want to be the weak link. Plus you just have to keep going. You don't have a choice.

Also, I had to renew my faith. I read Bible passages that give me hope, like "Out of the darkness shall come the light." I knew that this whole thing was bigger than me. I needed the Lord to help fix this and make it right. I had to have faith to bring this into a logical perspective. Otherwise none of it made any sense.

You are never treated well on death row, period. If guards are nice to you then other inmates will be suspicious. You don't fraternize with the guards. You keep your distance from them, and you almost have to have a sharp tongue or the rest of the inmates will think you are weak.

As far as conditions go, it is hot in the summer and cold in the winter. You are treated like an animal. You are in your cell all the time. You are let out only on Monday, Wednesday, and Friday for an hour on rec days, and you get three fifteen-minute showers a week, after rec. During the time when you walk to the shower you get any cleaning supplies that you might want to use in your cell. You might also get a health visit if are sick.

The worst thing was that you are never trusted. Before you left your cell you were always strip-searched. They stripped you down and spun and twisted you and bent you over, then they handcuffed you, belted you, and shackled your feet before you could even leave your cellblock. That treatment alone was incredible to me. I had top secret clearance in the military. In the post office I handled people's mail. In there I couldn't even have my hands loose.

The other thing that was really hard is that you are almost always alone. I'm a people person, but in there you had to keep to yourself. There were other deprivations, like the food was never warm. It was prepared in another yard and delivered over, and it sat out until the guards felt like delivering it. Sometimes they let the food get totally cold, causing a lot of strife and turmoil. Once in a while we stood up to the abuse and mistreatment. If all the inmates threw their trays the captain and sergeant had to come down and address the problem. But if one person did it you didn't get attention, and you might get in trouble.

We were allowed one phone call every two weeks. You could request for either A.M. or P.M. Since my family was all back east, it did me no good to make a phone call in the daytime because everybody was at work, but if you requested P.M. they were more likely to give you A.M. just to be spiteful. So I'd put down that I wanted A.M. If you complained about the time they'd say you had refused the call and walk away, and then it was another two weeks before you'd get another. I usually requested a weekend time, but that was when everybody else wanted to call, too. Since I never knew when I was going to be taken out for a call, my family would have to wait all day long until I called.

I tried not to cause the officers too much trouble. I caused just enough trouble to cover myself with the inmates, but didn't cause excessive trouble. I tried to treat the guards with respect. Being aggressive, you aren't going to win with them. I wasn't treated as bad as some of the inmates were. If the guards didn't like you, they would do things like not feed you for days. I just tried to take the path of least resistance. I tried to get along with everybody. You had to get along. These people could take your life or save your life.

I didn't go around talking about the fact that I was innocent. You got to act like you are the toughest dog in there. Everybody was always suspicious of everybody else. Jailhouse snitches are always telling on people. I didn't want people to think that I was going to be a snitch. Besides, it is hard to talk to people on death row at all. You have to yell out of your cell. But I did tell some people, and they believed me. I also met others who were innocent. You feel a type of bond and camaraderie. It helped make it easier to withstand it. When you see other people getting out, that gives you encouragement.

•   •   •   •

The family struggled to maintain hope and continually plotted how to help Ray. Their roots ran deep in York. Almost everyone knew the family or knew of them, and most people believed Ray was innocent. Jim Leming visited the editor of the local paper, the *York Daily Record,* with a stack of paperwork making the case that Ray was innocent. The paper took an interest and started covering it. Total strangers sent notes of encouragement, and entire congregations put Ray on their "prayer chain." Carolyn's employees made it a point to be kind—to give her hugs and supportive notes. In spite of all the support, there was never any respite from the situation. It was like living with a terminal illness: The fear and pain were always present.

CAROLYN: I would think about Ray all the time. When fixing dinner, I'd wonder what he was eating. Driving to work, I'd notice new construction and I'd imagine what Ray would think of it. It was hard for me sometimes, especially at work, to deal with other people's problems. I'm in charge of a department, and I found that I had little patience for all the petty problems and squabbles that would go on. It's hard to care about little stuff when your son is on death row for a crime he didn't commit. I tried never to show my impatience, but it was a challenge.

The thing that kept me going was my faith. I believed that God has a purpose for everything that happens, but it was pretty hard to figure out this one.

AMY: I felt helpless, but I never felt hopeless. You have this notion that you need to go rescue him, and then you realize those feelings are dumb because it was the legal system that has him. It wasn't like a bunch of criminals came and held him for ransom. It was shocking. It just kind of puts you into a state of numbness.

You can't really call up your friends and talk to them about it because no one understands what you are going through. There is nowhere you can go to talk. Even when you go to a counselor, it is not like that counselor has ever dealt with this problem before. There is not too much they can do for you. There is nothing they can say to make it any better. Basically you feel like you have stumped them. You came in with a problem they haven't heard before. There weren't any Web sites for family members of wrongfully accused people. In one way, you are really dealing with it all yourself. Our whole family lives in this area, and we are close, but we don't cry on each other's shoulders easily.

I got to the point where I couldn't sleep. I'd be lying on my comfortable king-sized bed getting ready to sleep, and then my next thought would be wondering where Ray was sleeping. I'd wonder if he was being treated badly, tortured or who knows what. Ray didn't complain, but sometimes he'd talk about prison and tell stories, and I knew there was a lot he didn't tell us.

Once I started thinking these thoughts, the night was done. I wouldn't be able to sleep. When this happens most nights, it really messes up your life and your kid's life and your relationships. Then I started taking sleeping pills because you can't survive without sleeping. I'd lie awake and think about all the things I could or should do to help Ray. Maybe I should go down to the courthouse and picket. Or maybe I should knock on every door in Phoenix, Arizona, and tell them that Ray should not be there. On days when I did feel happy, I'd feel guilty. It's not as though life isn't hard enough to begin with. I was a single parent, and I had a lot of trouble just keeping my head above water.

•   •   •   •

In the spring of 1993, Jim Rix, Carolyn's first cousin, called his eighty-year-old mother, Dorothy. They were chatting about nothing in particular when he mentioned to her a television program that he had seen the previous night about a person who had been released from death row after being wrongfully convicted. Dorothy said, "You have a cousin on death row that is innocent." Taken aback, Jim asked who. "Carolyn's son, Ray."

Carolyn's and Jim's mothers, Hazel and Dorothy, were sisters. They were born and raised in Pennsylvania, but Dorothy headed west, married a man from California, and settled there. She did not get back to Pennsylvania often. Jim had only met Carolyn a couple of times at family occasions and did not know her children at all.

Jim had worked in the high-tech industry and had started a successful business developing medical and dental software programs. He had raised three children from his first marriage and was living with his second wife and their child in Lake Tahoe, Nevada. Jim's business was comfortably established, and he found himself in the enviable position of having time to look into Ray's situation. Jim found it hard to imagine that someone in his family was on death row. As far as he knew, no one in his family had ever been in prison before.

JIM: Apparently Ray's family did not advertise the fact that Ray was in trouble until after he was convicted. My mom had heard about it, but I didn't hear about it until I mentioned this program to her and it triggered her memory. If I hadn't brought up the subject, I'm not sure she would have mentioned it. I called Carolyn and asked if she minded if I contacted Ray, and she encouraged me to.

I've always been interested and concerned about the issue of innocent people being wrongfully convicted. I followed the Ruben Carter case and I thought he got railroaded, so I knew that innocent people could get convicted. However, I never thought that would be the situation when I first got involved in the case.

Jim wrote Ray, who replied in June with a detailed explanation of what had happened. From what Ray told him, it seemed to Jim that Ray had not gotten a fair trial. He called an old friend, Gene Burdick, who was an attorney in Phoenix, and asked him what he knew of the case. Gene told Jim that he was familiar with the "bite mark" case, the case where the boyfriend killed his girlfriend at the bar. Jim asked Gene how he could learn more about the case, and Gene offered to get the trial transcripts for him. It took several weeks to receive the transcripts. Jim read all 1,425 pages. By the end, he believed that his cousin had been railroaded, too.

JIM: Except for the bite mark they had no evidence. It appeared that Ray had been railroaded. The lead detective ignored any evidence that didn't point to Ray. For example, there were tons of footprints at the crime scene. Initial police reports recorded the size of the prints as nine and a half. Ray is an eleven. In later reports the footprint size is changed to eleven. Instead of explaining why the killer has a different shoe size than Ray, they just changed the reports to make it fit with Ray.

Witnesses would suggest other leads, and the detective in charge never followed up on them. Once they realized the DNA testing was not consistent with Ray they didn't do further testing but just reported the results as "inconclusive." Instead of investigating Kim Ancona's murder, it became the "Ray Krone did it" investigation.

Since the bite mark was the basis of the state's case, Jim was particularly concerned about the fact that Geoffrey Jones had not called an expert witness to contradict the testimony of Dr. Rawson. Jim decided to hire an expert to examine the evidence. He started with Homer Campbell, the expert to whom Geoffrey had sent the video on the eve of trial. Dr. Campbell told him he needed to examine all of the evidence—the transcripts, the bite mark cast, the photographs, and the video—before he could render an opinion. Jim had the transcripts, but the rest of the material was housed in the evidence room in the basement of the Phoenix Superior Courthouse. To view the evidence, a person had to physically go to the courthouse, which would be difficult and time consuming for Dr. Campbell, who lived out of state. Gene suggested that Jim hire Mike Pain, a private investigator, to help. Mike hired a photographer to take pictures of the photographs and obtained a copy of the videotape from John Antieau, Ray's appeals lawyer. However, no one could figure out how to make copies of the dental casts.

By early 1994, Jim asked Dr. Campbell to evaluate the materials without the cast. He agreed but said he couldn't do it until he returned from the annual meeting of the American Academy of Forensic Sciences held that year in San Antonio. Jim suggested that he meet Dr. Campbell at the conference; that way he could learn more about bite mark evidence himself.

The Southwest Airlines flight to San Antonio went through Phoenix, so Jim decided to stop over and visit Gene and his wife, Carolyn, and also visit Ray in prison.

Jim rented a car for the trip to Florence. Having never been to a prison before, he was unsure of the procedures. He parked the car in a lot outside the prison complex and walked about half a mile to an outside window, where he was told that he had to leave everything in the car except his keys and driver's license. In the sweltering heat, he walked back to his car, deposited his possessions, and returned to the prison. After passing through a metal detector and security, he boarded a prisoner transport bus for death row.

JIM: The guards brought Ray in with his hands cuffed and shackled to a leather belt secured around his waist. They removed the handcuffs. I noticed that Ray kept smiling through this entire process. At first we reminisced about family, but Ray was more interested in hearing about my contacts with Dr. Campbell. I told him what had been going on, and he listened carefully and asked a few questions. I told him that I thought Dr. Campbell would exclude him as the source of the bite mark, and he said, "I couldn't understand how it was possible for the murderer and me to have the same teeth pattern." It hadn't occurred to Ray that Dr. Rawson had made a mistake. He just assumed that he had the bad luck to have the same dentition pattern as the murderer.

Throughout the visit I was impressed with Ray. He never complained about his situation. He didn't try to exaggerate the case. If I asked him a question and he didn't know the answer he'd say so, which made me have confidence in the information he gave me. We discussed his options. He could either wait for the appeal or attack the conviction by moving for a new trial, called a Rule 32 motion, based on the new evidence, assuming Dr. Campbell gave a positive opinion. Most people on death row wanted to wait for the appeal to finish before raising any new claims. That way the process took longer, thus prolonging the execution date. Not Ray. When I asked if he wanted to go forward with the Rule 32 now or wait he said, "Let's do it!"

Jim's trip to San Antonio was successful. Dr. Campbell reviewed the evidence and concluded the initial photograph of the bite mark had been improperly labeled, so that what Dr. Rawson was looking at when he opined that Ray was the biter was not even the correct configuration of teeth. Not only had Dr. Rawson misidentified Ray as the biter, he had misidentified the type of teeth that were in the photograph. Dr. Campbell showed the evidence to other colleagues. Many concurred that Ray was not the biter, or at the very least they determined that the evidence was inconclusive. No one concurred that Ray was the biter. However, Dr. Campbell refused to render a final opinion until he saw the dental casts. Jim offered to pay Dr. Campbell's expenses to travel to Phoenix, and he agreed to go.

Dr. Campbell also introduced Jim to a defense attorney named Christopher Plourd who was based in San Diego and an expert in DNA and forensic evidence. Chris kept abreast of the latest technological developments by attending forensic evidence conferences. Jim took to Chris right away and asked him for his business card.

On June 2, Jim and Dr. Campbell went to the evidence room of the Phoenix courthouse. All of the trial exhibits were carefully sealed in plastic and labeled. Jim removed the casts from the plastic bag so that Dr. Campbell could measure them. When he returned the evidence, the custodian noticed that the bag had been opened. On June 7, Carol Schreiber, director of court file services, wrote a memorandum expressing her concerns that Jim might be "tampering" with the evidence. She called the attorney general's office, and on June 8 Noel Levy went to the courthouse to examine the evidence. Although Levy concluded that the evidence had not been tampered with, he dispatched investigators to check out "Mr. Rix."[1]

Within a week, Homer Campbell issued a report excluding Ray as the biter. The following Sunday, Jim flew to San Diego to meet Chris Plourd.

Chris's office was in a renovated house, and among its homey features was a large outside deck. The two discussed the case over a beer. Chris was dressed casually and smoking a cigar. Jim liked Chris and found him very approachable. After Jim had a quick consultation with the family, they retained Chris to represent Ray in a postconviction new trial motion.

Since so little investigation had been done by the defense in the first trial, Chris wanted to conduct additional DNA tests. He met with Ray in prison and explained to him the risks of DNA testing. There were several types of evidence that could be tested—saliva from the bite mark and blood evidence from the victim's bra. Chris needed Ray to understand that if the tests came back positive, Ray would be in worse shape than he was now. Chris was impressed when Ray answered, without hesitating, "Test it all!"

Soon after being retained, Chris contacted a local forensic odontologist he worked with, Dr. Norman Sperber. Dr. Sperber told Chris that the case seemed familiar to him, and then he remembered that Dr. Piakas from the Phoenix crime lab had contacted him soon after the murder—and Sperber had told him that the bite mark evidence excluded Ray! However, prosecutor Noel Levy, who had a legal obligation to give the defense any exculpatory evidence, never informed Ray about his consultation with Dr. Sperber.

Chris filed several hundred pages of documents in support of his new trial motion. He presented affidavits from Dr. Campbell explaining how Dr. Rawson had actually misidentified teeth from the bite mark, thus invalidating his conclusion. Dr. Campbell's affidavit concluded by stating that "the video tapes are of no evidentiary value and obscure rather than enhance any analysis" and that he "totally disagreed with the analysis that was done and the conclusions that were reached."[2]

Chris even obtained an affidavit from Dr. Bruce Etkin admitting that he was incompetent to advise Geoffrey Jones about bite mark evidence.[3] Dr. Richard Souviron, another forensic odontologist, filed an affidavit concluding that "the defense provided no competent forensic dental expert" and that this failure to consult with an expert meant that "Mr. Krone did not receive fair representation."[4]

He also submitted affidavits from several other experts challenging virtually every aspect of the state's evidence against Ray, including one from Thomas Wahl, a senior forensic geneticist for the Analytical Genetic Testing Center in Denver, challenging the state's DNA evidence.[5]

Prosecutor Levy vigorously opposed the new trial motion:

The thrust of defendant's pleadings is based upon defense counsel's personal view, based upon a misstatement of the trial, the evidence, and in an attempt to misrepresent the facts in support of his pseudo-scientific conclusions, is to state that all the State's experts are wrong, the prosecution wrongly presented the case, and if only the defendant could get all of the evidence, then he would have his experts handle it and come up with the conclusion that the teeth marks are not Krone's, and none of the biological evidence are related to Krone. Thus, Krone is not the murderer but someone else, and by such a procedure, the defendant would have created newly discovered evidence, by which to justify future Rule 32 proceedings.[6]

Levy also argued that the defense could not file a new trial motion until the appeal was completed. He requested that the judge deny Ray's motion and asked for an order sealing all of the trial evidence, based in part on his claim that Jim Rix had tampered with it. Judge Hotham agreed with the state and denied Ray's Rule 32 motion and ordered all of the trial exhibits sealed, thus preventing the defense from conducting additional tests.[7]

Jim was frustrated and discouraged by the judge's ruling and decided to hire a private investigator named Tex Brown, who had gained notoriety working with the Drug Enforcement Administration in Mexico. Tex promised Jim that he would find the real killer, and Jim flew to Arizona in the fall of 1994. Tex requested a substantial payment up front with the remainder due when "Ray walks." After a few days, Tex claimed to have uncovered a ring of illegal message parlors that he believed was associated with Kim Ancona's murder. Tex was hot on the trail of two alleged witnesses, "Sugar" and "Hot Lips," when Jim decided to end their business arrangement.

As it turned out, the judge's adverse ruling worked to Ray's advantage, because the appeal of the motion went to the Arizona Supreme Court at the same time that the court was considering the appeal from Ray's trial. Although they were two separate proceedings, the judges learned of information from the Rule 32 case that had not been part of the trial record, such as the fact that the state had failed to disclose to the defense Dr. Sperber's opinion that the bite mark was not made by Ray. Meanwhile, Chris briefed Ray's appellate lawyer, John Antieau, on the new trial motion, and on December 12, 1994, Antieau argued Ray's appeal while Chris and Jim watched from the front row of the courtroom. Chris had so thoroughly convinced Antieau of Ray's innocence that he went so far as to call Dr. Rawson a quack and a charlatan.

The appeal focused on two issues: the discovery violation that resulted from the state not giving the defense the videotape until the last minute and the hearsay statement by Kate Koester that Ray was planning on closing the bar with Kim. Chris and Jim were heartened by the judges' questions, which intimated they had serious concerns about whether Ray had received a fair trial. The coup de grace came when a justice asked John Antieau if he had any evidence that Dr. Rawson's testimony was not based on sound scientific evidence and John referred the judges to Dr. Campbell's affidavit stating that Dr. Rawson's methodology was not accepted within the scientific community.[8] This evidence would not have been before the court had Judge Hotham granted the new trial motion. John finished his remarks:

> This is probably the most anomalous murder case in my experience. The defendant was advancing into middle age with never any problem with the law. He was a veteran gainfully employed for years and years. If in fact Ray Krone did murder Kimberley Ancona, it is the most aberrational murder I've ever seen. It was 180 degrees away from the rest of his life.[9]

The family felt optimistic after the hearing, but were told that it would likely be a year before the court came down with its ruling. However, as it turned out, they did not have to wait that long. On June 22, 1995, the Arizona Supreme Court overturned Ray's conviction and granted him a new trial, ruling:

> The State's discovery violation related to critical evidence in the case against the accused. We cannot say it did not affect the verdict. We reverse the convictions and remand for a new trial, where Krone will have an opportunity to meet the force of the videotape.[10]

•　　•　　•　　•

This time, Ray and his family actively participated in preparing for trial. Amy, Jim Leming, and Jim Rix learned as much as they could about forensic odontology, including attending a weeklong conference in New York City to meet with the country's top experts.

Carolyn and Jim made arrangements to take time off from work for the trial. They planned to drive a camper across country and live in it during the trial. Amy made arrangements to be there for as much of the trial as she could.

By the time the trial began, Chris Plourd had familiarized himself with every piece of evidence. He had catalogued every police report, every expert witness statement, and all the transcripts from the first trial into multiple notebooks. Although he was a very experienced defense attorney, Chris had never tried a case in Arizona. Colleagues told him to be careful of Arizona juries because they did strange things.

Superior Court Judge James McDougall's courtroom was small with limited seating—only three benches on each side of the room, each seating eight to ten people. Sitting on Ray's side were Carolyn and Jim Leming, Jim Rix, Amy Wilkinson, several of Ray's friends from Phoenix, and a reporter hired by the *York Daily Record* to cover the story. On the state's side were Kim's mother, accompanied by a victim's advocate, and a close friend of Kim's.

Jury selection began on Monday, February 12, and lasted until February 16. Immediately following jury selection, both sides made their opening statements.

Unlike Geoffrey Jones in the first trial, Chris had retained eight expert witnesses for the defense.[11]

The first witness called was FBI agent Chris Allen, a defense witness. Normally the state puts its case on first, but because of a scheduling conflict, Agent Allen had to testify at the beginning of the trial. He testified that there were two pubic hairs found on Kim Ancona and that they did not belong to her or Ray but were from an American Indian.

The state's case was essentially the same as in the first trial, but because Chris took so long cross-examining the witnesses, it took Noel Levy weeks instead of days to complete it. Levy did call one new witness, Dr. Moses Shanfield, a DNA expert who had examined saliva found on the bite mark and blood found on Kim's bra. Under cross-examination Dr. Shanfield admitted that the saliva on the bite mark was not Ray's. However, the blood on the bra was inconclusive, and he could not exclude Ray as a possible source.

While cross-examining criminologist Scott Piette, Chris asked if he had found blood on any of Kim's clothing besides the bra. The answer was no. Chris asked if any tests had been done to determine the presence of blood. Piette answered that he had not because it was unnecessary. Chris asked him if he would be willing to conduct a simple test called a Kastle-Meyer test, which would determine the presence of blood. Piette agreed and in front of the jury he conducted the test, which showed the presence of blood on Kim Ancona's jeans—blood that the police had never tested.

The state's last and most important witness was Dr. Rawson, who took the stand on March 18. As in the first trial, Dr. Rawson presented very engaging testimony, including the videotape. However, after Chris examined him for two and a half days, Dr. Rawson seemed less sure about his conclusions.

Although it was stressful, being in the courtroom gave the family an opportunity to visit Ray and got Ray out of his small cell. He was not in shackles, and he wore a suit instead of his prison uniform. George Schuester, the bailiff in charge of the courtroom, had serious doubts as to whether Ray was guilty and was much more lenient with him than he would have been with other inmates. He allowed the family to talk to Ray and even hug him as well as to give him things like pieces of candy. Each morning his family brought Ray clean clothes to wear to court.

AMY: One time Ray asked me to get him a package of salt from McDonald's. During a break he said to me, "You gotta get me a pack of salt. I need some salt for my food." The prisoners weren't allowed to use salt. "What am I supposed to do with it?" I asked him. "Stick it in the coat pocket of my suit before you give it to George." I told him I'd think about it.

The food was really horrible. Ray got very thin in prison. It never tasted good, and sometimes they served the prisoners bad food that made them sick. Once in a blue moon they'd give them produce. One time they gave Ray a hot pepper with his meal, and he somehow cut the pepper into fifty little pieces and he saved it and put one piece a day under his tongue just so he could taste something with flavor every day.

You can't imagine how I suffered over that decision. I didn't tell anybody because I didn't want anybody else to get in trouble if we got caught. You don't know how bad he wanted a pack of salt. He had done so much for me in my life and all he asked me for was a stinking pack of salt and I was freaking out about it. I was sure if I got caught they would test it for drugs and accuse me of trying to sneak drugs to Ray.

I never did get the pack of salt for him. I couldn't do it. I decided that if I gave him a pack of salt and got caught it might hurt his case and I wouldn't be able to live with myself. Plus my mom and the lawyers would have killed me. But not getting him a pack of salt was killing me, too. I felt like I should have done it without thinking. I still feel bad about that lousy pack of salt. When I told him I wouldn't do it he said,

"It's all right, don't worry about it." I don't think he realized how bad
I felt.

After Dr. Rawson's testimony, the defense opened its case on Thursday,
March 21, with the testimony of Dr. Norman Sperber, who told the jury that
he had advised the prosecution early on that Ray had not made the bite mark.
On Friday, the defense called Dale Henson, a street cleaner who testified that
he had seen a person going into the CBS Lounge at closing time and it was
not Ray Krone. On Monday, Art Epstein, an expert in blood spatter, testified
that the natural folding of the bra, not Ray's teeth, had made the blood pattern on the bra. For the remainder of the week, Chris called three more DNA
experts. Then he concluded his case with testimony from Dr. Campbell and
Dr. Gerald Vale, prominent forensic odontologists who both excluded Ray as
the biter, and a state's expert, who testified that part of what Dr. Rawson was
calling a bite mark,was actually a scratch mark that was made postmortem
during the autopsy.

Counsel made closing arguments on Tuesday, April 9, and the jury began
deliberations that day.

Every morning for five weeks, a group of Ray's supporters had shown up
at court, and every day the victim's advocate had brought Kim's mother,
Patricia Lou Gasman. The two families had not spoken in nearly two months
when Kim's oldest son approached Carolyn.

CAROLYN: It was obvious that Patricia hated Ray. I felt really bad for her.
She had lost her daughter, and she didn't seem to have that much support. None of her kids lived with her, and we heard that she had gone
through a period of years where she didn't speak to Kim and they had
only been back in communication for a matter of months before the
murder.

During the jury deliberations, Kim's oldest son, Chris, came over and
sat down on a bench next to me. I told him that I was very sorry about
his mother and I felt really bad because the person who really did it was
still out there somewhere and hadn't been punished. He told me that he
was not convinced that Ray did it.

With the exception of Carolyn, everyone in the family felt that the case had
gone very well. Carolyn, however, had a bad feeling about the jury.

CAROLYN: The third day of deliberations I couldn't sit still, so I started walking around the city. My husband was feeling positive, and my cousin Jim's wife and son had come down, and Jim had asked Ray where he wanted to have his celebration party. But I didn't want to talk about things like that.

The jury finished deliberating on Thursday evening, and the judge excused them for the night, ordering them to return the next day to read the verdict. Before dismissing the jury, the judge asked all the spectators to leave the hallway so that the jurors did not see anyone. All parties returned the following morning.

The family was already assembled when the jury was brought into the courtroom. Carolyn watched George walk up to Ray and whisper something in his ear. Then the foreman read the verdict: "Guilty."

Chris and Ray did not react at all. At first there was a stunned silence—even the judge looked surprised—but then commotion broke out. Kim's family cheered, and Amy yelled, "This is insane." As is customary, Chris asked to have the jury polled, and all confirmed that they agreed with the verdict, although the ten women of the jury were sobbing as they answered.

CAROLYN: I don't know if I could ever describe it. I heard it, but I didn't really hear it. Ray turned around and said, "It's okay, Mom." And then they took him out. We couldn't even say good-bye. They just took him out. It is like you are no longer human. And there was the prosecutor gloating.

AMY: I remember someone pulling me out of the aisle. The next thing I know, my mom and my stepdad and I were going into an elevator right outside, and a photographer was trying to get into the elevator with us, and everybody was shooting pictures. My stepdad pushed them out of the way. We kind of flew out the front door and down the steps holding hands. With all the craziness we could have gotten separated. I broke off at some point and went behind a sign and sat there for a while. It was kind of scary. I just couldn't believe that it had happened again. We had a bag packed for Ray with new clothes and a reservation at a nice hotel. We even had a dinner reservation. We didn't even remotely think that he would be found guilty again. We had no plan for that.

I had all this adrenaline pumping, and I wanted to do something like go talk to the judge, which you can't do. But we did wait for the jury to walk out of the courthouse, because we wanted them to have to look at us.

CAROLYN: After the jurors left I made a statement that our family felt bad for the victim's mother, but I said that we were victims, too, because Ray was innocent and we were the victims of false conviction. Patricia got very angry about that statement.

The family met at the investigator's office near the courthouse. Despite his intense disappointment, Chris tried to remain optimistic. "This isn't the end. There's more we can do," he told the family. No one said much at the meeting; all were in a state of shock.

AMY: The feeling of hopelessness was huge, because without a doubt we proved that Ray didn't do it. We pulled out all the stops, and the jury just said he did it. I was there for a lot of the trial, and I heard a lot of the evidence. I was completely 100 percent sure the jury was seeing the same thing I was seeing. When they said guilty I thought they misspoke. It was horrible. Here Ray had had a second chance with a good lawyer with all of us out there and all of the forensic odontologist support (with the exception of one idiot) and still he was convicted. What could we possibly do better? We presented everything. We proved him innocent. It took five weeks, what more could we possibly do to change anybody's mind?

We called his friends. The ones I was staying with came right down. We were all in a very big state of shock. We all pretty much lost it. We were all just saying things and doing things against each other. There wasn't any reason. We were just losing it. My mom exploded, and my stepdad and I did, too. I don't know if that is a typical reaction. We didn't all sit around and hold each other, because it was too big.

Jim and Carolyn went back to their camper. Jim Rix went back to his hotel room, Amy went back to Ray's friends' house. Ray went back to prison.

•　•　•　•

The next few days were a blur. Chris was as devastated as the family. He had become very emotionally involved in the case, and the verdict shook his faith in the system. Talking to the jurors after the verdict, Chris learned that they had discounted the expert evidence. They believed that the bite mark was the crucial piece of evidence—if Ray was the biter he was the killer—but they didn't believe either Dr. Rawson or the defense experts. Instead, they examined the photographs and dental casts on their own and decided that Ray was the biter. As his colleagues had warned him, Arizona juries do strange things.

The family tried to make sense of the verdict. Everyone had a theory. Maybe the jurors had been more influenced by Dr. Rawson because he was a Mormon and 40 percent of the population of Maricopa County was Mormon. Or maybe the fact that Ray was a postman influenced them. The prosecutor kept mentioning throughout the trial that Ray was a postal worker. A postal worker had recently shot up a post office, and everyone was talking about people who had "gone postal."

JIM: There are other ways to influence a jury. The simplest thing to do is that somebody drops the word that Ray confessed but it wasn't able to come into court. We had heard that Rick Romley, the county attorney, had been extremely upset that Ray's conviction was overturned. He had said in no uncertain terms that they had to do whatever was necessary to convict Ray Krone. Who knows what that meant? Of course, this is all highly speculative, but to anyone watching the trial the verdict didn't make any sense.

AMY: Of course we tried to figure out why this had happened. The second trial happened right after O. J. Simpson got off. That was not a good thing for Ray's case. The public was pretty much dissatisfied with that verdict. They didn't want to see anybody else "get off." And I really don't think they cared about the fact that the state was supposed to prove him guilty beyond a reasonable doubt. We had proven that Ray was innocent. I knew that the only hope we had of helping Ray was to find the person who actually did it.

After the verdict, I went out to some barrooms where people that knew Ray went. We had some ideas about who might have done it. I didn't tell anybody I was going to the bars. Some were really hardcore bikers' bars. I thought I'd get there and without telling people I was Ray's sister try to get them to talk. The trial was over. It was in people's minds, and they were talking about the guilty verdicts. I was a single woman going to a bar by myself; I figured some of these guys were going to talk to me. I never found out anything.

The *York Daily Record* also postulated an explanation for the verdict. Staff writer Scott Dodd wrote an article headlined, "Defense May Have Been Too Sure," in which he concluded:

Although defense attorney Chris Plourd ripped into the prosecution's main witnesses, he didn't always make it clear where he was heading or what conclusions he expected the jury to draw from his cross-examinations. Sometimes he seemed to be playing more for his audience of fans, Krone's supporters, than he did for his audience of skeptics, the jury. And when he gave his closing argument after a strong presentation of the evidence by Prosecutor Noel Levy, Plourd focused more on his conspiracy theories about the police and prosecutors than he did on the evidence that he thought would cement Krone's innocence.[12]

The article concluded with a surprising twist:

One thing will greatly aid Plourd's struggle for an appeal: a death sentence. Death row inmates have more automatic appeals and a better chance of securing a new trial. "We're hoping he gets the death penalty again," [Jim] Leming said. "That's Ray's wish," Carolyn Leming added.[13]

Before returning home, Jim, Carolyn, and Amy visited Ray one last time. They were not permitted a contact visit so they had to say good-bye through a Plexiglas wall.

AMY: It was a short visit. I wish that it hadn't been through glass. I couldn't understand why it had to be through glass. I know they have rules but we live on the other side of the country and weren't going to see him for a long time. Ray tried to stay upbeat but we were all depressed. We knew we wouldn't be seeing him for a very long time.

Jim and Carolyn drove straight back to York, taking turns driving around the clock. Amy flew back. Ray stayed in Arizona.

On December 10, 1996, Ray returned to court for sentencing. In a brief statement he said that there was a good explanation for the lack of evidence against him like hair, fingerprints, and blood: "I didn't kill Kim Ancona."[14]

Patricia Gasman stated that she had no doubt whatsoever that Ray had killed her daughter, and she asked the judge to impose whatever sentence was adequate "for this heinous and depraved murder."[15]

Judge McDougall read a seventeen-page prepared statement in which he announced that he would not sentence Ray to death, and he expressed doubts that Ray was even the killer. He pointed out problems with the state's case, such as the fact that the state had failed to disclose to the defense Dr. Sperber's opinion that the bite mark was not made by Ray. He sentenced Ray to twenty-five years to life for the murder and twenty-one years for kidnapping and concluded, "This is one of those cases that will haunt me for the rest of my life, wondering whether I have done the right thing."[16] At age thirty-nine, Ray would have to serve thirty-six years before becoming eligible for release. For better or for worse, he was no longer on death row.

•   •   •   •

Ray was lucky to come from such a resilient family, and to come from a community that believed so strongly in his innocence. After recovering from the initial disappointment, the family returned to the task of freeing Ray. Amy and two sisters who had been friends with Ray in high school organized a petition campaign. The *York Daily Record* ran a story on their efforts.

> Wade [Amy's last name at that time] believes that the jury ignored reasonable doubt in her brother's case, not to mention DNA evidence and witness testimony that seemed to prove his outright innocence. Apparently, many people in York County agree with her. "A lot of people are really outraged," she said. Everyone she talked to said they wished they could do something to change the outcome. "After hearing this night after night, I said we really ought to collect this energy," Wade said.
>
> So with half a dozen other people who believe Krone is innocent, including friends of the family and former school buddies, Wade has found a way to keep the fight going for her brother. The group has distributed hundreds of petitions all over York County, asking people to say they believe the justice system failed in Krone's case.[17]

The article also quoted the two sisters involved in the campaign:

"We just felt that after all of this that we had to get the word out," said Melinda Eppolito, who is writing letters with her sister, Laura Meagher. They followed the case "fully expecting the opposite of what happened to happen," Eppolito said.

When it didn't, they decided they needed to act. "The jury system, I mean, something's got to be done," Eppolito said. "We just want to get this out to people and open their eyes, show them this is what's going on."[18]

The article concluded with the text of the petition.

We, the undersigned, believe that the American justice system has failed greatly in the Ray Krone/Kim Ancona case in Phoenix, Arizona. In particular, it points out a severe problem with the current jury system. It puts too much responsibility on people who are uneducated in very technical evidence and who do not understand the law. We believe Ray Krone was wrongfully convicted of this crime and would like to see it solved as soon as possible for the benefit of all Americans who care about justice.[19]

•   •   •   •

For the second appeal, the court appointed James Kemper. As he had with John Antieu before the first appeal, Chris met with James to go over the evidence with him. Once again, the main issue on appeal was the hearsay statement of Kate Koester. And once again there was new evidence—the blood on Kim Ancona's jeans, which no one knew the source of. Chris suspected the blood was Kim's, but he wanted to make absolutely certain that it wasn't someone else's.

As before, Ray's case proceeded on two tracks: the appeal from the conviction and a motion for a new trial. However, this time, Chris thought it better to wait before filing the new trial motion. Emotions were running high after the second verdict and needed time to dissipate, and Chris did not think it likely that the state would pay for new DNA testing at the same time it was paying for Ray's appeal.

Unfortunately, this meant a long wait for Ray. It took five years before the appeal ran its course—first to the Arizona Court of Appeals, then the Arizona

Supreme Court, and finally the United States Supreme Court. All three affirmed Ray's conviction.

JIM: We had to cover all possible legal routes, but I did not think Ray would get any relief in Arizona courts. I thought that once we got out of state court and into federal court we might have some hope. I read a book written by Ruby Gerber, a retired Arizona judge who knew Gene. The book was all about how the system in Arizona gives prosecutors so much power. Many of the judges are former prosecutors. Judges are afraid they will lose their jobs or get really bad assignments if they go against prosecutors. The first judge, Hotham, was the worst. He was nothing more than a prosecutor in a robe. He never made a favorable decision for Ray in the whole case.

•   •   •   •

The weeks stretched into months that stretched into years. The family did all they could to keep hope alive. Since Ray was no longer on death row, the rules were less strict. He was allowed to have a television, so Carolyn sent him one. Phone calls were more liberal, so Ray had more contact with friends and family. In most ways, prison life improved for Ray.

RAY: Unlike on death row, we didn't have to stay in our cells all the time. In maximum security, they'd open your door up and let you out of your cell for breakfast, lunch, and supper. And we had rec once a day. It's not like you could walk just anywhere, but at least you got out of your cell each day. You could put in for a visit at the law library and go over there.

Of course, when interacting with that many people there are more problems: egos, violence, people looking to cause some type of trouble. You had to be involved with prisoner politics. Prisons are very segregated. You don't cross those lines without severe repercussions. You have to be a lot more careful about your physical safety. If you are walking down the hallway or chow hall you might get stabbed, or raped.

There were stabbings of inmates if not daily then at least weekly. I've been stabbed, lived through riots. It's just part of life. You just hope they don't get you in the neck or the throat. On death row there was not the same racial segregation or tensions. We knew they were going to kill us all.

Ray's hometown community continued to support him. Old friends sent Ray letters including pictures of their kids. A Sunday school teacher told her class about Ray, and many of the young children wrote Ray letters with drawings they had made. Everyone put Ray on their "prayer chains." Amy and her friends continued their campaign, meeting once a week to write letters on Ray's behalf. They wrote to everyone they could think of—politicians, movie stars, news shows—and got a lot of form letters back.

AMY: The media didn't want to cover the story until it was over. They always wanted an ending. "Contact us when the case is resolved." They didn't seem to think their role was to bring attention to the case. The only paper that covered it regularly was the *York Daily Record.*

Desperate enough to try anything, Amy contacted a psychic she had seen on *The Montel Williams Show* who had helped police departments solve crimes. The psychic had a web page and for $750 promised to answer one question.

AMY: I spent a long time trying to come up with one question to ask and decided I'd ask her if Ray would ever get out of jail. They had rules against asking things like what is the name of the killer. That cost a lot more money. I tried to get the money together, then I went through in my head how I would feel if the answer was no. When I thought about it more I realized that if she said no I was going to be devastated, and if the answer was no then I didn't want to hear that answer. I guess I thought if she would have said Ray was going to get out of jail that would have given me more desire, more power to keep going. In the end I didn't pay to have it done. I don't know, maybe subconsciously I needed reassurance that we were working in the right direction. I never told anybody that I had been doing that.

After Ray lost all his appeals, Chris believed it was time to request to have the blood found on Kim's clothes tested. He wanted to have a local lawyer handle the motion both because it was easier to have someone local and because he thought it would help Ray if he stayed in the background. In July of 2000 the family retained Phoenix lawyer Alan Simpson, who, like Chris, was an expert in forensic technology.

Chris's instincts proved to be correct. On April 16, 2001, five years and four days after the second jury found him guilty, the court released the bloody jeans for DNA testing. The judge ordered that the blood on the jeans be tested and that the results be run through the CODIS databank (a national database with DNA records of convicted offenders) to check for matches. It was six months before the state got around to testing the blood, but the family was not given any results.

At the beginning of the year, the family learned through a lab technician who knew Chris that the state had results that it had not turned over. Chris began making inquiries, but it took until April 4, 2002, before the police released a report that confirmed that the blood on Kim Ancona's pants was not from Kim or Ray but from Kenneth Phillips, a man serving time on a sex offense, due to be released in July. The defense contacted Kenneth Phillips in prison. He admitted that when he heard the news of Kim Ancona's murder he wondered if he had killed her, but couldn't remember because he was in an alcoholic blackout. At the time of the murder, Kenneth Phillips had been living six hundred yards from the CBS Lounge.

On April 5, 2002, Alan Simpson petitioned the court for Ray's immediate release. The judge denied the request but set a hearing for April 29 to hear testimony on the new evidence. Alan Simpson was quoted in the press, "This proves with certainty that Ray Krone is an innocent man. Every day from this point on that Ray spends in jail is a day the county acts at their own peril."[20]

Three days later, on April 8, the Maricopa County Attorney's Office called a news conference and announced that it was petitioning for Ray's release pending the April 29 hearing. That afternoon, Ray, pale and thin, and wearing sunglasses to protect his eyes from the bright light, walked out of prison accompanied by Chris Plourd. Standing outside the prison, Ray said in an interview with KPNX-TV, "For ten years I felt less than human. This is certainly a strange feeling, and I think it'll take a while for it to set in."

AMY: None of us really expected anything to come from the DNA testing. There had been so many times when we had gotten our hopes up just to have them dashed down again. I thought this would be one more time.

On April 8, I was over at my dad's with my daughter picking up sticks in the front yard from the oak tree. I had spent most of the day with him. The three of us were having fun. A van pulled over, and I realized it was a lady that my mom worked with and she yelled at me, "Where have you been—your mother's looking for you!" She's still yelling from a distance and I think I hear her say, "They are going to leave your brother out of jail! They're going to leave your brother out of jail!" I said, "Dad, I've got

Jim Rix (left) with attorney Christopher Plourd.
Provided with permission of Jim Rix.

to go, I'll let you know." By the time I got to my mom's place, there was a reporter there already.

Everybody was there with big smiles on their faces, and they started telling me the details that at that moment they were sending a fax that would order Ray's release. It was kind of weird having a reporter there to capture every detail of what you are thinking. I was still past disbelief until I watched him on TV walking out of jail and then he called on the phone.

Carolyn and Jim packed the car immediately to drive to Arizona. Dale offered to come along and help with the driving so that they could drive straight through. Amy wanted to go, but she had a two-year-old daughter, and someone had to stay behind to handle all the media questions.

AMY: I didn't mind dealing with the local media. They had always been really good. The people around here totally believed in Ray. But then I started getting all these calls from other people that I had written to about Ray's case, and I felt like saying, "You know what? I wrote a letter last year, and if you show me that letter maybe I'll talk to you about it. If you had paid attention you would have had the story long before anyone else." I tried not to let that attitude come through too much.

For the next five or six weeks there was someone from the media around all the time. It was strange to have a house full of cameras and an interview scheduled every day and night. Because the rest of my family wasn't here, I was the one they had to talk to. It did get frustrating. Sometimes you think the questions are kind of dumb. Like, "Were you excited to hear he was getting out?" It still didn't seem real. I thought that the prison would find some way to keep him. They'd realize a mistake had been made and put Ray back in prison.

Two days later, Carolyn, Jim, and Dale arrived in Phoenix after a record two-day drive across the country. The three had slept only four hours during the 2,400-mile journey. Carolyn brought some of Ray's possessions that she had been holding for him for more than a decade: a leather bracelet, a necklace, his driver's license and Social Security card.[21]

Ray spent the next couple of weeks relaxing with his family, enjoying the freedom of things like eating whenever and whatever he wanted and swimming in the pool. Only one piece of news marred his happiness—his grandmother, ninety-three-year-old Bertna Mae Krone, died in her home in Dover Township before he had a chance to see her again. Ray had desperately hoped to see her before she passed away, but he could not leave the state until his case was resolved, and she was too sick to travel. Fortunately, she had lived long enough to learn that Ray had been released from prison.[22]

On April 24, 2002, Maricopa County Attorney Richard Romley dismissed the charges against Ray and charged Kenneth Phillips with Kim Ancona's murder.[23] Ray was going home.

Before the family returned to Pennsylvania, a local television anchor arranged a meeting between Carolyn and Patricia Gassman.

CAROLYN: Patricia told me that she had believed all the things that the prosecutor had told her about Ray. She now realized that she had been lied to. She apologized for all the things she had said about Ray. I told her that I felt bad for her because now she would have to go through another trial and hear and see the murder all over again.

The family loaded up the car and left the state, for good. They estimated that they would be back in York by May 3. The media were particularly interested in covering Ray's release because he was the one hundredth innocent person to be released from death row since the death penalty was reinstated in 1976.

> **AMY:** Relatives and friends and the media all gathered together at my house. It was a circus until he finally got here. I didn't know what I would do or how I would react. My stepdad pulled into the driveway, and Ray got out of the car. It seemed like nobody moved, and I said, "I'm not standing here!" I ran down the yard to the side of the car and I hugged him for I don't know how long. Ray looked skinny and very pale, white as a ghost, an unhealthy look, like he had cancer or something. Then I introduced him to my daughter, Hannah Rae, named after him.

Two days later the entire community welcomed Ray home at a party organized by Amy and his supporters held at Quickel's Lutheran Church picnic grove. The theme was "Christmas in May"—the idea was to make up for all of the Christmases and birthdays Ray had missed while he was in prison. Half of the room was decorated for Christmas and the other half for a birthday party. People brought wrapped presents and placed them on either side of the room. Barbecue was served, which was a thrill for Ray; he rarely ate meat all the years he had been in prison, either because it wasn't served or because when it was, he feared that it was spoiled.

The party brought together the people who had continued to believe in Ray and kept him going through his ordeal. Everyone signed a guestbook with warm, welcoming words. There were a couple of fund-raising events, too, to help Ray get back on his feet financially. Someone organized a $^{50}/_{50}$ lottery—the winner was to split the pot with Ray—but both winners of the lottery refused their share of the cash. Ray's television that he had watched while in prison was auctioned off to the highest bidder.[24] The party helped Ray make the transition back into "real life" by reminding him of how much love and support he had.

• • • •

More than a year after his release, Ray is still unsure of what the future holds. He lives in an apartment owned by his mother. He spends most of his time traveling and speaking about his experience and speaking out against the death penalty. Although he had no experience in public speaking, Ray is proving to be a natural. He inspires audiences with his quick wit and upbeat attitude. Unfortunately, these engagements are not earning him regular income. When at home, he helps his family and works for a friend who owns a plumbing business. He has tried to get his job back at the postal service, but so far has been unsuccessful.

AMY: It is amazing how well Ray has held up. However, I wonder if he will ever really be back to "normal" again. I have met various people that this has happened to, and I checked into some of the statistics before he got out. A lot of them become drug addicts, alcoholics, or homeless or are back in jail.

I worry about him. It's not like it is over. I know deep down he is damaged like no one can imagine, but his spirit and his attitude are outstanding. Anybody who meets him and talks to him is pretty much amazed. It's been that way since he got out. He was that way when he got home. He hasn't shown any anger or bitterness.

• • • •

CAROLYN: It's hard to know how Ray is really doing. We know and he has told us that only about 15 percent of the guys who come out make it okay. A lot of guys have a lot of trouble. He considers himself one of the very lucky ones. I'm sure there are scars that will never heal and there will be things that he has to deal with for years. His attitude is certainly commendable. I know that the whole time that Ray was in prison he'd call us and say, "I'm fine. I'm doing okay." He always tried to protect us, and I feel sometimes he is still doing that. He is not really opening up. He doesn't have a lot of time to himself. When he visits us his cell phone is ringing off the hook. You can't even have a meal without lots of people calling, but he has a good attitude about all of it.

Our family is deeply religious, which helped us get through this ordeal. I believe everything happens for a reason. When Ray was released, he became the one hundredth innocent to be released from death row. That has given Ray a lot of opportunities to speak. Ray seems to have the knack and natural ability to talk. One pastor at a church where Ray spoke said Ray put him to shame because he doesn't talk with "ahhs" and "ums." All Ray has ever wanted to do was get out and start his life again, but maybe God has other plans for him.

Ray can also speak with credibility because he has never been in trouble with the law before. Many of the people that you hear about that were wrongfully convicted had been in trouble before, which is why the police focused on them. But in Ray's case there was no reason to suspect him of murder. They made a case out of nothing. They needed to find someone to convict and they chose Ray.

Ray lost all of his possessions while in prison, except the Corvette his friend saved for him. However, with any luck, Ray may receive some financial compensation for his lost years and for the untold resources spent untangling himself from the legal nightmare. A year after his release, Ray filed a $100 million lawsuit against the Maricopa County Attorney's Office and the Phoenix police alleging police incompetence, fraud, misconduct by prosecutors and perjury by witnesses. Ray is not looking to get rich. Any money he gets will be used to repay his family, especially his parents, who depleted their retirement and other savings to pay for his defense.

Before he returned to Arizona to file his suit, people warned Ray to be careful of the police who were very angry at him and might try to tarnish him in some way. However, public sentiment appears to be on Ray's side. The *Arizona Republic* published an editorial called "Pay Ray Krone His $100 Million," that stated in part:

> We should pay the $100 million not because his conviction, as the lawsuit alleges, was based on prosecutorial and police misconduct, altered evidence, evidence not tested, exculpatory evidence not disclosed to the defense or a prosecution that shopped for and got an expert who said what it wanted. We should pay because we should collectively be held accountable for the mistakes made in our name, particularly when they cause such great harm.[25]

•　　•　　•　　•

The people of York, Pennsylvania, who pride themselves on being good law-and-order citizens, no longer have blind trust in the system.

CAROLYN: We always believed in an eye for an eye. When we heard about a horrible thing, like a kid being brutally killed, we'd say we wanted justice. Now when I hear about a horrible crime I don't automatically assume the person is guilty. The system is not designed for justice, it is about showboating and notches on the belt. There are people who are completely innocent and are treated like Ray. The death penalty does not deter anybody from doing anything. Too many people won't admit that it doesn't work.

•   •   •   •

JIM: From a practical point of view the death penalty serves no useful purpose. It is very expensive. It serves only our animal instincts for revenge, retribution, and retaliation. If they could get the right person I probably wouldn't have a problem with it. But too often they get the wrong person. We'll never have a perfect system, so some innocent people will always be convicted. The best thing to do is eliminate it. But there are many more changes that need to be made besides getting rid of the death penalty. Prosecutors and police can get away with anything. They have blanket immunity. They pay an expert an amount of money to say it is their guy, and then if it turns out they are wrong they just say, "I just believed my expert." That is the immunity they get. What incentive do they have to play by the rules when nothing happens to them? In our case they knew for months that the DNA showed Ray was innocent, but they spent all that time trying to come up with some connection between Kenneth Phililps and Ray to cover up all their mistakes. To them it was nothing. To Ray, it was another six months of his life in prison for a crime he didn't commit.

CHAPTER 2

A Hero's Life

In the fall of 1980, Viet Nam veteran and war hero Manuel "Manny" Babbitt moved to Sacramento, California, to live with his brother Bill, Bill's wife, Linda, and their three children. Bill worked as a pipefitter for the Southern Pacific Railroad, and Linda worked for the State Department of Motor Vehicles. Bill's mother, Josephine, and sister Donna had already moved to California and could help support Manny.

BILL: I was excited about having my younger brother live with me. Despite his troubles, he still looked like a kid. He was handsome—clean-shaven and well built with penetrating dark, childlike eyes.

I was seven years older, and Manny had always looked up to me. But I was proud of him, too. We grew up on Cape Cod in Wareham, Massachusetts, in the Oakdale area. Our family had emigrated from the Cape Verde Islands off the African coast. My dad worked shucking oysters, and my mom picked cranberries. We grew up poor. Manny was born in 1949. He had a hard time in school. When he was twelve, a car hit him while he was riding his bicycle, and doctors told us he might not recover. His head injury made it even more difficult for him in school, and he dropped out at seventeen, never making it past the seventh grade.

Not having many options as an uneducated African American man, at eighteen, Manny enlisted in the Marines. He was functionally illiterate, but a recruiter helped him pass the entrance examination. Since his return from Viet Nam in 1969, Manny's life had deteriorated. He had turned to drugs and alcohol for comfort in dealing with his demons. He had had two failed marriages, spent time in a psychiatric hospital and in prison, and had lived on the streets.

The family thought that moving west might help Manny make a new start. Linda used to be a corrections officer, and we had good jobs, so it made sense for him to live with us, at least until he got himself established. I had high hopes for Manny. I didn't realize how ill he was.

Manny's Marine career began at Parris Island. After basic training, he joined the Third Division of the Twenty-sixth Marine Regiment and was shipped out to Khe Sanh, which would prove to be the site of one of the war's bloodiest battles. On January 21, 1968, a siege began that lasted for seventy-seven days. The Marines were trapped on their tiny base surrounded by more than forty thousand enemy troops. American pilots flying B-52s bombed the periphery of the base every three hours with half-ton bombs, dropping a total of 150,000 bombs. In a single day in February 1968, thirteen hundred rounds of mortar fell near the perimeter of the base.[1]

BILL: A former Navy man, I had been following the action in Viet Nam. I asked my mother where Manny was, and she told me "some place that begins with a *K*." I asked her to spell it for me. She got out Manny's letter and spelled Khe Sanh. I didn't have the heart to tell her what was going on there—that Manny was in an active combat zone where hundreds were dying.

Nearly one thousand Americans died at Khe Sanh, and another fifteen hundred were wounded. Fifteen thousand North Vietnamese died as well. By the end of the siege, the once-thriving town of Khe Sanh was decimated. Gone were the lush trees, French villas, and village huts. The land looked like a bloody moonscape. Those soldiers who survived Khe Sanh did not do so unscathed. For their "extraordinary heroism, indomitable will, staunch endurance, and resolute courage," President Johnson awarded Manny's unit a Presidential Unit Citation.

Manny worked on an Ontos, an armored vehicle that rode on tracks like a tank and carried six recoilless rifles, three mounted on each side. The rifles fired armor-piercing shells as long as an arm and "beehive shells," casings loaded with a hundred thousand tiny darts.[2] He volunteered for dangerous assignments like checking for land mines. Promoted twice to the rank of lance corporal, Manny was made commander of his own Ontos.

During his first tour of duty, Manny was wounded twice and stung by a deadly scorpion while he was on the Ontos. Flying shrapnel nearly severed his thumb. Manny tied it back in place with a piece of cloth, thereby saving it. Another time Manny was knocked off the Ontos during battle and a piece of incoming shrapnel penetrated his skull, lodging in the folds of his brain. While going for help, Manny lost consciousness on the airstrip and was mistaken for dead. The operators of a helicopter carrying dead bodies loaded him onto a pile of dead bodies and body parts. Manny regained consciousness in the hull of the helicopter surrounded by severed limbs and heads and bloody bodies.

> BILL: Manny told me about waking up in the helicopter lying on top of a stack of body parts. He had nightmares about those bodies for years. His head wound would have qualified him to be returned to the States, but a week later Manny asked to return to Khe Sanh. As soon as Khe Sanh ended, Manny got transferred to Con Thienh, another hot zone. Altogether Manny fought in five major campaigns. Besides the presidential citation, Manny also received the National Defense Service Medal, the Vietnam Service Medal with five stars, the Vietnam Campaign Medal, the Combat Action Medal, and an award from the Vietnamese government called the Vietnamese Cross of Gallantry.

Manny saw dozens of people killed during combat and developed rituals for handling the bodies of fallen comrades. Before bagging the body, Marines tied something around the ankle for identification, usually the soldier's dog tags. If the body was too heavy to move, they covered it to prevent it from being hit again. Another custom was to remove items from the body. Sometimes Marines entered enemy villages on intelligence missions and took personal items, which they called "souveniring."[3]

Despite his injuries, Manny signed up to extend his tour in Viet Nam. The Marines gave him a thirty-day leave in October 1968, and he flew home and married Lorraine Estelle, whom he had met while working at the Wareham shoe factory before joining the Marines. He wanted the wedding to be special, so he spent $350 of his $500 monthly pay on her wedding gown.[4]

Nine months later, in July 1969, he returned stateside to take a post at Quonset Point in Rhode Island, where he could live with Lorraine, who was pregnant. Manny arrived stateside in July 1969. While waiting for a ride at the bus station in Providence, Manny spilled a soda. He went to the restroom to

Manny Babbitt. Provided with permission of the family.

get paper towels to clean it up and returned to find that someone had taken the bag filled with presents he had brought back for his family—kimonos for his mother and sisters and pool sticks for his father and brothers.[5]

The homecoming incident foreshadowed events to come. Manny's life started unraveling. He couldn't concentrate on his work. He developed strange habits like playing with the pull tabs from aluminum cans, rubbing them like castanets. He walked for hours by himself playing with the tabs. He drank alcohol and used drugs, which often made him act crazy. People sometimes gave him drugs surreptitiously to watch his reaction. After not showing up for guard duty several times, and leaving without permission, Manny received a general discharge.

BILL: Unfortunately, the Manny that returned from Viet Nam was not the Manny that had gone over there. Manny never reintegrated into civilian life after the war. He'd meet someone and right away start talking about the war. On job interviews, he talked about the war. He just couldn't leave it behind; it overshadowed his life. Decades later Manny would cry when talking about his experiences there.

Manny started having flashbacks—moments when he was back in Viet Nam, at least in his mind. Sometimes he lost consciousness and ended up in strange places, unaware of how he had gotten there. At those times, Manny felt that he was in danger. Once, Lorraine found him lying on the bathroom floor crying. Manny had no idea how he got there. Another time, he wandered onto the beach during the middle of the night, and friends found him sleeping in his underwear.

Sometimes his strange behavior threatened others. He tried to jump out of a car traveling at sixty miles an hour. Another time a young woman approached him at a party unexpectedly, and it startled him so much that he spun around and nearly hit her before realizing what he had done.

He couldn't sleep at night and went out at all hours. One particular evening he was in the car with two acquaintances when they decided to hold up a convenience store. Manny was charged with armed robbery. Without legal representation, Manny pleaded guilty and was sentenced to eight years in prison. He started serving his sentence at the Bridgewater drug addiction center. While there, he acted crazy, jumping on tables and threatening fights. This got him transferred to Bridgewater State Hospital, where he spent eight months.[6]

BILL: I visited Manny at Bridgewater in 1974 and was shocked at the conditions. I remember the smell of urine and vacant faces. Manny was so doped up on Thorazine he didn't recognize me. He sat in his cell with a vacant stare. When he saw me he sized me up and said, "I could take him."

Manny was transferred back to the drug facility and soon learned that Lorraine, no longer able to deal with his behavior, had left him. He rummaged through a utility closet and mixed together lacquer, pine oil varnish, and ammonia, then drank the mixture. He broke a bottle and swallowed glass. Then he stripped a television wire, wrapped it around his waist, stood in the toilet bowl, and plugged it in.

Manny's suicide attempt got him transferred back to the psychiatric facility where he was diagnosed as a paranoid schizophrenic. Without having received proper treatment, Manny was paroled on Halloween night 1975. Riding back to Providence, Manny thought the people dressed up in Halloween costumes were Vietnamese villagers. He closed his eyes to block out the sight.

In Providence, Manny got a job working for his brother Charlie Babbitt, a local entrepreneur who owned a steak house and a strip club. When that didn't work out, he tried several other jobs, all of which ended unsuccessfully.

He met the daughter of a Providence police officer, Theresa Guertin, and the two lived together and had two children. Things were good for a while, but then Manny began acting increasingly bizarre. He would yell at Theresa for using black garbage bags, saying they reminded him of body bags. One night he ran around the house yelling, "The bombs are coming. The baby's going to get killed. We've got to get out of here." Theresa took the baby and left.

Manny began living on the streets, sleeping in a cardboard box in the doorway of Charlie's restaurant. He roamed the streets at night wearing fatigues and carrying a flashlight, as if patrolling for enemy combatants. The flashbacks continued.

Manny stopped showering. His hair was wild and his clothes torn and dirty. Friends of Charlie's told him that Manny was nuts, "a time bomb ready to go off."[7]

The bomb exploded in January 1980 when Manny assaulted a prostitute, stole money from her, and covered her with a wooden pallet as he had done with slain bodies in Viet Nam. Manny was prosecuted for rape but found not guilty by the jury, who questioned the prostitute's veracity. Although he was set free, a state psychiatrist warned that without treatment Manny's prognosis was guarded.

BILL: When Manny came to live with us, we did not know about the psychiatric prognosis. We set out to try to help him get a job. Linda took Manny on a number of job interviews, mostly restaurant jobs, but Manny was never successful. He couldn't seem to act appropriately. Sometimes she waited outside the interview room and listened as Manny answered the interviewers' questions by telling inappropriate and irrelevant tales of Viet Nam. Manny was not able to find work.

Besides his behavior during interviews, Manny was acting strangely in other ways. One day, I returned home early from work to find Manny riding my bicycle around the neighborhood wearing cutoff jeans over a pair of dress pants with a bright orange shirt. He had placed flattened aluminum beer cans in the bicycle spokes. When I asked him what he was doing, Manny said he was earning money by collecting cans. Another time, Manny, Linda, and my mother went to a bar to have a drink and Manny got on top of a pool table, sat in a lotus position, and started humming and chanting.

I noticed that there was something about him that was antisocial, like he was ready for war all the time, and he sometimes looked at people as if they were an enemy. One time when he was out with me, we ran into a friend of mine. Manny was rude and obnoxious, like he wanted to pick a fight. My friend told me, "If it weren't for you I would have laid this [beer bottle] out against the side of Manny's head."

By mid-December, Bill and Linda had come to the sober realization that Manny would probably not be able to live on his own.

BILL: Linda was the first one to realize that things weren't going well with Manny. I was busy at work and had gotten involved with a church group and was traveling out of town, so Linda was actually around Manny more than I was.

It was around Christmastime that we realized that Manny was not going to be able to fit in and be self-sufficient. Linda and I decided that it was not going to be enough to help him get set up in California; we were going to have to care for him ourselves—make sure he had a roof over his head, a bed to sleep in, and food and money to spend.

We knew he wasn't well but had no idea of the extent of his illness. It seemed like as long as Linda or I was around, everything was fine. We had heard about post-traumatic stress disorder, although not much was known about it then. We decided that after the holidays we would take him to the VA and get him some help. Unfortunately, we were already too late.

In the early morning hours of December 19, an elderly woman named Leah Schendel died of a heart attack after an intruder robbed her and beat her in her apartment at a senior citizens' complex on North Manor Drive in Sacramento. A neighbor discovered Mrs. Schendel's body on the bedroom floor covered from the waist up with a mattress. Her bathrobe and pajama top were pulled above her breasts. A teakettle was sitting on top of her pubic area, and a leather strap from a tefillin—a sacred object worn by Jewish men—was wrapped around her left ankle.

The furniture was in disarray; playing cards, broken dentures, and pieces of glass were lying on the living room floor. The television was turned on to channel 40. A pillow by her head was heavily soaked in blood. The house had been ransacked, but the only things missing were a few rolls of coins (Mrs. Schendel had recently returned from a trip to Las Vegas, where she had played the slot machines), two wristwatches, and a silver engraved cigarette lighter.

According to the pathologist, Mrs. Schendel died from a heart attack brought on by a severe beating. The wounds themselves were not fatal. The police suspected the intruder might have attempted to rape Mrs. Schendel, although experts later disputed this claim, and the evidence indicated that she had not been raped.

Late in the evening of the nineteenth, Mavis W., a woman who lived in the same vicinity as Mrs. Schendel, was returning home when she was grabbed from behind. The assailant demanded her car and then dragged her behind some bushes and struck her until she lost consciousness. Mavis was found by her daughter lying unconscious on the grass with her pants pulled down and the contents of her purse strewn across the lawn.

BILL: Right before Christmas, Linda called me at work and asked if I had given Manny any money. I said no. She said that Manny had money and he was giving the kids coins that he kept hidden under a rug.

I got home and started snooping around the house. I found a bunch of nickels in a Choo Choo piggy bank. I went into a closet in the room where Manny was staying and found an old leather jacket of Linda's that had a peace symbol on it. I picked it up and a cigarette lighter hit the ground.

I picked up the lighter and saw it was engraved with the initials L. S. That night I got up in the middle of the night because I couldn't sleep. I was shaving when I started to put together the pieces of the puzzle. Without even wiping off the shaving cream I rooted around in a pile of old papers and found the articles about the crime that happened in our neighborhood. I had the taste of fear in my mouth. The name of the lady was Leah Schendel, and the article said that she had just gotten back from a trip to Reno.

I went into the bedroom and got down on my knees near Linda and said, "Wake up." She said, "Oh my God, Bill, what is wrong?" I said, "I think Manny might have done something terrible." It was horrible. It was the longest morning that I have ever spent. Linda and I prayed.

The next morning, December 21, I called a friend of mine, Diamond Jim, who was a bail bondsman. I told him the story and my suspicions and asked if he could bail Manny out if I turned him in. He said, "No, Bill, this would be a capital case." [Bail is not available in capital cases.] I went over to his house to talk it over with him and called the police from there.

Turning Manny in to the police was one of the hardest things I have ever had to do. I had become involved in the civil rights movement and saw what some police were doing to civil rights and other political activists, and I had developed an intense mistrust of the police. But I decided that I couldn't live with myself if Manny did something that hurt someone else. When I called, I told them, "I think my brother Manny is involved [in Leah Schendel's death]. My brother is ill. He is not well. He is still a Marine in Viet Nam. He never did come home. The officer I spoke with told me, "We'll get him the help he needs, but he's gotta be off the street."

The police picked me up from Diamond Jim's house and brought me to my house and asked us to show them the evidence: the lighter, the nickels, the shoes he had worn [to check for footprints]. Manny wasn't home. I gave my wife instructions to get the children out of the house. Linda loaded them into our van and drove around for hours waiting until Manny had been arrested before returning home.

They took me downtown and interrogated me. I cried. They told me that I was doing the right thing and that Manny was going to get the help he needed. They brought me coffee and a bologna sandwich. I trusted them.

I volunteered to take them to find Manny. I told them I thought he might be at our sister Donna's house. I watched the four police officers and one prosecutor load up their guns. It was raining cats and dogs as we drove from downtown to south Sacramento. It was thirteen miles to Donna's place, but it seemed like it took us forever to get there. We got to the complex, and I told them I would go on up and bring Manny down. I said, "Don't kill my brother." I was worried about Manny getting shot during the arrest.

Manny was inside playing with Donna's two boys, making tents with chairs and sheets and blankets. Kids always liked Manny because he liked to play. I suggested to Manny that we go play some pool, and he came with me.

When we got outside, the police arrested him without incident. Manny had always had respect for authority. They asked me if I wanted to ride with him, but I said no because I couldn't get control of my emotions. I was crying and didn't want to upset Manny. I said to Manny, "Please forgive me." And he said, "You're forgiven." Even though I felt terrible about turning him in, I knew it was going to be better for him because he was going to get the help he needed.

I rode back to the station in a separate car. When we got there, the police put Manny in an interrogation room and asked if I would help get a confession. It never occurred to me to ask for a lawyer. They said to me, "It's not like he is going to get the death penalty. If he cooperates, he'll go to Atascadero or Napa [psychiatric hospitals]. I was so naïve, I believed them."

When I went in to speak with Manny, he was barefoot and shivering because the police had taken off his shoes and socks so that he couldn't use them to hurt himself. I asked an officer if he would get Manny a pair of socks. He said, "We're not supposed to do that," but then he found a pair. That was the only nice thing the police ever did for my brother.

They kept trying to get Manny to confess, but he kept saying that he didn't remember. He didn't deny it; he just said he didn't remember. I believed he was telling the truth. During the taped interview, Detective Terry Brown said, "You know you're not going to the gas chamber or anything like that."[8]

Contrary to Detective Brown's pronouncement, the State of California immediately sought the death penalty, which shocked Bill. "We thought he would be taken to a psychiatric hospital where he could not hurt himself or anyone else. I felt totally betrayed by them."

The court appointed attorney James Schenk to represent Manny. James was a tall, good-looking blond man with blue eyes who had an office across the street from the courthouse. James's appearance initially inspired confidence, which turned out to be misleading. Years after Manny's conviction, James would resign from the bar after being convicted of embezzling money from a client trust fund. Paralegals who worked for James would testify that he drank heavily during Manny's trial, sometimes as much as four double martinis at lunch.[9] The Babbitts would also later learn that Schenk had been sued by an African American employee for race discrimination.

BILL: Dealing with the criminal justice system was a nightmare. Initially I was impressed by James's appearance. He looked like one of those high-profile lawyers you would see on TV, and I thought that appearance was important. But as time went by, I lost all confidence in him. I gave him all kinds of information that he never followed up on. I couldn't see that he was doing much to help Manny.

I called the prosecutors and police, and after a while they stopped returning my calls. I kept wondering when we would get to the part where Manny got some help, but that never happened. When they needed me for something, they treated me like I was the best thing since popcorn. I felt that they respected me. They said that I had "done the right thing" by coming forward. But when they didn't need me, they ignored my requests. I tried to give them the benefit of the doubt—they're just doing their jobs, they aren't really out to kill my brother—but I was sadly mistaken. I kept telling Ma that everything would be okay, that Manny would get help. I just couldn't say to her, "Ma, they're going to try to kill your son, and I am the one who gave him to them."

·   ·   ·   ·

Manny's trial began in March 1982 before Superior Court Judge Joseph A. DeCristoforo. Deputy district attorney for Sacramento County C. T. "Kit" Cleland represented the state. During jury selection, Cleland preempted all the African Americans in the jury pool without objection from defense counsel. Not a single African American was picked to sit on the jury. (In criminal cases lawyers are able to have a certain number of jurors preempted, or removed from serving on the jury. While lawyers can preempt jurors for no particular reason, they cannot ask to have them removed because of their race.)

BILL: When I asked James about getting blacks on Manny's trial, Schenk told me that he didn't want any niggers on the jury. He didn't trust that they would come to court or understand the complexities of the trial. That didn't make sense to me, but I thought that I should trust him because he was the one with experience. But later on it became painfully obvious that Manny did not have a jury of his peers. Now I wish I had said something to him about it.

Leah's daughter, Hellen Park, and her two daughters, Kathie Rizzotti and Laura Thompson, attended the entire trial sitting conspicuously in the front row.

The state established that on December 1, 1980, Manny had spent the day at the Stix bar drinking beer and playing pool. Jeffrey Kato, an acquaintance of Manny's, testified that the two smoked a "sherm" (a marijuana cigarette laced with PCP) in his van sometime after 10:00 P.M.[10] He said Manny appeared to be acting normally when he left him.

Manny left the bar walking through dense fog back to Bill's house on Sixty-sixth Avenue. His regular route would have taken him by Leah Schendel's housing complex. The defense believed that when Manny reached a major intersection, the lights and noise, combined with the fog, reminded him of nighttime reinforcements landing on the airstrip at Khe Sanh. Manny lost consciousness, and when he regained it he was lying on a lawn next to a cigar box with "stuff" in it.

The defense tried to establish that Manny had a diminished mental capacity based on three theories: (1) Manny's childhood head injury in the bicycle accident caused organic brain damage; (2) Manny suffered from post-traumatic stress disorder (PTSD) as a result of being in combat; and (3) Manny suffered from psychomotor epilepsy, a condition that renders people unconscious of acts committed during a seizure. Two psychiatrists, Dr. Joan Blunt and Dr. David Axelrod, testified for the defense. Unfortunately, PTSD had only been officially recognized as a mental disorder in 1980. At the time of Manny's trial, many professionals were not familiar with the dissociative state that sometimes occurs when people with PTSD experience a flashback.[11]

BILL: I couldn't watch the trial because I was a witness, but I went to court every day and sat outside. First, the prosecution called me as a witness to establish that Manny had taken Mrs. Schendel's possessions. I was very scared. My mouth was dry and I was thirsty.

Later in the trial, the defense called me as a witness to testify about Manny's history of mental illness. During cross-examination, the prosecutor made hostile remarks, and if I couldn't come up with the answer he kept badgering me. I felt like I was being accused of doing something wrong.

The judge admonished him several times, "Let him finish," and all the time I'd be looking at Manny's lawyer and he would hunch his shoulders like he didn't know what I should do. I had to look to the judge for sympathy.

I sensed hostility in the courtroom coming from the jurors. I searched the jury looking for a face that seemed sympathetic and trying to figure out if they were listening to what I was saying, if they could understand our family's situation, but I felt like I was in a foreign land. I wanted the jurors to know that I was one of them, that I believe in the law. I believe that if somebody is dead, somebody else has to be accountable. But I felt like once I served the prosecutor's purpose he tossed me aside like old dirty rags.

The worst part was when the prosecutor used information that I had given him to argue for the death penalty. I had told him about a time when Manny was fourteen and he and some of his friends took my car out for a ride and then abandoned it when it ran out of gas. Manny didn't tell me he had done this, and I thought the car had been stolen until I saw it at a junkyard. Then Manny told me what he had done.

The prosecutor kept harping on this story as proof that Manny had a long criminal record going back before Viet Nam and that he had victimized his own brother. I didn't really see what a teenage boy going on a joy ride with his friends had to do with deciding whether to execute him many years later. But the defense attorney didn't object.

I wanted people to know that Manny had been a good kid. He cared about people. He chopped wood for old people and shoveled snow. He brought the old people food. He liked old people. Why would he pick on an elderly person? The state claimed he tried to rape Mrs. Schendel. If he attempted to rape a seventy-eight-year-old lady, why didn't he succeed? But the jury wasn't getting a good impression of Manny, because his lawyer was letting the prosecutor make him look like a monster.

I had turned in Manny and now was helping the state convict him, but my goal had always been to save him. At this point, I still believed that Manny would end up getting the help he needed, that the trial was just something that had to be gotten out of the way before Manny could get help. I kept telling my family that Manny would go to a hospital, maybe for a long time, but it would be a good hospital, not someplace like Bridgewater. But my mother and sisters and their families were sitting in the courtroom watching the trial, and it didn't look to them like the state was going to send Manny to a hospital. They kept coming to me for answers, and I didn't have any.

One thing that was very painful for me was that after I testified, the bailiff escorted me back to my car because the Schendels said they thought I would try to hurt them. The bailiffs watched me get in my car and waited until I drove away. I had seen the prosecution change the story of my brother's life around to make him look like a monster. Now the same thing was happening to me.

Rulings by Judge DeCristoforo stymied Manny's defense. Judge De-Cristoforo forbade the introduction of key pieces of defense evidence including records of Manny's hospitalization for his head injury, a volume of the combat history of Viet Nam describing battles that Manny fought in and mentioning Manny by name, testimony from Theresa recounting some of Manny's bizarre behavior while he lived in Providence, and evidence that a movie about Southeast Asia was playing on channel 40 at Leah's house the night of her death, which may have exaggerated Manny's flashback. The judge ruled the evidence irrelevant, claiming it would distract the jury.

In addition, the prosecutor mocked the defense's assertion that Manny suffered from mental illness, calling as a witness Dr. Lee Coleman, a psychiatrist, who expounded at length on his view that psychiatrists and psychologists had no business in the courtroom. Dr. Coleman stated that psychiatric and psychological diagnosis is unreliable and that doctors perform nothing more than guesswork and are no more able to evaluate human behavior than the average person. Coleman told the jury that they should give "no weight" to the expert opinions of the defense witnesses.[12]

During closing argument, the prosecutor made numerous references to Dr. Coleman's testimony, reiterating the weaknesses of the psychiatric profession and going so far as to say, "In a sense we have a social cancer in our community now, and it is this very process of allowing psychiatrists to come in and make their moral pronouncements disguised as medical opinion in the hopes of persuading jurors to let people off the hook . . . and . . . the way that social cancers are removed is [that] people like Lee Coleman have the courage to stand up and be heard."[13] James Schenk did not object to these remarks. The appellate court later ruled that the prosecutor's remarks "approached misconduct," and noted "that the courtroom was not the proper forum to challenge the propriety of this system." However, the court held that any error did not prejudice the defendant's case.[14]

Despite the wealth of evidence of Manny's long-term psychiatric problems, the jury was not persuaded. After deliberating for three hours, the jury found Manny guilty on April 20, 1982.

The next stage of the proceeding was to determine whether Manny was sane. A finding that he was insane would have meant treatment in a psychiatric hospital instead of jail. James Schenk would later acknowledge that he was unsure how to defend Manny in the sanity phase or sentencing phase of the trial. He said his strategy was "to throw mud on the wall and hope some of it would stick where I threw it."[15]

The jury found Manny sane on May 8, then moved to the final phase of the trial, the sentencing phase, where they would decide whether to impose the death penalty. During closing argument, James argued for sparing Manny's life. He asked rhetorically, "Will Manny's death help?" Leah's daughter and granddaughters enthusiastically nodded their heads for the jury to see. The trial concluded on May 14, and Bill and Leah's family were in the courtroom to hear the verdict.

The judge asked the jury foreman, William Hampton, to pass the verdict to the court clerk to announce. When the clerk announced that the jury had decided to impose the death penalty, Laura Thompson said, "Yes," and happily squeezed the hands of family members. Bill, sick with shame, felt like a traitor for turning his brother over to the executioners.[16]

Outside the courtroom after the judge announced that Manny "shall suffer the penalty of death," Bill angrily lashed out at one of the granddaughters, "Show me one instance where a white man has gone to the gas chamber for killing a black man." The granddaughter said, "I don't view him as being black. I view him as a human being who committed a murder . . . a brutal murder."[17] Bill told her that she was "ghoulish," but then immediately regretted it.

BILL: The state didn't give a rat's ass about Manny's background. To them, he was a creep and a scumbag. People in the media had even called him that.

The prosecutor had asked me all kinds of questions about Manny's background, but somehow he only ended up using the bad stuff. They used the story about the joyride to tell everybody in California that I had been victimized by Manny. They didn't care who they were going to hurt. Of course, they didn't use any of the stories about all the ways that

Manny did nice things for old people. They used my words to sentence my brother to death.

There were two other capital cases going on at the same time as Manny's. One guy kidnapped two women, raped them both, and killed one outright and left the other for dead, throwing them into a hole and burying them with rocks. One of them dug herself out and got a ride back to town, naked. The other guy had also kidnapped a woman and shot her in the hip, and she bled to death in the trunk of a car.

I had spent long hours outside the courtroom and had gotten to be friendly with some of the reporters. The reporters were taking bets about who was going to get what penalty. They bet that these two guys, who had both killed more than one person, would get death, and that Manny would get life in prison. But it didn't turn out that way.

In Manny's case, there was no evidence that it was premeditated murder. He didn't plan to go into Leah's house. Nobody can honestly tell me that this was a more heinous crime. It took quite an effort on the part of the state to paint Manny as a monster, but they succeeded.

I felt that I had failed my family. Manny had been my responsibility. I had wanted to help him get his life together and protect him. Instead, I wasn't around when he needed me and when he killed Leah Schendel, I turned him in, thinking it would help him get the help he needed. As it turned out, I helped put him on death row.

Most of my family did not blame me—Manny never did, neither did my mother or siblings—but I constantly asked myself what more I could have done to help Manny or what more I should have done to prevent the crime from ever happening.

It didn't help that I was surrounded at work with people hassling me about Manny. Co-workers said things like "They ought to take everyone on death row out into the yard and put a bullet in their head. That would save the state a lot of money." I'd complain to my supervisor, who'd just say that everybody had a right to express their opinion.

•   •   •   •

Bill determined that he was going to do everything possible to save Manny's life. He believed that Manny might win his case on appeal or might succeed at getting clemency.

Manny's luck started to improve when the Sacramento office of the state public defender's office got involved in his case. The entire staff took an interest in it. Barry Melton, the "Fish" from Country Joe and the Fish, organized a benefit reunion concert to raise money for Manny's case. Jessica McQuire thoroughly researched Manny's life, including taking her family on vacation to the Cape Verde Islands to better understand Manny's family heritage. Jesse Morris Jr. coached Bill on how to deal with the media. Wilbur Haines provided all-round support, and Ellen Eggars reached out to Vietnam veterans.

One veteran she contacted was Ernie Spencer, who had written a book called *Welcome to Viet Nam Macho Man* and edited a newsletter for Khe Sanh veterans. Ernie knew Charles "Chuck" Patterson, another Khe Sanh veteran and managing partner of one of California's largest and most conservative law firms, Pillsbury, Madison, and Sutro. Chuck had been hired as a special prosecutor to investigate Bill Clinton in the Whitewater case and had authored the famous Pillsbury Report that cleared the president of any wrongdoing. Chuck usually fetched large fees for his services but agreed to work on Manny's case pro bono. They also brought on board Gregory Pipes, a highly decorated military officer.

Chuck strongly identified with Manny. He, too, had experienced post-traumatic stress. When he returned from Viet Nam, Chuck found that nobody wanted to talk to him about it. "Those who favored the war wanted to hear about what a good job the men were doing over there; those who were against it didn't want to talk at all."[18]

Chuck put away his medals and went on to become a successful attorney, but privately he suffered. Sometimes he heard helicopters or smelled napalm when nobody else did. He burst into tears for no reason. He entered therapy and was diagnosed with post-traumatic stress disorder. He stayed in therapy for eleven years. "Compared to Manny Babbitt," Chuck said, "I had a super goddamned life and childhood. But it [Viet Nam] got to me. It certainly hit me hard. You pour hot water into a coffee cup, it'll stay in there. But if that cup's got a crack in it, or a ding, or a flaw, then it's gonna break, and all the hot water's gonna spill out. And that's what happened to Manny Babbitt."[19]

BILL: Chuck was able to understand Manny in a way that James never could. He pointed out to us a lot of additional information that could have been brought up at trial about post-traumatic stress disorder. In fairness to James Schenk, PTSD was very new at the time of Manny's trial. But James should have done more to explain Manny's behavior to the jurors. He could have brought in veterans to testify about what the war had done to them.

The last thing that Manny remembered about that evening was seeing a bright light, which was probably coming from passing cars. Chuck thinks that when Manny crossed the major intersection he had a flashback that put him into a dissociative state. When he saw the vehicles coming at him, he thought it was an aircraft carrier landing at Khe Sanh. When planes landed at Khe Sanh, the enemy would lob shells—Manny had seen C-130 cargo planes full of troops get hit while they were coming in for a landing.

So when Manny saw what he thought was a plane landing, he took off running and ended up in Leah Schendel's house. She probably yelled at him, so he thinks there is an enemy in his bunker. He attacks her, but then tags and covers her body.

Covering Leah Schendel's body with a teakettle and a mattress made sense to Manny. A Marine would never leave a fallen comrade uncovered and unidentified. Tying the leather strap to her ankle is another thing Marines did—they tied dog tags to the boots for identification. Also, Marines took personal possessions of their comrades for safekeeping or took small items from the enemy as souvenirs.

Frankly, Manny's behavior only makes sense in the context of Viet Nam. Why else would a cold-blooded killer act so strangely?

Although they worked tirelessly on Manny's appeals, his new attorneys believed that their best chance to save Manny's life was through clemency. Governor Gray Davis was also a Viet Nam veteran and at the beginning of his term had made promises to help veterans. Maybe he would help Manny.

Chuck and his firm, along with Jessica and Ellen and other lawyers at the public defender's office, organized a sophisticated clemency campaign that included a public relations effort organized by renowned publicist Lee Housekeeper of San Francisco, the production of a high-quality clemency video, organizing public rallies and concerts, and a petition drive targeting veterans.

Another service that Chuck performed was filling out the necessary paperwork for Manny to receive the Purple Heart, a medal awarded to servicemen killed or wounded in the line of duty. On March 20, 1998, Marine

Corps officers performed a small ceremony in a private boardroom next to the warden's office at San Quentin. Bill and his mother attended along with four Marines who had served with Manny at Khe Sanh, including Lynn Dornan, who credited Manny with saving his life during that campaign.

No longer the young man who had entered San Quentin, Manny had acquired the nickname "Bear" because of his massive body, bulked up from weight lifting. People considered Manny more of a teddy bear because of his serene personality and friendly face, with its graying mustache and soulful eyes. Four correctional officers escorted a handcuffed and shackled Manny to the ceremony. As the sergeant major pinned the shiny purple metal on his freshly pressed blue prison uniform, Manny tried to salute him, but because the guards refused to unshackle him, Manny bowed his large body to touch his forehead to his shackled hands. Josephine wrapped her thin arms around her son and said, "I'm so proud of you."[20]

> BILL: After the ceremony, they gave my mother the Purple Heart. She opened up the case and the medal fell out and hit the ground and it chipped the heart. The medal itself is purple; it must have hit right on the roundness, and it put a little ding, a little scufflike mark. The Purple Heart got a purple heart, so to speak. My mother picked it up and said, "Maybe that purple heart needed to be scratched."
>
> If you go to my mother's house, she has pictures of four Marines on her wall—Manny, Stevie, and two nephews. And she has pictures of me and her brother, the two Navy men. And she has that medal on display for everyone to see.

When news of this award reached the Schendels, they contacted Senator Dianne Feinstein (D-CA) to complain. In May, the senator introduced the Military Honors Preservation Act, a bill to prevent members of the armed forces from entering a prison to present medals to persons serving time for violent felonies. Speaking about her bill on the floor of the Senate, Senator Feinstein said, "For Mrs. Schendel's family, this medal ceremony was a slap in the face."[21]

In spite of the fact that the defense team had refused to allow press to cover the secret ceremony, the Schendels felt that the ceremony was merely a ploy by defense lawyers to generate sympathy for Manny in their efforts to save his life.[22]

BILL: When the Schendel family heard about Manny receiving the Purple Heart, they were very, very angry. They thought Manny didn't deserve anything like that. They couldn't take away his medal, but they wanted to make sure Manny was not afforded other military awards.

Senator Feinstein may as well have called it the "Keep Manny Babbitt from getting a medal bill." Then she made her statement about how Manny Babbitt getting the Purple Heart was like a slap in the face to the Schendel family. What about the fact that the Babbitts felt like we got a big slap in the face because Manny had had to wait decades for something he had earned long ago? What about the fact that he risked his life for his fellow Marines and was hauled out on a pile of dead bodies and then went back to Viet Nam for another tour? Manny had been dealt too many cards from the bottom of the deck; a medal was the least that the government could do for him.

Where were Senator Feinstein and others when Manny was walking the streets of Providence as a crouched figure playing Viet Nam at night? Where were they when he was living in cardboard boxes in doorways, like so many old, gray, tired-looking men in their fifties, casualties of Viet Nam? I had supported Dianne Feinstein for years, ever since she first got involved in California politics. I don't vote for her anymore.

Additional help came from another quarter. David Kaczynski (the brother of Ted Kaczynski, "the Unabomber"), executive director of New Yorkers against the Death Penalty, made a public statement in support of Manny Babbitt and criticized the role of race in the criminal justice system. Like Bill, David had made the painful choice of turning in his brother, whose campaign of letter bombs over nearly twenty years killed three people and injured twenty-eight others. And the government had initially sought the death penalty against Ted, as it had against Manny. However, the ultimate resolutions of the cases differed greatly, as David wrote in an article to the *Sacramento Bee:*

Whereas I was proclaimed a "hero" by Robert Cleary, who prosecuted my brother's case, Bill Babbitt was forced to testify in court against his brother, and his brother's prosecutor took advantage of the opportunity to make Bill himself look bad so that the jury would not sympathize with him. Whereas my brother was sentenced to life in prison without the possibility of parole, Bill's brother, who is black, was sentenced to death at the recommendation of an all-white jury. Evidently the justice system does not work the same for everyone.[23]

Manny's lawyers arranged joint speaking engagements for Bill and David. They appeared together on several national programs including *The Today Show, Sally Jesse Raphael, The John Walsh Show,* and *Good Morning America.* They spoke together at a rally on April 22, 1999, attended primarily by African American activists. Alice Huffman, former president of the Black American Political Association of California, said, "Manny Babbitt's death sentence was determined by the color of his skin. The conviction of a black man for murdering a white woman by an all-white jury is racist."[24]

Manny's case received national and international attention, but the television coverage abruptly ended on April 20.

BILL: David and I had gone to New York together to be on a talk show. We had taken our wives with us. When we got to the green room, the producer told us that the host was sick and had to cancel.

David knew Mike Wallace pretty well and got us a meeting with him at the CBS studio. He is a very compassionate man. He was familiar with Manny's case and seemed to genuinely want to do something to help. Then he gets a phone call from his secretary telling Mike to check on the wire. He turns on his computer, and we see the pictures coming from Columbine. Mike says, "There's the story now." At that point, it would be difficult to get national coverage for anything besides Columbine. However, Mike offered to call Governor Davis on Manny's behalf.

David was an incredible support to me. He was one of the few people who understood how hard it was for me to turn in my brother. We both felt a responsibility to society to prevent further violence, but we also wanted help for our brothers. We both felt betrayed when the death penalty was pursued.

David knows what it is like to have your entire family history paraded out for public consumption. Both of us come from proud immigrant families whose parents worked hard to make better lives for their children. To have a child end up on death row is a terrible tragedy.

But the contrast between the two cases is stark. Ted killed three people and injured many others and is serving a life sentence, Manny beat up one woman who died from a heart attack and was sentenced to death. Race plays a role in these things. Everybody who has their eyes open knows that.

•   •   •   •

On April 26, 1999, the Board of Prison Terms was scheduled to hear Manny's petition for clemency. If granted, Manny's sentence would be commuted from death to life in prison. Governor Gray Davis would ultimately make the clemency decision, but he would rely on the board's recommendation.

Before the hearing, the Babbitt family sent a letter of apology to the Schendels. They had wanted to apologize for years but had been advised by Manny's lawyers not to make contact. In April 1999, the family wrote to the Schendels through Leah's granddaughter Laura Thompson.

Dear Mrs. Thompson and Schendel Family,
On behalf of the entire Babbitt family, please let us convey our pro-found sorrow for the tragic and unexpected loss of your dear grand-mother, Leah Schendel. We know words will never bring your grand-mother back, however, let us express our deepest apologies from the bottom of our hearts to the depths of our souls, we feel the pain and share the sorrow.

We were precluded earlier by the suggestion of trial attorneys from contacting you. Also, it was awkward to speak or write to you in the past and it will become more awkward in the future, so we write this now.

We fully know your family was victimized by this crime but we also want you to know we tried to do everything possible to atone by turn-ing in Manuel to the police.

Please accept our deepest apology on behalf of the entire Babbitt family. The deep remorse my family feels is joined by Manuel.

May God bless both of our families.
Bill and Linda Babbitt and the Babbitt Family

Chuck, Jessica, and Ellen had been preparing for two years for this day and had garnered significant support from some unlikely quarters: movie stars, veterans, former jurors, a prominent death penalty prosecutor, Death Penalty Focus, Murder Victims' Families for Reconciliation, and civil rights organizations. Furthermore, much more was understood about post-traumatic stress disorder in 1999 than in 1982, at the time of Manny's trial, a fact that supported clemency. Most of the major California papers had editorialized in favor of it.[25]

The day before the hearing, Chuck delivered petitions signed by several thousand veterans to Governor Gray Davis.[26] Writers Tobias Wolff, Robert Stone, Michael Herr, and Yusef Komunyakaa, all of whom served or worked in Viet Nam, wrote to Davis in support of clemency.

Bill walked into a packed hearing room with about two hundred observers. Clemency supporters wore tiny framed photographs of Manny in his uniform. Opponents wore buttons with an image of Leah smiling during a family photo. Manny did not attend.

BILL: I felt tremendous pressure to save my brother's life. I believed that we had a good shot at clemency, but a positive recommendation from the board was extremely important. I had to make the board understand how unfair it was to execute my brother.

When I walked into the hearing room, most everyone had already sat down. I saw Laura Thompson and her uncle, Leah's brother, Aaron Weinberg. Laura came over to me. At the time of the trial she had been a young college student; now she was a mature woman with silver in her hair.

Of course, I'm also a lot older and fatter. I have fewer teeth, walk with a limp, and have a big stomach. I'm a grandfather now. Laura said to me, "I want you to know it's not about you. We are separating you from Manny. We are glad for what you did." I said to her, "I must tell you this. Your family can separate me from Manny, but my family is not going to separate your dear grandmother from Manny. We feel your grandmother's demise was the result of the effect of the time when Manny was at war."

Aaron joined us and held out his hand to me. I grabbed his hand— and I swear I'm not going to tell you no tales—and I kissed the back of his hand. I wanted to really show him that my family did not hate them, even though they were calling for Manny's murder. He had tears in his eyes.

Since Manny had filed the petition for clemency, his witnesses spoke first. Corporal Lynn Dornan testified. He had written a letter to the governor:

Dear Governor Davis:

My name is Lynn W. Dornan and in the spring of 1968, I was a corporal in the United States Marines Corp, at Khe Sanh, Viet Nam, with Alpha Company's 9th Motor Transport Battalion. I met a fellow marine at Khe Sanh, near the gate along Route 9, where we were staging trucks for a convoy back to Dong Ha. That fellow marine was Manny Babbitt. He and his crew were attending to their Ontos combat vehicles, and I had walked over to talk, to see if they knew of a friend of mine who was assigned to 3rd Anti Tanks.

We spoke for about twenty minutes, standing next to the Ontos. As we talked Manny heard the incoming NVA artillery and yelled for everyone to get down, but I was slow to react, so he grabbed me and threw me to the ground. The shells hit within seconds and were close, within 100 yards. You could feel the concussion and hear the shrapnel and debris fly over our heads as we lay on the ground. We were lying out in the open road and Manny said there was a trench line just 25 feet away that would give us better cover.

I wasn't as sure as he that we should try to make it. Manny said, "After the next barrage we'll make our move." The next assault came in a matter of seconds, but this time much closer. Manny yelled, "OK, let's go!" But when I hesitated, he grabbed my flack jacket and pushed me up the road yelling, "Go!" As I ran along the road, Manny pushed me into the trench line just as the next rounds of artillery came in, hitting the ground where we had just been. We spent the next twenty minutes in the trench, as the shelling continued.

I never thought you could fit your whole body under a flack jacket and helmet, but you can if you are scared enough. I can remember lying there, the fear so great that small unrelated memories would flash in and out of my mind like still pictures of my past. This was the only time, in my whole tour in Viet Nam, that I accepted the fact that I was going to die. For some strange reason it seemed to give me peace.

When the shelling stopped you could hear marines calling out for corpsmen; they had been hit. As we left the trench, Manny looked at me, smiled, and said, "That was close." He went back to work checking his Ontos and I went to my truck. We never spoke again after that day, but I have never forgotten him, his name or his face, in all these years. I know that if it had not been for Manuel Babbitt, I would have been killed that day.

Instead, I came home to a loving, supportive family, became a police officer, had three wonderful children, and lived a productive life. Sadly, not all of us did. Who can ever know, ever predict how each of us will be affected by the horrors of war, and the angst that many Viet Nam veterans felt. Each of us deals with it still, in his or her own way. Perhaps I was the lucky one in more ways than the obvious. I had the retreat of my family and a job with fellows who understood and knew. But many of my brother veterans were lost in their own haunting punishment and subsequent self-medication. It was the only way they knew.

You must understand why an honorably retired police officer would ask that you show mercy and not execute Manual Babbitt, commuting his sentence to life in prison without the possibility of parole. For my own part, I have seen the victims and aggressors of this world and know that Manuel Babbitt is not a one-dimensional villain. He was a man of worth and merit; a young 19 year old who risked his own life to save another human being, a stranger to him.

My deepest sympathy and condolences go out to Leah Schendel's family and I hope in time that they can forgive and find peace, as we all must.

Respectfully yours,

Lynn Warner Dornan[27]

Gary Dahlheimer, another Khe Sanh veteran, told the board that he still suffered from post-traumatic stress disorder. He said, "I smell the blood in my nose every day, all of the rotten, stinking smells." He explained that he could not sleep in the same bed with his wife because he had nearly killed her while having nightmares in which he was fighting the enemy.[28]

Two of the jurors who served on the jury that sentenced Manny to death, Mary Ann McCollum and Lyle H. Iverson, asked for clemency, saying that they had not gotten a full picture of the post-traumatic stress syndrome at trial. Mary Ann said, "I think taking a life in this case is unjust because we didn't have the whole picture. There was information available that could have given a fuller picture of this man. I had no idea of the extent of the war in his background. It was not adequately presented. . . . I sincerely believe that if the jury had heard all of these facts about Mr. Babbitt, we would have concluded that there were mitigating factors that justified a sentence of life with-out parole rather than death."[29] Lyle said that Babbitt's service was only men-tioned; it was not elaborated on or made a key argument in his defense. "I know that I certainly would not have voted for the death penalty had I been presented with this evidence."[30]

Brian Engdahl, a psychologist at the Veterans Administration, testified for clemency:

> In times past, it was easier for critics to dismiss flashbacks. We know a whole lot more now. We have actually looked at activity in people's brains when they experience flashbacks. You lose the sense that it is here and now, and you are utterly convinced it is back there and then. It's a psychotic-like state in which you would not recognize that the person standing in front of you is not an enemy soldier.[31]

The head of the local NAACP wrote an editorial in support of clemency, saying, "If you can't give Manny clemency, give Bill and his family clemency."

Florida prosecutor Harry Shorstein, who led his state in putting the most people on death row, told the board that executing Manny "would be wrong." In comments after the hearing he told reporters, "In my thirty-four years' experience, this is the most compelling case for life in prison I've ever seen."[32]

Pro-death-penalty victims' rights advocates Collene Campbell and Scott Henderson supported Manny's clemency petition. "I'm certainly not op-posed to the death penalty, but I have a lot of compassion for a man [Bill Bab-bitt] who did the right thing," said Campbell. "He certainly was also a victim in this crime. And I don't want him to carry the guilt."[33]

Manny's children attended the hearing. His son, Manuel Babbitt Jr., spoke tearfully, pleading for his father's life. His twenty-year-old pregnant daugh-ter, Desiree, sat clutching a stuffed white rabbit.[34]

Bill testified about how difficult it was for him to turn in his brother and how he did so because he believed Manny would be helped. "I'm up here shaking like a leaf because while I'm running out of patience for justice, my brother is running out of time for his life. I'm pleading, I'm pleading, please spare my brother's life."[35]

Despite the warm interaction with Bill before the hearing, members of Leah's family spoke firmly against clemency, denouncing Manny's claim of post-traumatic stress disorder. Aaron Weinberg told the board that Manny was not reacting as if he were in Viet Nam but was "out to rob and got caught. I don't have a sister anymore. When I want to see my sister I've got to go to the cemetery."[36]

The prosecutor told the board that the claim that Babbitt was suffering from a combat-induced flashback on the night of the slaying was "wishful thinking based on psychiatric guesswork."[37]

John Rizzotti, Leah's great-grandson, testified. "His career as a criminal began long before the war in Viet Nam did. . . . Leah Schendel did not die for her country, nor should she be made out to be a casualty of war. This so-called man was then and is today someone who deserves to die. . . . Babbitt is not a national hero. . . . He is a man who murdered a grandmother. He deserves to die."[38]

BILL: It was hard to listen to the Schendels advocate for Manny's execution. Aaron said, "Where was Bill Babbitt when his brother was killing my sister?" When he said that, you could hear a gasp in the room. The parole board members shuffled in their seats and looked bored. The chairperson admonished him.

It seemed like the Schendels could only see Manny as the person who had done something horrible to their grandmother and could not see that there were other aspects of Manny. For them, Leah's death had wiped away any good that Manny did before or after that night.

I blame the government for the hard feelings the Schendels have towards my family. It was almost like the Schendels were doing what was expected of them. I see it as the result of the government's campaign to kill Manny. They were promised closure, but to get it they had to bring out the worst in themselves—the hate and revenge. The government encouraged them to cry out for murder.

After the hearing, Manny's supporters waited on pins and needles for the governor's decision. Manny, however, continued with his life, spending his days the way he had during his seventeen years in prison—corresponding with family and friends and the hundreds of supporters who had written letters (Manny taught himself to read and write while he was in prison), writing letters to school kids emphasizing the importance of not getting involved in crime, shining other inmates' shoes, reading and writing poetry, and cooking meals for the guards and other inmates. (Manny had a hotplate in his cell and was renowned as an excellent cook. Although it was against prison regulations, the guards made an exception in his case.)

At the advice of his attorneys and family members, Manny consented to press interviews. He told reporters that he hoped his death (if he didn't get clemency) would give Mrs. Schendel's family the peace they sought. He said, "I've never begged for my life—it's just a life. For the time I have been on this planet it hasn't been a very happy situation."[39] He also said that he would respect whatever decision the governor made. "Whatever he decides, he can decide and forget about it the next day. I hate it when people take that road of pity and sorrow. I'm not going down that road. I'm not going to freak out. I'm not going to scratch the floor when I'm dragged away. My last words will probably be, 'Strap me down and leave me alone.'"[40]

Manny also expressed the pain and sorrow he felt for what he had done saying that he cried nightly for the Schendel family during and after the trial. "I know how sad and nerve-racking it was for them to go through this. I've requested to meet and talk with them. I've had sleepless nights. How many times can a person say he's sorry and wish that it reaches the ears that want to hear it? I'm very, very sorry." He praised Laura Thompson for the courage and strength she had shown and "for not carrying any hatred toward my family for something I have done."[41]

Last, Manny praised his brother for turning him in. "I feel he did the exact thing I would have done if the tables were turned. I know his sense of decency transcends his relationship to me. He may have saved many lives by turning me in."[42]

On April 26, the board unanimously recommended denying clemency. By statute, all clemency recommendations are secret, but word of the board's recommendation was leaked to the press before Governor Davis announced his decision. In his fifteen-page written opinion, he stated:

Honorable service to the United States in the United States Marine Corps and the other military branches is service to the country and worthy of the highest commendation. However, Mr. Babbitt's service in the Marine Corps does not justify nor excuse the brutal killing of a defenseless seventy-eight-year-old woman. We pay high homage and deep respect to those servicemen who have served honorably, to those who have sacrificed their lives and others who have suffered life threatening and permanent war wounds for our country.

Our society properly recognizes veterans' sacrifice for their country with parades, monuments, G.I. education benefits, mortgage assistance, lifelong medical attention for the injured and employment return rights. We expect our veterans to act honorably both in war and upon their return home. In any event, even the most honorable military service would not excuse the savage beating to death of an innocent and defenseless grandmother.[43]

Manny accepted the news calmly. He spent his last days saying good-bye to family and friends in person and on the phone. He began a fast. He told a San Francisco Chronicle reporter, "I'm not bitter. I have no fear of going. I've made my peace, and I hope it reaches the hearts of those who seek to take my life. God bless you. Semper Fi."[44]

Although Manny had made his peace, his lawyers were not ready to give up. New evidence about James Schenk's performance was revealed, including the fact that he had told Manny not to testify at his trial because he was "too ignorant and incoherent to take the stand and tell the jury [his] story." Two of Schenk's former law clerks came forward to say that he drank heavily during Manny's trial and that they believed that his drinking had affected his performance. Manny's lawyers also learned that Schenk's former secretary Pam Doli had filed a discrimination complaint against him because of his frequent use of racial slurs. Manny's lawyers used this new evidence to try to open up Manny's case again. Leah's son, Don Schendel, blasted Manny's lawyers for "raising the race card."[45]

Manny's execution date had been set for midnight, May 4, 1999, one minute after his fiftieth birthday. The Schendels wanted to make sure that Manny was not accorded any other military honors, so they publicly spoke out against his being buried in Arlington Cemetery.

BILL: Newspaper stories started to come out about how Manny shouldn't be buried in Arlington. I don't know if it's true, but I heard that Benedict Arnold was buried in Arlington. If there is room for him, there is room for Manny. Manny was not a traitor to his country—it was a traitor to him.

Several days before the execution, Bill and Linda went to San Francisco in order to spend as much time as possible with Manny at San Quentin, located in an unusually idyllic coastal setting in a quaint historic district.

Bill and Linda Babbitt. Provided with permission of the family.

They stayed at the home of Lee Housekeeper, with whom they had become friends. Bill, Linda, and Paula all started fasting before the execution to atone for their part in the tragedy. Bill consumed nothing but water for five days.

BILL: The day before Manny's execution, which also happened to be his birthday, the prison authorities moved him from his regular cell on death row to a special holding cell near the death chamber. I spent the day coordinating visits with my sister Donna. He must have had about fifty visitors that day. I had a short visit with him, not as much time as I would have liked, but I wanted everyone to have a chance to say good-bye. During that visit, Manny told me that he wanted me to take the high road. He asked me not to do or say anything to disrespect the Schendel family. And he told me that he did not want me to beg for his life.

Manny sat in the visiting area shackled at the waist and handcuffed. My mother went in for a visit, and before they parted for the last time, Manny wanted to hug and kiss his mother good-bye. Manny always liked to cup Mom's face when he kissed her, but he couldn't do that with handcuffs on. I asked the sergeant if they would unlock Manny, but they said they couldn't do that. I thought, "This monster isn't going to be with you much longer. Can't you let him kiss his mother good-bye?" Some of the other visitors started to protest, but Manny asked them not to give the guards a hard time.

One of his last visitors was an old girlfriend, Patty, who Manny had become reacquainted with through his former fifth-grade teacher, Beverly Lopes. Patty went to California to spend Manny's last thirty days with him. Patty was in a wheelchair because she had lost her legs and hands from diabetes. During one of their last visits, she somehow managed to scoot up in the wheelchair and reached out to kiss Manny with her arms with no hands. Manny leaned over towards her, also not being able to use his arms or hands because he was shackled, but somehow they managed to touch each other. I thought that was one of the most poignant things I had ever seen in my life. It was like God just wanted to show me what happens when there is love.

They both needed somebody. They were torn bodies. He had been young and handsome and she had been pretty, but they both had their misfortunes. At least Manny got a little shot of love before he died.

That night I couldn't sleep, so I spent a lot of time looking out at the city. Lee's house was on a hill and had a spectacular view of the city and the Bay Bridge. The city was all lit up. I felt blessed because so many people were helping Manny and showing our family so much love. It was like the city was all lit up for Manny.

The next night, Lee arranged for his driver to take me to the North Gate of San Quentin to a back entrance, where I met Chuck Patterson. The execution was scheduled for 12:01 A.M., but we got there several hours ahead of time. There were people outside the East Gate protesting, including my eighty-year-old mom, who was wrapped in a large wool blanket to stay warm.

The prison guards searched us and took our wedding rings and wristwatches and made us take off our shoes, and we sat down waiting to enter the death chamber. A person from San Quentin came and told us what to expect. They loaded us onto a white van and drove us to a part of San Quentin I had never seen before. When we arrived and started unloading, I saw the Schendel family being unloaded from another white van.

Twelve correctional officers were standing at parade rest with their arms behind their backs. I had to walk between them. I remembered Manny's words about taking the high road, so I looked at each and every officer. I wanted them to know I wasn't bitter and I had seen tears in

told reporters: "I know what he went through. I woke up today and I knew I had to go out of respect. No matter what he did, we're brother Marines and brother post-traumatic stress syndrome survivors."[49]

Laura Thompson issued a statement on behalf of the Schendel family:

Crime is not pleasant. We cannot expect that justice will always be pleasant. Our hearts and prayers go out to the Babbitt family. We know how much they have suffered. Our family has suffered for eighteen years.

It is a terrible thing when two good families are thrown on the opposite sides of such a devastating issue. We hope and pray that they will find the way to heal their wounds as we strive to heal our own.[50]

BILL: Manny had forgone his traditional last meal. He had fasted three days before his execution and requested that $50 meal money be donated to the hungry, but the prison wouldn't do it. Instead, supporters donated money in Manny's name, and we donated the money to Loaves and Fishes in Sacramento. A year after Manny's death, they held a dinner for four hundred homeless people where we served food. Many of them came up to me and shook my hand and told me they had served in Viet Nam. A lot of people society considers bums risked their lives for this country.

A memorial service was held the next day. About three hundred people crowded Sacramento's largest Catholic church. Two of Manny's attorneys, lead defense attorney Jessica McQuire and her public defender colleague Musawwir Spiegel, gave moving eulogies about Manny, and Manny's children spoke.

BILL: People from Death Penalty Focus and the state public defender's office arranged for my brother's body to be taken to Sacramento to a black funeral parlor. The lady who works in the parlor is a friend of my wife. I later learned that the funeral director's wife died the day Manny's body was brought in, but he still serviced it anyway.

I was so grateful to the Catholic Church for giving my brother a funeral because my mother is still Catholic. The priest's remarks were kind and sympathetic. It was a very good service. The news media was across the street, and several of my nephews were getting upset because they didn't want the funeral covered. I told them that it was good for people to see what had happened. I told them if they got a chance to talk to reporters they should, but that they should always take the high road because the world is watching us as a family to see how we react to all of this.

Desiree did a beautiful job speaking. Manny's children had been estranged from their dad, but they made an effort to get to know him before he died. Manny Babbitt Jr. didn't want to come out to California. He said that he hated Manny. But he finally made up his mind that he was going to come, and when he did he fell in love with his dad. He only had a month or so to know his dad. He cried all the time. Now he wanted his dad and he wished that he had communicated with his dad and come and seen him more while he was living. I was so proud that he came out and got to know his dad.

The day after Mother's Day, the family buried Manny in Wareham at St. Patrick's Cemetery at a site donated by Beverly Lopes. The cemetery is on the Agawam River, not far from the clam flats where Manny played as a boy. In the background stood the Tremont factory, which made cannonballs for the Continental Army during the Revolutionary War.

Nearby, buried in that same cemetery, were Manny's father, his father's father—who died on the day Manny was born—and other family members going back a century. Manny was buried in a Marine Corps uniform that had been donated by a veteran who had offered it for Manny's burial. The full military service was conducted by a Cape Verdean veterans' group and included a flag-draped coffin, a rifle salute, and a bugler playing "Taps."

Chuck Patterson spoke. Later, he eulogized Manny in an article for *California Law Magazine:*

> When I came into the case, I had some doubts about the man I was going to represent. I had been involved in murder cases before, as both a prosecutor and defense counsel. I knew that the pleadings I had read, the products of the conventions of advocacy, were rarely indicative of the person.
>
> None of that prepared me for what I found when I met "this" man. No one had him right. I was first aware that something was different when the guard at the visitors' gate at San Quentin asked me if I was "Babbitt's new lawyer." When I said I was, he said, "I hope you can help him. He's one of the good guys."

He would prove to be right.

Manny Babbitt was a good man, a decent man who contributed to the death of another human being without intent to kill, without pre-meditation. Yet he was executed with a cold and deliberate intent to kill. . . .

Throughout Manny's case, people would characterize a judge as pro– or anti–death penalty and the "luck of the draw" was an oft-mentioned talisman. We were even told how unfortunate it was that Manny was coming up for execution so early in Gray Davis' term; after Davis had a few executions "under his belt" he could grant someone clemency. But not yet. The politics of the death penalty overshadowed everything. . . .

I knew Manny Babbitt the man. I loved him as my brother. I believe that Leah Schendel, if she had known Manny Babbitt the man, would have liked him too. As long as there may be men or women like Manny Babbitt who deserve mercy, who deserve humanity despite the crimes they may have committed, I can no longer support the death penalty.[51]

Altogether, Chuck and his firm donated more than a million dollars' worth of services to Manny's case. Chuck's work earned him recognition by the California State Assembly in the form of a resolution, one line of which read, "The extraordinary efforts of Charles Patterson on behalf of Manuel Pina Babbitt exemplify the finest qualities of the legal profession."[52]

BILL: I keep asking, why did my brother have to die? There wasn't any need to kill Manny. When he was in prison he had stopped smoking and doing drugs. He started doing artwork and corresponding with people all over the world. He was basically rehabilitated. He was well liked by the staff and the inmates of all hues—white, Asian, Hispanic, and black. He had only been in one fight the entire time he had been in jail. Manny could have continued to thrive in a highly structured environment under constant supervision. He did well in prison. He did well in the Marines.

When I first moved to Sacramento County, the last person from there to be executed was a guy named Aaron Mitchell, who was executed in 1966. Aaron Mitchell was also black. Thirty-three years go by before anyone else from Sacramento is executed and that person is Manny. During those thirty-three years there had been many more heinous murders in Sacramento.

I feel like I failed Manny by not getting him the help he needed before the crime. I tried to make it up to him while he was in prison by saving his life, but I failed at that. Now I am compelled—it is a commission from on high—to tell what happened. I need to let people know that murder hurts right across the board regardless of what side of the courtroom you are sitting on.

Everyone is always talking about closure. There is no closure for me. The only way there will be closure is when we get rid of the death penalty for good. I have a mission to recover the Babbitt family name. It wasn't just Manny that was hurt. The experience brought shame to my family. Journalists told stories about our "dysfunctional family," about my crazy mother and alcoholic father, and how we were dirt poor. Many of these stories were exaggerated. But I went along with all of it to save Manny's life. We may have been poor, but our family is very strong and there was a lot of love. We are as dysfunctional as most families, but we did get a worse break.

We are truly grateful for all the wonderful people who came to Manny's defense—Mike Farrell and other Hollywood celebrities, writers, and Mrs. Martin Luther King. My family is very grateful for that. Most death row families don't get that kind of help nor have those sorts of resources. I had people who buoyed me and helped me talk to the press, and Manny's case got covered on national news. But the person who has buoyed me more than any other is my wife, Linda. She has kept me going through times I wanted to give up. And she was the first person to really understand that something was wrong with Manny.

Most people think that something like this could never happen to them, that they would never have someone in their family end up on death row. But it could happen to anyone, and you better hope if it does happen that you aren't black, or poor, because you'll get a different kind of justice in America.

I have not forgiven everyone who supported killing my brother. I am still very angry at Governor Gray Davis and Jan Scully, the Sacramento County district attorney. I feel like the system used the Schendels to help kill my brother, but I have forgiven them.

But I do not want to soil my brother's memory by holding on to hate. I will not. I've got to keep working for other people. The death penalty makes anguished victims out of both sides, and my fight will not be over until it is.

having killed a man in a bar fight when he was seventeen. The state took the case to the grand jury, and on October 15 the jury indicted Cornelius for first-degree murder, felony murder, conspiracy to commit murder, and two counts of possession of a deadly weapon during the commission of a felony and conspiracy to commit murder. The State of Delaware gave notice of its intent to seek the death penalty.

A year later, in a two-day trial on November 2 and 3, Cornelius was convicted on all the counts except conspiracy to commit felony murder. On November 16, 17, and 18, the sentencing hearing was conducted, and on a vote of twelve to zero, the jury recommended the death penalty. Cornelius's mother, Lydia Jones, and his sister Tammy were in the courthouse when the jury came back with its verdict.

On December 1, Superior Court Judge Richard Gebelein sentenced Cornelius to two death sentences, a five-year prison sentence, and six months in a halfway house. In a separate proceeding, Tyrone pled guilty to a second-degree murder charge in exchange for a fifteen-year sentence.

TAMMY: I had just had my third child when my brother Cornelius got charged with murdering Troy Hodges. He hadn't been out of jail too long since his last charge. I tried to follow the trial, but it was hard getting to the courthouse. I had three young kids, and I had a lot of problems at that time in my life. My mother, Lydia, tried to go, but she works long hours and couldn't always get there. I did go to hear the victim's mother testify. His mother made it look like Troy was an innocent person and that my brother was a cold-blooded murderer, but her son was a drug dealer, and his drug dealing probably killed people, too. My brother was living a fast life. He had a death threat against him, and he was always paranoid. I think he panicked and that was how it happened. He didn't mean to kill Troy.

I wasn't actually in the courthouse when they sentenced him to death. It took a long time for the whole thing to set in. I was living a life that was not the life I would want to relive.

•   •   •   •

In October 1995, Lenora Long took a job as director of adult offender services at the Delaware Center for Justice, working with inmates in Delaware correctional facilities. The job was vastly different from her previous jobs, where she had worked with crime victims, not criminals. In fact, she had applied for a different position altogether—director of the HIV/AIDS education program—but when she didn't get that job, she agreed to the other.

While getting acquainted with her new position, Lenora discovered several letters that had been sent to the center from a prisoner on death row at the Smyrna Correctional Center named Abdullah Hameen. Abdullah Hameen was Cornelius's Muslim name. Although he had been a Muslim before he went to prison, Abdullah became more active once there and legally changed his name.

As far as Lenora could tell, the letters had never been answered. Being a hands-on kind of person, she decided to visit. During one of her regular visits to the Smyrna Correctional Facility, Lenora requested a visit with Hameen, but he declined. She tried again on another trip to the prison, but Hameen refused again. Determined to meet him, Lenora visited a third time. This time he met her and explained that the reason he had refused the visits before was that he had been meeting with his lawyer.

LENORA: There was something about him when I first met him. He was so powerful, so intelligent, I found him very interesting. He had an execution date, but he was really concerned about the other guys on the row. He asked me what our agency was going to do to help all of the guys on death row. He wanted to know if we could do things like help with legal research or contact the families of people on the row.

The fact that he was thinking of others when he had his own execution date already scheduled really impressed me. I was also impressed because he knew about everyone's case on the row. He gave me a brief rundown of everyone's situation, explaining where their cases were in the process. I knew nothing about the death penalty.

Lenora continued meeting with Hameen regularly. He kept her informed about what was happening in the prison and educated her about capital punishment.

LENORA: The job was a challenge for me, but once I started getting to know the inmates and getting to know their problems I wanted to change the world, change the prisons, and stop the death penalty. I facilitated victims' groups. I brought victims into the prison to tell their stories to the offenders who were in prerelease so that they would develop empathy towards the victims. I developed a life skills class. I started going to the parole and Board of Pardons hearings.

At the time she started her job, Lenora had an active social life and was living with someone in Center City, Philadelphia. After a few months she felt restless, and she and her boyfriend started arguing a lot. She felt very disconnected from him, and the two broke up. Lenora realized that she was developing romantic feelings for Hameen, but she didn't want to admit it to anyone, even herself.

LENORA: I tried to hide my feelings because I thought that people who loved inmates were a little off, and I certainly wasn't like that. But I had felt very comfortable with Hameen from the first time I met him. I never saw him as an inmate—I saw him as a person. Over time I started sharing personal experiences with him. I had been raped when I was sixteen and had never really told anybody about the experience. He was a good listener. We would talk for hours, and he always made me feel very comfortable.

Although she dreaded dealing with the situation, eventually Lenora could no longer hide her feelings from herself. She believed that her feelings prevented her from having a professional relationship with Hameen.

LENORA: I could no longer deny my feelings for him. I prayed about it and talked to my mother and children about it and decided I had to tell Hameen how I felt. Sometime at the end of the summer, probably August, I told him that I loved him. He laughed and told me that he didn't want to be involved with anyone. He said he was in an impossible situation and getting involved meant hurting too many other people. He said that he didn't want to take anyone on this trip with him.

Although Hameen had told her he was not interested in a romantic relationship, he soon changed his mind, and on September 4, 1996, he proposed marriage. Lenora became increasingly uncomfortable continuing in her professional position. She explained the situation to her employer, and although they encouraged her to stay on, in November she gave notice and by the end of December she left. Fortunately, she was offered a position directing a welfare-to-work program through the Philadelphia YMCA. Lenora also told Warden Robert Snyder about her feelings.

LENORA: Warden Snyder said to me, "God dang it, girl, what are you doing here?" He then asked me all kinds of questions. Had I thought about the implications of this? Was I prepared to love someone who was going to be executed? Did I have another way to support myself? He was quite good about it, really. However, Paul Howard, the bureau chief of prisons, was not so good about it. He told me that I couldn't visit Hameen while I was working.

The director at the center, Janet Leban, was really good about it, too, but some of the other employees were not. They were very judgmental towards me. I had crossed a line, and they could not forgive me or forget about it.

· · · ·

Soon after Lenora left her position, she and Hameen entered into a romantic relationship. Lenora moved to Smyrna and lived right around the corner from the prison. They could not visit at first, so Hameen wrote her letters using an assumed name. However, the prison officials started to soften the no-visiting rule. In January 1997, the prison hosted a big event to honor Project Aware, a program in which prisoners serving lengthy sentences worked with kids who were starting to get into trouble with the law. About forty-five people attended the event, including Bureau Chief of Prisons Paul Howard and the district attorney. Hameen and some other prisoners had raised a thousand dollars to give as a scholarship to a kid who had turned his life around. Lenora invited her parents to attend with her.

LENORA: Hameen was so nervous because I was bringing my parents to meet him. But they connected with him right away. My mother said that from the moment he opened his mouth she knew that he was a good person.

After the Project Aware event, Lenora had permission to visit Hameen at the prison. However, it was much different from her professional visits; then, all she needed to do was flash her ID and she would be taken to a private vis-

derstand who we were and how we are each others' mate (soul mate). So my love I am very thankful that neither of us gave up along the way, even though we couldn't see up to this point we still forged forward praying and hoping for the best outcome we could receive. Al Hamdulliah.

Shakeerah, my love, when I brought up the subject of Delaware's law, please don't mis-understand my deep concern as anything other than just that. I don't want any one to say that you are not my wife, and if and when someone does say it you can present your proof with a smile of security and faith. That's where I am at my loveliness, no where else.

So my love, tell me what has been running through your mind since taking our vows? Baby you don't know bad I wish I could have been standing next to you, holding your hand and telling you that I love you at that very moment to hear those famous words: "You may kiss your bride!!!" . . .

In closing I say to you: "My beloved wife, I thank you for accepting me as your husband and life long mate."

Your husband,

Hameen[1]

Any concerns that prison officials originally had about Hameen and Shakeerah's relationship dissipated. After Shakeerah visited regularly for several months, Warden Snyder asked her to consider returning to her old job. He told her that her replacement was not working out so well, so Shakeerah offered to come back and train the replacement. When that failed, Shakeerah agreed to return to her old job, and in October 1997, less than a year after she had left, Shakeerah was back at the Delaware Center for Justice.

SHAKEERAH: I had stayed in touch with the administration of the Department of Corrections, even though I wasn't working there any longer, because I was following up on some grievances that I had brought on behalf of some of the prisoners. Warden Snyder told me that he was tired of the bullshit, and he told me I needed to come back. Janet wanted me back, but I had coworkers that did not. They hated that I was allowed to come back to work, because you just don't marry inmates. I consider myself very lucky that I was able to continue to work, to marry him and be able to support him and other inmates. It was a blessing because it was something that just didn't happen.

• • • •

The couple settled into their marriage, visiting once or twice a week, speaking on the phone regularly, and writing letters daily. Despite Hameen's incarceration, their two families became very involved in each other's lives.

SHAKEERAH: Hameen had a fifteen-year-old son, Hameen Carroll, who everybody called little Hameen. Little Hameen would go through phases of seeing his father. Sometimes it would be a couple of times a month, sometimes it would be every other month, but they had an excellent relationship. Hameen told me that if we were going to be in a relationship he needed me to be involved with his son. He wrote to Pam, Hameen's mother, and asked her to allow me to be a part of her son's life. We liked each other right away and soon started coparenting little Hameen. She lived near Philly, and we visited often.

When Hameen first got sentenced to death, his son flipped out and started getting into fights. The first time I met little Hameen I went with his mother to pick him up at a juvenile detention center. He had gotten in trouble for something. I'm not sure what. Whenever something happened with Hameen's case, he would do something—like assault someone—to get into trouble.

When I first met little Hameen he was resistant. He didn't trust me. It took several months for us to become close.

Shakeerah wanted her family—her two sons, John and Harley, and Harley's daughter, Jasmine—to know Hameen, too. Harley visited regularly, often bringing along Jasmine. John did not get to know Hameen, although he supported Shakeerah's relationship with him. Shakeerah's parents visited sometimes, and her mother, Lenora, corresponded regularly with Hameen. Later John married a woman named Erin, and she, too, became part of Hameen's life.

SHAKEERAH: Jasmine went to the jail all the time to visit her "Pop Pop." Whenever there was a special function, like the Ramadan feast, I took

Shakeerah Hameen, little Hameen, Jasmine,
and Abdullah Hameen. Provided with permission of the family.

her with me. She sent Hameen cards and letters. One time when Jasmine was about six, we took my aunt with us to visit Hameen. Jasmine told my aunt not to be afraid. She said the people in the prison were really nice.

Shakeerah also got to be close with Hameen's mother, Lydia, who lived in Media, Pennsylvania, and usually spent at least part of every weekend with her. Shakeerah also got to be close with Hameen's sister Tammy.

TAMMY: When I first found out that Hameen was going to marry Shakeerah, I kind of thought she had lost her mind. But then I thought that everyone deserves someone, so I thought it was okay. My brother teased me about it when he told me he was getting married. He said, "You didn't think I could love a big girl, did you?" He was kidding me because I'm heavy like Shakeerah.

I tried to visit Hameen as much as I could, but it was hard to get down there. But each time I visited him I got stronger and stronger. He really encouraged me along the way. He was strong because he had overcome anger, which had been a big part of his life for a long time.

LYDIA: When I got to see Hameen, we had good visits. It wasn't anything dramatic. We tried to enjoy our time together.

Through her visits to the prison, Shakeerah got to be friends with Katherine Nevin, who was married to Jack Outten, who was also on death row. Shakeerah knew Jack through her job, and he had suggested to Katherine that she meet Shakeerah. The two immediately hit it off and quickly became each other's confidants. After a few months of friendship, Shakeerah took Katherine to meet Hameen:

KATHERINE: When I met Hameen I instantly felt that I was in the presence of somebody very wise. I knew he had been through a lot. It was kind of a combination of toughness and sensitivity that he had that made Hameen so interesting as a character, because you knew that he had come from the roughest of the rough, and you knew that he had it in him to be the roughest of the rough. But this other person had emerged who was balanced and loving and knew his faults completely.

I attended an awards banquet for Project Aware where Hameen received an award for his work with young people. I remember the look of humility that I saw in Hameen when he got up to receive the award. The kids looked at him with such affection. It struck me that he was someone who was doing so much good. He was showing young people who were headed in the wrong direction what could happen to them. They respected him for that.

This may sound strange, but I saw Hameen as kind of a prophet figure. I went to him for advice. I ended my marriage with Jack because of things Hameen said. He was so clear and helpful to me in sorting it through spiritually. He was attentive, intelligent, respectful, the qualities that you would seek out in a spiritual leader. I tried on Islam around that time. I had one foot in the Episcopal Church and one foot in Islam. The Islamic prayers are very calming. Seeing Hameen was kind of like going to prayer because he had that same calming effect on people. Most of the guys that I have seen in prison are jumping out of their skin in one way or another. Not Hameen, he was always centered and calm.

Shakeerah and Hameen had a very special relationship based on shared life experiences and spiritual beliefs. It is not easy to love someone on death row. It is an odd sensation to look at someone you love in an environment that is hateful. It is horrible to walk into this place that is designed to crush spirits. You know you are walking into this huge monstrosity, yet you have this love in your heart. As soon as you enter the prison you just want to make a beeline and connect with the person you love.

Besides sharing the people in their lives with each other, they shared work. Both were active in criminal justice reform, especially in efforts to oppose the death penalty in Delaware. Hameen edited a newsletter called *Just Say "No" to Death Row*. In the March/April 1997 edition he wrote an article describing the first execution in Delaware after the death penalty was reinstated.

In the year of one-thousand and nine-hundred and ninety-two the state of Delaware began to reengage in the conspiracy of murdering and assassinating her citizens, where she had set her sight upon one Steven Pennell, whom was to be her first victim since the United States Supreme Court in 1978 reopened the gates of the Slaughter-houses of death and destruction for the fifty children. . . .

D.C.O.D.P. [Delaware Citizens Opposed to the Death Penalty] seeks to educate and promote an understanding among Delawareans of the realities associated with capital punishment, by focusing on its philosophical and practical inadequacies, while encouraging non-violent alternatives for the punishment of crime which does not denigrate the value of human life.

In coalition with other organizations and groups engaged in the struggle through the activities of Education, Community Outreach, Public Awareness, Legislative Action, and Litigation they inform all Delawareans that:

1. The death penalty is unjust in its application;

2. The death penalty is ineffective in dealing with crime;

3. The death penalty is a destabilizing element in community life, while at the same time reminding Delawareans that they are very concerned with the rising crime rate which touches all our lives.

So aren't we as Americans suppose to be the most advanced and civilized of all nations? How so, if we have failed to maintain true equality and justice for all our citizens regardless of race, class, or where we find ourselves in society.

So let us join forces with D.C.O.D.P.; B.L.A.C. [Because Love Allows Compassion]; and J.S."N" D.R. [Just Say "No" to Death Row] and other such organizations in doing what other developed countries have done, by finding alternatives to the death penalty, racism, and classism and plain-old injustice, and then the ills which plague our fellow citizens shall begin to disappear from our societies. So get involved![2]

Hameen was also a member of Respect for Life, an ecumenical organization of inmates and noninmates working for nonviolence that met at St. Dismas Parish within the Delaware Correctional Center at Smyrna. Sally Milburn-Steen from the Newark Delaware Friends Meeting (Quakers) wrote of her first impression of meeting Hameen at a Respect for Life series on the death penalty:

When the prisoners started arriving, many of them flocked towards a stocky man with a wide smile who reached out to them with hugs and handshakes. He radiated warmth and hope, composure and love. This was my first impression of Abdullah T. Hameen, the only Muslim member of the Respect for Life Committee.

We started the evening off with a worship service, during which Hameen gave his reflections on the death penalty. He bared the burden in his soul. He had taken life, but God had been merciful and had led him through suffering, remorse, and penitence to a profound understanding of the preciousness of life. As an expression of his faith, he was doing all that he could to preserve life and end violence in the time he had left before his execution.[3]

Shakeerah joined an organization founded by her friends Anne Coleman and Barbara Lewis, Because Loves Allows Compassion—an organization composed both of people who had lost loved ones to murder and people who had family members on death row. Anne Coleman's daughter was murdered in Los Angeles, and the killer was never found. Barbara Lewis lost an uncle and a nephew to murder. Despite these losses, both opposed the death penalty. Barbara and Shakeerah had another connection: Hameen's cellmate was Robert Gattis, who was Barbara Lewis's son. Robert had been sentenced to death for a domestic homicide.

Shakeerah actively spoke out against the death penalty. She wrote letters to the governor and her elected representatives. She attended demonstrations in Washington. She gave interviews. She even wrote articles about the death penalty. One essay, "Living with Death," was published by Biddle Publishing in a book called *Frontiers of Justice.* The following excerpt is from that essay:

It's three P.M. and I have been busy all day, but as my day winds down, my thoughts return to death row. Don't get me wrong—they never actually escape—but as long as I stay busy, I can hide from them. You see, my husband is on death row, and every day, every minute, I live that sentence with him.

I am the victim that society would like to forget about because I have no rights. I don't have the right to hurt, because, after all, my husband committed the crime. The courts said they had no alternative but to sentence him to death. Was there an alternative, and if there was, would they have shown mercy? I have always felt the death penalty is a way for society to purge itself of its own failures, because had someone intervened earlier, would my husband be on death row today? The crime that brought Abdullah to Delaware's death row was an accident. No one cared or wanted to hear that, because my husband's past is not unblemished. He was the perfect sacrifice, the perfect candidate for death in the name of justice. . . .

The man I love and the man I know is active in the Muslim community, and in Project Aware, a group that works with juveniles in the hope of deterring them from a life of crime. He is co-editor for Just Say "No" to Death Row, a bimonthly newspaper. He is a caring father and grandfather, and he is a supportive husband and friend. He is, as society says, rehabilitated. Abdullah chose to change.

No one forced him, and no one encouraged him.

When I visit with Abdullah, I don't see a monster. I see a man who has had a lot of hurt and rage in his lifetime. I see a man who is struggling to maintain his relationship with his family. I see a man who deserves a chance to live, because he can give so much to society. He can help kids not make the same mistakes he made.

His sixteen-year-old son constantly asks if his father is going to be put to death. How do I prepare him for that? How do I prepare myself for that? I go through each day trying to keep it together, and trying to stay strong. There are days that all I can think about is my husband being executed. There are times when I don't know which way is up, and how I'm going to get through another day.

I sometimes feel like I am walking with death, and that it's going to jump out and attack me when I least expect it. Abdullah is a breathing, healthy young man that the state may escort to his death one day. How do we, as a family, prepare for that? Please know that we have not forgotten the victim or his family. We feel their pain, and we wish that what had happened could be reversed, but it can't.

I don't want to lose this man, and neither does his family. We cannot bring back the victim, but is creating more victims the answer? I ask you to let my husband live so you can see the spark in him that I saw. Know him as I do and you will know his life is worthy to be saved.[4]

· · · ·

In April 1996, John Malik and Kent Jordan were appointed to represent Hameen during the last stage of his appeals. Both Shakeerah and Hameen liked the lawyers very much and trusted their judgment. Unfortunately, John and Kent were limited by decisions made at trial by Edmon Hills and James Bayard, who had not zealously represented their client. They failed to raise his self-defense claim at trial and had not put forward much mitigating evidence at his death-sentencing hearing. Admittedly, Hameen's previous convictions for homicide and aggravated assault influenced the outcome.

Shakeerah became immersed in the details of her husband's case and was involved in every decision that affected it. She played go-between, passing messages from the lawyers to Hameen and vice versa. Shakeerah attended meetings at the lawyers' offices, and with his power of attorney acted on behalf of her husband, who could not leave the prison walls.

In 1997, Hameen lost his appeal in the federal district court. Little Hameen, as had been his pattern, got into trouble with the law, and on May 4, 1998, he was sentenced for an aggravated assault charge against Keith Green. The crime was particularly tragic because Hameen's victim, Keith Green, committed suicide.

Shakeerah did not give up on little Hameen, but instead wrote a letter to Judge William R. Toal Jr. asking permission for the young man to spend weekends with her while he was living in the halfway house. Shakeerah wrote:

> Since Hameen's [the son] incarceration I have noticed tremendous growth and change. He is active in the Islamic Community, has been in various programs including Anger Management, has attended school, plays basketball on one of the Institution's Leagues and has had an exceptional Institutional record. I have spoken with his counselor who speaks very highly of him.[5]

•   •   •   •

Things did not improve with Hameen's case. On May 17, 2000, he lost his appeal before the Third Circuit Court of Appeals, the penultimate appeal in the legal system.[6] His lawyers filed a petition for a rehearing, which was denied on June 15, 2000.[7] Their only remaining appeal was to the United States Supreme Court, which only accepts a few death cases from the hundreds filed each year. Even though it was a long shot, on August 17, 2000, John and Kent filed a five-hundred-page, two-volume petition. If the Court declined to hear Hameen's case, their last resort was to ask the governor to commute his sentence from death to life in prison. Hameen was an excellent candidate for clemency because of his extraordinary efforts to rehabilitate himself, but the Delaware Pardons Board had never in its history recommended clemency for a death row inmate.

SHAKEERAH: When we lost our arguments in the Third Circuit, the reality of the situation slapped me in the face. It is hard to explain. I had always known that his execution was possible, but never believed it. It was kind of like when I lost my brother. He was thirty-eight and he had cancer. The doctors gave him six months to live. I had a healthy brother who didn't smoke or drink, so the thought of him dying was not a reality to me. That's what it was like with Hameen.

Little Hameen started going downhill again. He had been doing pretty good for a while. He had been active in Islam and played on several teams. His coaches loved him, but then he'd stop doing those things and just kind of hang out and not be productive. Between the stress of having his dad on death row and the stress of being a dad himself and just trying

to grow up, he'd get overwhelmed and give up. He couldn't seem to follow through with anything to completion.

•   •   •   •

In December 2000, the state of Delaware opened its new nine-hundred-bed
supermax correctional center—a high-security prison designed to house the
most violent and dangerous offenders. All the men on death row—about
twenty—were transferred to the new facility and put on one wing.

Whereas previously all the death row inmates shared cells with a roommate and were allowed to participate in all the activities of the prison, now
they were isolated nearly all the time. They stayed in their cells twenty-three
hours and fifteen minutes a day. Besides the forty-five minutes a day they
spent outside their cells, they were let out two or three times a week for recre-
ation and showers.

The prisoners could still have visitors, but contact visits were prohibited.
All visits were behind glass, and before and after each visit the inmates were
strip-searched, and during the visit their hands and ankles were bound.

SHAKEERAH: The supermax unit was separate from the rest of the prison.
It had nine hundred beds. Delaware doesn't even have three hundred of
the worst of the worst offenders, let alone nine hundred. But the legislature gave them all this money to build it. So now they are filling it up
with people who have no business being there.

At first Hameen said everything was fine, but by mid-January the conditions at the supermax had started to affect him. I think what affected
him the most was the total loss of control. It was also terrible not being
able to have contact visits. At the time when we most needed to comfort
each other, during his last appeals, we could never touch. It was also
hard to be strip-searched all the time. It was hard to understand why he
had to be strip-searched after a noncontact visit at which his hands and
ankles were bound. It was really just a way of keeping the inmates under
total control.

For the whole ten years he had been on the main compound, he was
active taking classes, and being involved in projects. Now everything he
did was solitary. He read the Koran, prayed, wrote letters, studied. He
wasn't that much into TV. Everything he did was either spiritual or working on his case.

I worried about his mental health. We started arguing about stupid stuff. He started to nitpick little things that he would never have complained about before.

When they moved him from the main prison he had had a television that he didn't want anymore so he asked his mom to come get it and take it home. She works a lot of hours and was having a hard time getting over to pick it up and he asked me about that television a million times, and one day I just cussed him out. But then I realized that the television was the only thing he had control over in his life, so that explained why he was obsessed about it.

The rules at the supermax unit prohibited anyone who was not a prison counselor at the unit to counsel or advocate for the inmates, which meant that Shakeerah was no longer permitted to visit any of the prisoners she had worked with before. This was quite a blow to the prisoners; they were naturally reluctant to talk openly with the prison counselors, who reported what they said to the prison officials.

•　　•　　•　　•

The New Year arrived, and with each passing day Shakeerah became more anxious about hearing from the Supreme Court. If the Court took his case, that meant there was still hope. If not, he had only the pardon board left.

The clerk of the Court had promised to call John once the Court made a decision in Hameen's case, so Shakeerah frequently called John's office asking for news.

SHAKEERAH: It was sometime in March, I was surfing the Net with Erin and went to the Supreme Court page. Every Monday the Court posted a list of cases it had accepted or denied on its Web site, but I had just called John's office and they told me there wasn't anything new so I shouldn't worry about it. Still, I decided to check it out.

The Web site had a humungous long list of people whose cases the Court had not accepted, and I saw Hameen's name. I was so devastated I couldn't believe they hadn't called John. All I could think about was that I needed to tell Hameen. I didn't want him to hear about it from somebody else or read about it in the paper.

I called Anne and she dropped everything she was doing and came over. I was hysterical. I just lost it. A part of me knew he was going to be executed, but a part of me still couldn't believe it would ever happen.

In April, Hameen had a scheduling hearing at which the judge would formally set his execution date, which was typically set for several months after the last appeal was completed. Normally, the scheduling occurs at a time when only the prisoner's case is being heard, but on this date, Hameen's court time was scheduled in the middle of the regular time set aside for probation revocation hearings. The courtroom was packed with people attending the probation hearings, besides all Hameen's supporters,

SHAKEERAH: There was a big group of us: Harley, Erin, Lydia and a friend of hers, Anne, and myself. The judge was calling up all these probation revocation cases, and most people were getting sentenced to community service or maybe thirty days in prison. Then they walked in with Hameen. He was not shackled or handcuffed. He stood at the podium and the judge said, "I sentence you to death by lethal injection on May 27, 2001. May God have mercy on your soul." Hameen said, "Thank you, Your Honor."

The judge went right back to what he had been doing without skipping a beat. People in the courtroom started talking. The room was abuzz with people wanting to know what was going on.

We were all shocked. We had expected maybe he would get a date in July or August. We were not prepared for May 25. It was only six or seven weeks away. David Dawson was scheduled to be executed in April, and we figured there was no way the warden would want to do one in April and one in May.

Little Hameen looked at me and said, "Ummi [Arabic for Mom], are they really going to kill him so soon?" I said, "I don't know, Hameen."

•   •   •   •

Thirty days before a scheduled execution, the prison system in Delaware relaxes the rules and allows death row prisoners three visits a week and two phone calls every day.

During the thirty-day period, little Hameen took an overdose of drugs in a suicide attempt. His mother found him unconscious on his bedroom floor after breaking down the door when she didn't get a response from him. He was taken to the hospital, where his stomach was pumped. He stayed for seventy-two hours and was released with orders to go to counseling.

SHAKEERAH: Hameen went to counseling, but he didn't talk. He didn't say much. He didn't want to talk to anyone, although he would talk to me. I think he expected me to fix the situation. He couldn't understand why no one was doing anything to stop his father's execution. He asked me details about how his father would be killed, and I told him as best as I could.

During that thirty days I was having a hard time trying to deal with little Hameen's emotional needs, Lydia's emotional needs, and my own. All I wanted to do was spend as much time as possible with Hameen. I didn't want to share him with anybody, but of course, I didn't say this to anyone except Hameen.

I felt annoyed with some of his family members. I had been telling his siblings for years that they needed to go see their brother, but they hadn't. When it got down to the end, everybody started popping out of the woodwork wanting to see him. I felt very resentful. Why hadn't they come to see him more before? He had one visit with his five sisters and brothers. It was terrible. Everyone was going through their own stuff and had their own way of dealing with it.

TAMMY: I was the oldest sibling, so I had to keep it together during the visit. My other siblings expected a lot out of me. Eric was a year younger than Hameen. Aretha started to cry before we even got to the visiting room.

He was chained and behind glass. In all the years I had visited him I had never had to talk to him behind glass. He kept looking down, and I said to him, "Why are you looking down?" and he said, "What else is there for me to do?" He was ashamed for us to see him like that. He said to me, "Don't cry." And I said, "Are you okay?" He said, "Who, me? Sure I'm okay." Then he told me, "Life has choices and I want you to make choices that will make you strong."

At that point I was looking for him to be commuted to life without parole, so I never said good-bye to him. I just didn't feel like that was the thing for me to say at that particular time. I went home and wrote him a letter and I asked him to forgive me for all the times that I hadn't been there for him and all the times I might have been selfish. I told him how I was trying to get my life together and how I finally conquered some things. He told my mother later that parts of the letter made him laugh and some made him cry.

•   •   •   •

Hameen's last chance for life was a commutation. In Delaware, the governor has the power to commute a death sentence to life in prison upon the recommendation of the Board of Pardons. The process involves a meeting of the Parole Board, which makes a recommendation to the Board of Pardons. Shortly after he lost his appeal, the Parole Board voted three to two in favor of clemency for Hameen.

On May 18, at 9:00 A.M., the Delaware Board of Pardons convened at Smyrna prison in a small conference room. The board was comprised of five state officials: Lieutenant Governor John C. Carney, serving as president; Secretary of State Harriet Smith Windsor, serving as secretary; Chancellor William B. Chandler III, Delaware State Treasurer Jack Markell; and Auditor of Accounts R. Thomas Wagner Jr.

At the front of the room was a long table where the five members sat. There were two tables—one for the prosecutor and one for Hameen and his attorneys—and between them a podium to speak from. Reporters and the victim's advocate sat in the front row, and behind them the spectators. Shakeerah sat surrounded by supporters; she was wearing a black crepe dress that she had had made especially for the hearing.

Hameen spoke about the things that he had done in his life. He talked about where he was in his life and where he had been. He talked about all the things he regretted and said how sorry he was for his crime.

John and Kent, Hameen's attorneys, and Shakeerah had arranged for a number of witnesses to speak and had coordinated their testimony so that all would not be saying the same thing. Sally Milbury-Steen spoke about her work with Hameen on the Respect for Life Committee. Kim Book, a friend of Shakeerah's and Hameen's whose daughter had been murdered, spoke about forgiveness and mercy. Janet Leban talked about how Hameen had met the requirement for exceptional rehabilitation. Pam, little Hameen's mother, did not attend but sent a statement saying that even though Hameen had been incarcerated he was her best friend and that he was always there for her and little Hameen. She said that he was a better father than many who were out on the street. Lydia talked about her relationship with her son.

Little Hameen sobbed as he begged the board to spare his father's life. He talked about visiting his father and how much he relied on him for advice and support. He ended by saying that he couldn't live without his father. Harley hadn't planning on speaking, but after hearing the others, he decided to. He said that when Shakeerah first told him that she was going to marry, he found it hard to believe until he met Hameen, and then he understood. Hameen had made his mother a better person, he said, and the strength that he got from watching their relationship made him realize how important marriage and commitment and family were. He wanted Hameen to be around to be a part of his life.

Then a surprise witness came forward. One of the cameramen covering the hearing for the local cable station turned out to be the nephew of the man that Hameen had killed when he was seventeen. He hadn't realized that Hameen had killed his uncle until he heard the name Cornelius Ferguson. He said that after listening to everything that had been said, he wanted Hameen's life spared.

SHAKEERAH: When it was my turn to talk, I talked about how grateful I was for the growing I had done with Hameen. I said he was my best friend. I cried through most of it. I said that I felt empathy for the victim but I didn't want to become a victim myself. By the end I was blubbering. They probably just wanted me to sit down at that point. Hameen was crying. He was bent over holding his head in his hands.

When the prosecutor spoke, he said that Hameen was not really rehabilitated because his writings were inflammatory. Hameen had called the criminal justice system racist and unjust.

The board asked Hameen about his writing, and he said that he had just spoken the truth. Then a pardon board member asked the prosecutor, "Are you saying that we should deny him clemency because you don't like his writing?" That brought the prosecutor up short.

Katherine also attended the hearing and testified.

KATHERINE: The pardon hearing was really bizarre. Watching the ease with which the members of the board spoke about life and death was very strange. To do what they do, they have to be half-cocked. The best way to describe it is surreal. One of the members was wearing sunglasses so you couldn't see his eyes.

Hameen's son was slumped over, tears rolling down his face and there wasn't anything anyone could do to comfort him. He had to sit there and hear horrible things being said about his dad. I wanted to scream and say you are not seeing all these other parts of him. You are denying his full personhood. He is someone who has committed a terrible crime, but there's more to him than that. The cavalier way they discussed the decision about whether Hameen should live or die was really shocking. It seemed to me that they were the sociopaths, not Hameen.

The board listened to four hours of testimony. All the witnesses, except the state's attorneys, argued in favor of granting clemency because of the extraordinary efforts Hameen had made to rehabilitate himself and because of the good work he was doing with the younger inmates. The family of Troy Hodges was not present. An employee from victim's services said that she had left eleven messages on the Hodges' answering machine but had never heard back. The Board of Pardons deliberated for four hours but at 4:00 P.M.—seven hours after the hearing started—announced that it was going to adjourn for the day and would continue deliberating over the weekend.

All the local media outlets reported on the hearing. Tara Hodges, the victim's sister, told a reporter covering the hearing that the state had not contacted her family for input into the clemency decision. When the reporter broke this story, the Board of Pardons scheduled an emergency follow-up hearing for May 23. The second hearing was also open to the public, but only three people were on the agenda—Troy's mother and sister and the director of rehabilitation at the Delaware Correctional Center. They also contacted John Malik and asked to see samples of Hameen's writing, which Shakeerah hurriedly put together.

SHAKEERAH: At the hearing, Tara Hodges blasted Hameen, describing him as "garbage" that should be disposed of. "You're not sorry for killing my brother, you're sorry that you got caught," she told him. "You are evil. You cannot change and you haven't changed."[8] The mother described the terrible toll her son's death had exacted. It was hard to listen to them, but I could understand their pain. But the worst was when Ron Holsterman, the director of rehabilitation, testified unequivocally that Hameen was not rehabilitated. He said that after having worked in the prison system for thirty years, he had never seen any inmate become rehabilitated.

The board asked him some hard questions, and you could tell they weren't buying that. Ron really made people angry. His staff was angry. I mean, if he hasn't seen any improvement after thirty years maybe he should get a new job.

TAMMY: I didn't go to this part of the hearing, but I heard it on the radio. I wasn't ready to come face-to-face with the victims a second time. I still remembered their testimony from the trial. I wasn't really angry at them. I felt remorseful and I know my brother was very remorseful. But the victims said that he was an animal, he could change his name but he could not change who he was. But that wasn't true. He was a totally different person—not only from my point of view, but other people who had been incarcerated and had gotten free said that my brother had impacted their lives. And I know he headed up a few things when he was in prison. He started a father-and-son program helping some of the guys that were in prison and didn't have a relationship with their father. And then the young juveniles program, Project Aware. I know a few teenagers that went through that program and told me that it helped them.

The members recessed to deliberate for an additional two hours and returned with grim expressions. The board concluded that although Hameen had shown genuine remorse for his crimes, they could not overlook the fact that he had previously killed another person and wounded two others. They announced their decision to deny clemency.

SHAKEERAH: When they denied him clemency, I had an out-of-body experience. I think that God just put me in this protective place. I remember them saying that they were denying, and I shut down and don't remember anything else. People were trying to talk to me. Erin was talking to me but I didn't even recognize her. All I wanted to do was see how Hameen was doing. I couldn't believe that he was going to be executed in a couple of days.

His lawyers came over and helped me up. They told me that the guards had said I could spend some time with Hameen by myself. The lawyers walked me back to where he was. The guards took us to a private room, shut the door, and left us alone. I lost it. I was hysterical. I broke down, cried and cried and cried, it was horrible—this was at the prison.

Hameen told me that the he was ready to die. He had decided that if Troy's mother wanted him to die, then he would willingly go, because that was her right to seek his death. The hardest part for him was having to leave me. He told me he didn't want them to see me cry anymore, that I had to be strong. I had to be there for his son and mother.

Then he told me that I had brought so much meaning to his life and I was a gift from God.

The visit lasted about an hour and a half. We held each other. Let's just say we had a real contact visit. I think the decision was hard for the guards, too, because I worked there, so they knew me, and they respected Hameen, which is why they gave us so much privacy. That was very unusual.

I think the board would have recommended clemency if the victims hadn't shown up. But if the board is going to rely on what the victims want, why bother to have a parole hearing. It was very emotionally draining to go through that process for everybody. You are begging for someone's life of these human beings who are not God. Who are they? They are just people. They don't know him, me, or his family. Who gives them the right to make judgments about someone's life?

Plus the whole thing was kind of a sham. What does the lieutenant governor, the state treasurer, or the auditor know about rehabilitation? They don't have any knowledge of criminal justice, how it works or anything. The people who have experience thought that Hameen should get clemency. When John submitted the clemency package to the Board of Pardons, Judy Smith, who works for the board, said to Lieutenant Governor Carney, "I think this is our first commutation." She told me that she just knew that Hameen's sentence was going to be commuted. Lieutenant Governor Carney also called Paul Howard asking about Hameen, and Paul told him that he thought Hameen had met the criteria for exceptional rehabilitation. But the board ignored Paul and listened to Ron Holsterman instead.

The other death row prisoners were very upset that Hameen did not get clemency. The month before, the board announced at David Dawson's clemency hearing that they would consider clemency for a person who had been exceptionally rehabilitated. Hameen had done everything he possibly could have done to rehabilitate himself. All the prisoners knew that if Hameen didn't get clemency, they didn't have a chance, especially now that they all lived in supermax, where no one had an opportunity for rehabilitation. There were no more classes, no more interactions with young people. There was nothing for them to do.

•   •   •   •

Two days later, Shakeerah was back at the prison, this time to say good-bye to her husband for good. Hameen had been transferred to the death house — a special area where prisoners were taken to await execution. The area was high security, and no contact visits were allowed.

Prison officials had forbidden the local imam from acting as Hameen's spiritual advisor. Hameen's attorneys challenged the decision but were unsuccessful at getting it reversed. The North American Islamic Foundation had sought to stay the execution on the grounds that his religious rights were being violated, but the Superior Court ruled that the group did not have standing to seek a stay.[9] Hameen was told that he could have the Christian prison chaplain or no one.

SHAKEERAH: It was the most bizarre day. It was surreal. I had to call the prison to find out what time I could come. I went at 10:00 A.M. I was met by the deputy warden and another high-ranking correctional officer, who walked me over to the death house. Hameen was in a room that was basically a cage. There was a slit that we could talk through at the bottom. They recorded everything we said.

The visit was an hour, and then I had to leave the prison for a couple of hours and was allowed to come back. I did that a couple of times, and then his mom came with me for a last visit. Hameen was pretty upbeat. We were trying to keep it light. When we went into the death cell Lydia said, "Oh, son, they gave you a cell all to yourself." We laughed. Hameen made a joke about Lydia needing to take her Prozac. The last time that his mom and I saw him might have been about five or six and then we had to leave and come back to the prison at 7:00 P.M. At that time they met us outside the prison, and we had to be escorted in. A female guard completely searched us, including going through our underwear.

They locked us in the backseat of a car and drove us to the death house. I don't know where they thought we were going to go. The car stopped next to the death house, and there was a bus with the warden and deputy warden and all the reporters. The deputy warden asked the guards if everything was on schedule, and they said yes. The deputy warden said, "That's really great," and gave the thumbs-up sign.

The prison had arranged to have food prepared for the state's witnesses. It was like a party. We were sitting watching all these people dressed up because there was media there, and they were bringing food back and forth. I wished it would just be midnight so it would get the fuck over. I couldn't stand watching these people act like the execution was a party.

While Hameen was inside eating his last meal of lobster, crab legs, a baked potato with sour cream, a mango, and ice water, his lawyers were filing futile last-minute appeals, and supporters were gathering outside to protest the execution. The crowd started gathering around 7:00 P.M., and their numbers continued to grow. All of Hameen's brothers and sisters and his mother came, along with Pam and little Hameen, Harley and Erin, Anne Coleman and Barbara Lewis, and many others. By 11:00 P.M., about seventy-five people were protesting, many holding signs, including one that read, "Governor Ruth Ann Minner — Serial Killer."

SHAKEERAH: At 11:59 they got us out of the car and let us into the room first. We were surrounded by guards. Behind the glass Hameen was lying on a stretcher spread out like a crucifix. Chaplain Parnell was standing there with his Bible, looking like he was scared to death. He was lying in there, and I'm on the other side of the window and watching him die and knowing there was nothing I could do to prevent it. It was horrible. I felt stupid that I was standing there letting them kill my husband. It was unreal. Then they brought in the victim and I was thinking, *This is the most bizarre thing I have ever experienced.* Hameen looked at us and we locked eyes and he smiled. I started praying. The warden asked him if he had anything to say. He said, "Tara, I hope this brings you comfort and eases your pain some. Mom and Shakeerah, I love you. I'll see you on the other side. That's all."

The warden put his hand up and they did whatever they do. I just kept looking at him. His body lifted up off the table, he gasped. The warden shut the curtain and pronounced him dead at 12:07. A girl behind us offered a tissue, which I didn't take. At that point I think I was in shock. We walked over to the car and they gave me some of his things and told me that I had to go to another building to get the rest of them.

When a prison official announced shortly after midnight that Hameen was dead, many people screamed, "Murderers!" Little Hameen and Harley clung to each other, sobbing. The Delaware Coalition Opposed to the Death

Penalty rang a huge bell. Half a dozen police officers were trying to keep the crowd in one area. Some yelled that the overtime pay they got for supervising the protest was "dripping with the blood of Hameen."[10] Phyllis Pautrat, a counselor from Philadelphia who attended the protest, commented, "We should be outraged. A murder is taking place tonight." Turning to one of the guards she asked, "What are you going to tell your kids when you go home tomorrow? Last night I killed a man?"[11]

TAMMY: I didn't feel comfortable with a lot of what was being said outside the prison. I didn't think people should speak badly to the guards. Their remarks were ironic, and I didn't think my brother would like some of the things that they were saying and doing. Even though his life was in their hands, he had forgiven them. I didn't think it was necessary to be rowdy. I knew that he had made peace with God, so I had to make the decision to let him go so that he could go peacefully.

SHAKEERAH: After it was over, they took us to Building 26, where we met up with Kent and John. We hugged for a long time. It was hard on them, too. Up until the last minute they were trying to talk Lydia and me out of being witnesses because it would be too hard for us. They said they would do it. But it would have been hard on them, too. Hameen said that the last time he saw them they couldn't even talk because they were crying. He was much more than a client to them.

At a brief press conference after the execution, Governor Ruth Ann Minner issued a statement:

The State of Delaware this morning carried out Abdullah Hameen's penalty for the murder of Troy Hodges. I pray that the completion of this sentence, recommended by a jury and imposed by a judge, will bring some amount of closure to Mr. Hodges' family. May God have mercy on Mr. Hameen.[12]

Tara Hodges issued a statement and answered questions. The *Wilmington News Journal* reported her remarks:

"The nightmare, this chapter is over. I wanted to know he was paying the price. This should have happened 10 years ago. I needed to see this happen to make sure he was really dead. I hope it sends a message to

people that you can't kill 1, 2, or 3 times and expect to get away with it."
A reporter asked her if Hameen's last words brought her any comfort.
Hodges replied, "It was meaningless to me. . . . I felt comfort, not from
what he said, but the act brought me some comfort."[13]

A reporter asked Shakeerah how it felt to watch her husband die and she
said, "It hurt to see my husband die, but I know that one day, inshallah [God
willing], I will meet him again."[14]

Katherine did not attend the protest; she feared retaliation from prison
officials who could prevent her from visiting Jack, claiming that because she
had taken part in a demonstration she posed a "security risk." However, she
was there for Shakeerah every step of the way and saw the effects it had on her
friend.

KATHERINE: The execution was horrible. Shakeerah tried to appear strong,
but it was outrageous the way that she was treated prior to the execution.
She had to jump through all the hoops of leaving the prison and then
coming back, and each time she came back she was strip-searched. It was
humiliating. But she went in there with a mission. She was there for
Hameen's soul. She bore it with a great deal of dignity.

I wrote this poem after Hameen's execution:

> *The Execution Party*
> The night after they killed you
> the carnival came to town.
> I could hear it in my room,
> ghost noises going up
> then down
> in the dark.
> Grown-ups with children,
> their mouths full, rising
> and falling.
> What if we had "death by ferris wheel"
> instead of death by lethal injection?
> What if they loosened all bolts
> and you took your chances,
> came crashing down.
> Or what if you just got stuck,

to be hoisted down weeks later
like a tattered flag?
I know you're beyond all speculation,
but still, I try to find a way
for you to cheat the machinery, get
your life back,
get free.[15]

•   •   •   •

Hameen was buried the next day in New Jersey at a Muslim cemetery owned by an Italian who had been following the case and donated the plot to Hameen. The Muslims at the prison paid for the funeral. They raised money by selling bean pies—a Muslim food something like a sweet potato pie. It is Muslim tradition to have the burial within seventy-two hours of death, but because Hameen had died on a Friday his family wanted to have his funeral during the Jumal service (the regular Friday afternoon Muslim service). Hameen was buried at 1:00 P.M. One thousand people attended the burial, and two thousand others not in attendance had committed to praying at that time for the speedy passage of his soul.

Grief and illness overcame Shakeerah, who did not go to the funeral. Her asthma flared up and turned into an upper respiratory infection, which turned into bronchitis. Harley and Erin stayed with her and took care of her. She was hardly getting any oxygen to her lungs and her doctor threatened to hospitalize her, but after a couple of weeks she improved.

SHAKEERAH: He was killed at midnight and buried before the day ended, and physically I fell apart. I woke up and had an intense migraine; my blood pressure was up; I had diarrhea. I was physically sick, and then I just got worse. I had asthma, and I got really sick with my asthma, and that turned into a bronchial infection. I was sick for three months. I couldn't go to work. I was fortunate that my job paid me while I was out; I was on short-term disability. I think that I teetered on insanity for a minute. I couldn't pray. I couldn't function. I think at some point during that time I made a conscious decision that I had to get myself together and move forward. God wasn't ready for me to be a nut.

Then I started to pray again. I remembered conversations with Hameen before he died, and my faith started to come back to me. In

Islam we believe that your date with death is already set the day you are born. Hameen's death was May 25, 2001. If Hameen was supposed to die on that day then he would have died of a heart attack or something else if he hadn't been executed. You make choices, but everything that happens happens because it is the will of Allah. Hameen was so ready to die that he was completely at peace. I think he had such a good basis in his faith at that point that he was okay with it. Still, for me, it would have been easier to accept Hameen's death if he had been sick or going through an illness. His death certificate said homicide. That was harder to accept.

In retrospect I probably shouldn't have witnessed the execution. For months I kept seeing that image of him spread out on the table, helpless, and there was nothing I could do. But I wanted to be there. I had married him until death do us part. I wanted to be there to say the Muslim prayer that we say when someone is dying.

After a few months, Shakeerah and Lydia drove to New Jersey to visit Hameen's grave. It was a lovely, peaceful cemetery, but Shakeerah found it hard to believe that Hameen was really buried there.

SHAKEERAH: I kept wanting to dig up his body to see if he was there. I know it sounds crazy, but I just kept thinking that maybe none of it was true, maybe he was still alive. But then I calmed down and talked to Hameen. I told him about what had been going on and how much I missed him.

• • • •

A year after the execution, the family was still suffering the effects. Little Hameen had attempted suicide again—another drug overdose.

SHAKEERAH: The one I worry the most about is little Hameen. Right after the execution, I was talking to him and seeing him on a regular basis, but that stopped. I am angry with him because he is being a brat and feeling sorry for himself. His girlfriend is pregnant again. He is only twenty-one and is on his fourth child. He is not working or taking care of these kids. He lives with his girlfriend, Victoria, and works sometimes. I offered for him to come live with me and go to school and told him he wouldn't have to pay any bills, but he didn't want to do that. He has just spiraled downhill.

When Hameen was alive, little Hameen still feared and respected his father, so he wouldn't do anything really off the wall. He would do things, but there were always limits. Now that Hameen is gone, there are no more limits. I worry about him because he was really involved in Islam and now he is not. The last time I spoke with Pam she said that he reminded her of his father; unfortunately she meant during his father's younger years when he got into a lot of trouble.

Lydia was angry about Hameen's death for quite a while and then she got angry at Shakeerah, who in January 2002 married an Egyptian man named Elsayed Haykal.

SHAKEERAH: I am very impulsive sometimes. I knew Elsayed through mutual friends, and when he found out I was a widow he asked me to marry him and I said yes. I got married because I really thought I needed to move forward. Sometimes the pain of Hameen being gone was so incredibly strong that I really thought that this was a way to make it go away. But it didn't work. It was a disaster. I compared him and every-thing he did to Hameen. Everyone told me I was crazy. They were less supportive of this marriage than of my marriage to Hameen, who had been on death row!

Elsayed is a really good person, and he deserves a wife who loves him and not one who is marrying him because she is trying to get over a dead husband or because she doesn't want to die alone. I thought marrying Elsayed would be like starting all over again. But I think what I realized is that I still love Hameen. He is dead, he is gone, but he is still a part of my life that I can't run away from.

Afterwards I felt incredibly guilty. First, because I had hurt Elsayed, a nice and decent man who didn't deserve to be hurt, but then I felt I had betrayed Hameen. His last words were that he would wait for me. How is he going to see me on the other side if I'm married to someone else? I wrote to him after he died and told him all about it. But truthfully, I don't think Hameen would have minded. If he could talk to me, he would probably advise me to get on with my life.

TAMMY: I don't think either my mom or Shakeerah is what you would say "recovered." I think sometimes we have a tendency as women to push things down, suppress them. My mom has been sick off and on since then. She has lost weight. I think she covers up a lot of things. I think it was rocky in the beginning. Everybody has their moments. I'm not always around to keep the laughter going.

Nine months after the execution I lost my husband. He was hit by a car. That was another tragedy in my life. I believe that my brother had prepared me for my husband's death. Maybe each tribulation makes you more determined to look forward. There were some things I set out to do before they died. One was to go to college. I am now in my second semester. One day hopefully I'll be able to obtain my master's degree in sociology. They encouraged me to go for it even though they aren't here. I still have something to look forward to because of their encouragement. My kids are okay—better than I would have expected. They have their moments, but they are open to expressing how they feel, which makes it easier to cope.

I still have things all the time that remind me of Hameen. Just a few weeks ago I met this guy, Owen Renkin, who had known my brother in jail. Hameen had talked with him, and he was also there when my brother was executed, and he said it was one of the saddest days even for the guards. It was doom and gloom. It was not the same as when he was alive.

• • • •

In December 2002, Kent Jordan was made a federal court judge. He invited Shakeerah to his induction ceremony and gave her a reserved seat in the front row.

SHAKEERAH: The place was packed. When I walked in, Kent's secretary told me I had a seat in the front. I met his wife, and she said she and the kids felt close to Hameen because he was so much a part of Kent's life. Kent told me he thought of Hameen during the ceremony. He told me that Hameen had had a tremendous impact on his life.

• • • •

In the spring of 2003, Shakeerah left her job at the Delaware Center for Justice when recurring health problems made it impossible to keep up her busy schedule. She moved back to Philadelphia to live with Harley and Erin. She spends a lot of time with her ten-year-old granddaughter, Jasmine, and her mother-in-law. Her parents live in Langhorne, Pennsylvania, and she sees them or talks to them every day. Her siblings live nearby, too.

SHAKEERAH: I have hepatitis C that the doctors think I probably got from a blood transfusion when I had my son over twenty years ago. I don't have a spleen and I don't have any tonsils, and because of my weakened immune system I get sick all the time. My joints ache, and now I have sleep apnea, which only aggravates everything.

I have never applied for unemployment before. It is a long drawn-out process. I am trying to figure out what I am going to do when I grow up and wishing Hameen was here to give me advice. He would probably tell me to buck up and move on. Whatever happens happens because it is the will of Allah. But I am forty-eight and feeling old. The only thing I have ever done is human service work. I think I'd like something a little easier, like customer service or something.

I still feel close to Hameen. When I can't sleep, I'll sit down at my computer and write to him. My oldest son called me the other night and asked what I was doing, and I told him, "Writing to Hameen." He asked me if I sent the letters. As strange as it may sound to some people, Hameen made me very happy. Even though we never lived together, Hameen was a part of my household. I included him in my decision-making, and our psyches were so connected. I would be upset and he would call me and know just from hearing the sound of my voice what was bothering me. I miss him terribly.

May 25, 2003, is the second anniversary of the execution. Lydia and I are going to mark the day by going to the cemetery. His mom and I usually talk to him for a while and then go out to eat. This year I think we will plant an azalea bush or something. He likes flowers.

LYDIA: When you have someone on death row, you are just waiting for them to die. The difference is that you know the time, the hour, the day, the year and the month. I knew he was going to die. I had the opportunity to be there and be with him. We did what we could do to stop it. We did everything humanly possible. We had lawyers, we prayed, we did everything. I sum it all up that it was his time to leave. It was a terrible way to go, but what can you do?

I don't think it is fair that they killed my son. It bothers me, but I don't know what more I could have done about it. Some things we have no control over. I did everything I could. I prayed. I think what they did was crap. Partying the night they were killing him. They'll pay for what they did. Everything you do you'll pay for. As far as I'm concerned it is not God's will for us to kill one another. I don't care how you do it. I don't want to dwell on it now. He's at rest and that is how it should be.

Katherine wrote another poem after the execution:

After Justice?
May will be turning itself into a memorial.
She will always think of May as a headstone,
A place to visit, to sit on, cry on, beat with her fists.
May will bring her his lips, the curve of his nose.
She will get to touch him one more time, taking
In the grasp of his fingers, feeling
His hand on her neck.
(They let you touch again before executions.
Just a little while.)
Then she'll find him again only on the news,
Only as a loss.
It will be a while before May will turn
Into a way of winning back spring
Before she can take comfortable swallows of anything
When even her tongue feels like a punishment
When waking up means being on an island, but the lights in the sky
Come from a thousand cameras.
May will eventually refashion her self.
It will twine around her in an easy chair
The way cats do
And she will spend every spring
Knowing he's always ahead of her,
The bronze of his back and arms
Always on the lids of her eyes
Moving away, out of reach of the machine that kills.[16]

·   ·   ·   ·

On September 7, 2003, which would have been Hameen's fortieth birthday, Shakeerah and Lydia visited his grave. Shakeerah is still having a difficult time dealing with his death.

SHAKEERAH: It is hard to say, but I think that there is no way to get closure around his death. It's not like he died because he was sick or anything, he was murdered, but nobody is being held responsible. Nobody is acting like anything is wrong. But I am just left missing him.

Little Hameen is doing okay, not great, but okay. He went to jail again over the summer, for allegedly stealing a kid's wallet, but the charge was dropped when he went to court because the victim said Hameen hadn't done it. But they kept him in jail for six weeks. Lydia is doing better than everybody. She gets angry, but she gets through it.

CHAPTER 4

From Revenge to Reconciliation

On May 11, 1979, Dempsey Wolfenbarger went to the Mableton Precinct of the Cobb County Police in Georgia, about forty miles outside of Atlanta, and reported to Corporal J. E. Davis that he was worried about his stepdaughter, Linda Gilreath. Linda had recently moved out of the house that she shared with her husband, Fred, and had taken their two children, eleven-year-old Felicia and eight-year-old Christopher (Chris), to South Carolina to stay with relatives. Fred was angry at Linda and had made threats against her. Dempsey told the police that earlier that day Linda and her father, Gerrit Van Leeuwen, had gone to the house to pick up some of Linda's belongings and had not returned when they were supposed to. Dempsey told the police that he feared there might be some domestic trouble.[1]

Corporal Davis and Officer Roy Rogers went to the Gilreath residence at about 5:00 P.M. They knocked on the door and got no response. They walked to the back of the house and entered a screened-in porch. From there, they saw a man's body. Entering the house, they saw Linda's body lying between a coffee table and a love seat, with a pink towel covering her face and a white suitcase by her side. She had been shot five times from approximately two to three feet away.[2] Gerrit was lying nearby and had been shot at close range in his thigh, chest, and head. Gasoline had been poured on and around the victims and on the kitchen floor.[3]

Police interviewed a water department workman who had been in the neighborhood fixing a broken water main. The workman testified that he saw a light blue Dodge Duster car pull up and two people got out, one an elderly man. A short time later, sometime between 1:30 and 1:50 P.M., he heard five rapid-fire shots.

adult area and children's area; I kept going back and forth between both. I was still in shock. It hadn't really hit home. When we were first told what happened, my brother started crying, but I didn't. I guess I was just expecting it.

Everybody knew it was coming. Several family members that were in a position to help her financially had done so repeatedly. I wish there had been a battered women's shelter or some organization that could have taken her in. But maybe she couldn't be helped. She loved him and kept going back to him. You read about cases like hers all the time—in the obituary section.

Other people in our town were terrified of him, too. I remember one incident from the fourth grade. The principal announced that Christopher and I needed to go to the principal's office. I was shaking so bad I couldn't even breathe. It was 8:15 in the morning, and my father was there holding a stick, a tree really. Christopher had forgotten to brush his teeth. Fred told the principal to get out of his own office, and then he beat the hell out of Christopher. I learned you couldn't rely on adults to help you.

After a week, Christopher and Felicia went to live with their grandmother to finish out the school year.

FELICIA: On my first day back, I got there early and I went around to all the sixth grade teachers to get the assignments that I had missed. I walked out of a classroom and saw the entire sixth-grade class following me. It was wild. I wasn't mad about it. I was embarrassed by all the attention. People weren't mean, but it made me feel funny and awkward. It soon wore off within a day or two.

Felicia and Chris spent the summer going from the home of one relative to another, visiting both their mother's and their father's families. They ended up living separately. Chris went to live with a paternal uncle in Virginia who was in the Navy, and Felicia lived with a maternal uncle who lived nearby and had a daughter her age.

• • • •

In the year between their mother's murder and their father's trial, Fred did not see either of his children. Before the trial began, the prosecutor offered

Fred a plea bargain—plead guilty to the crime and be sentenced to life in prison instead of the death penalty. Fred's attorney advised him against taking the plea, telling him that by pleading guilty to first-degree murder he was admitting that the crime was premeditated. Fred did not want to make that admission: It wasn't true, and he didn't want his children to think that he had planned to kill their mother.

Fred went on trial for capital murder in May 1980. On the first day, Linda's family went to the courtroom to watch, bringing Felicia along and sitting her in the front row for all of the jury to see.

FELICIA: They brought me right into the courtroom and sat me down in the front row. Dad turned around and looked at me, and when he saw me his face lit up, he was so happy to see me. He hadn't seen me in fourteen or fifteen months. He was shackled and handcuffed and he held up his hands gesturing to me. I wanted to get up and run to him. It was horrible. Dad's lawyer immediately had me sequestered from the courtroom, claiming he might call me as a witness. They never had any intention of calling me as a witness, but they didn't want me in the courtroom.

He was right and my mother's family was wrong. During the trial they showed very graphic pictures. I'm glad I didn't see them.

Fred had a difficult time during the trial. Seeing the photographs of his wife's and father-in-law's bodies was very hard for him. By the end of the trial he had had enough. The jury convicted him. Anxious to finish the process, Fred asked his lawyer not to put on any evidence during the sentencing phase of the trial. The lawyer had investigated Fred's troubled past and identified witnesses who could have testified about it, but Fred asked him not to call the witnesses.[5] The jury never heard about his childhood fraught with deprivation, nor of his chronic alcoholism, which was so advanced he had experienced multiple hallucinations such as pink elephants and little green men that were so real to him that he shot up the furniture he saw them coming out of.[6] Given Fred's state of mind due to the stress of the trial and recovering from alcoholism, he was probably not competent at the time he advised his lawyer to forego calling witnesses at his sentencing trial.[7]

Left with only the impression that he was a cold-blooded killer who tried to burn the bodies of his victims before fleeing town, the jury sentenced Fred to death.

it, for her sake. I guess I was probably jealous of their relationship, too. She had always been daddy's little girl, and growing up—before he went to jail—I wanted his attention, too. I wanted his affection, and approval but he never gave it to me.

•   •   •   •

After the year at Stone Mountain, Felicia moved back to the Atlanta area to live with her mother's brother and his family. She stayed there until age seventeen, when she argued with her aunt, who slapped her in the face, and Felicia decided it was time to leave. She moved in with her boyfriend Craig's stepfather, who had taken in a number of teenagers who were having problems with their families.

Chris was also having problems. He was an angry teenager. He was a good student, but had a hard time getting along with people.

CHRIS: I always made it clear to the people around me that I didn't need them. I always wanted them to know that I would be perfectly happy whether they were in my life or not. This was particular true with girls and women. It was also a trait of my father's.

I knew that I was like my father in a lot of ways. I guess I realized that it was inevitable that parts of me would be like him. But I never tried to fight who I was. I had a lot of testosterone in me, and I never tried to alter it because I was my father's son.

FELICIA: I think if our father hadn't gone to jail, Christopher might have ended up killing him. Chris has told me many times that he would have. He still struggles with his anger, but he is a lot better now.

At sixteen, Chris developed Crohn's disease. He became close to the doctor who was treating him. The doctor eventually adopted Chris, and Chris took his name, Kellett. It helped Chris to have a male role model other than his father.

While Chris sought fatherly guidance elsewhere, Felicia continued a relationship with her father. She visited him a few times a year, and he called a few times a year. She sent him gifts at Christmastime and did nice things for him like paying for subscriptions to newspapers and magazines.

As Fred's case progressed through the system, the lawyers sometimes contacted the two asking for their assistance. Chris told the lawyers that he hoped they were electrocuted along with his father. Felicia agreed to help. At nineteen, she signed an affidavit, which Fred's lawyers had prepared for her. It said in part:

> My father was a wonderful father. He instilled in me good values and morals. My father never mistreated me. To my knowledge, he never mistreated my younger brother or my mother.
>
> My mother, father, brother and I were a very happy family. There was a lot of love in our family. My father always showed a lot of affection. He and my mother had a loving relationship. We did a lot of things together as a family. The whole family would go to North Carolina almost every weekend to visit my grandparents. We went to Sunday school fairly regularly.[8]

As they grew older, Felicia and Chris became close. He usually spent at least one day a week with her and her boyfriend, Craig.

After being together for six years, Felicia and Craig separated. Felicia attended college and graduate school, and both she and Craig married other people. However, eventually both marriages ended and they got back together and married. Felicia says of that time, "It was obvious to everybody, even us, that we were meant to be together, but I guess we needed to be apart for a while." As of 2003, Felicia and Craig have been happily married for seven years and have two daughters.

· · · ·

Beth Zogg was teaching chiropractic courses at Life University in Marietta, Georgia, in 1996. One of her students was Chris Kellett. Chris was a large man—tall, well built, and exceptionally good-looking. He was outgoing and had a sense of humor. Chris did well in class; he was a quick learner and always came prepared. Beth thought he was a man who seemed to "have it all together."

BETH: It was around Christmastime, and I asked my students what they would be doing for the holidays. Chris didn't say very much. He acted funny, so I just dropped the subject. Then a couple of days later he came up to me and asked to talk to me. He pulled me aside and told me the story of his life. He told me his father was on death row for murdering ration in May 1979. That time, she picked the children up at the school and, without Fred knowing it, secreted them away in South Carolina. Fred must have known then that Linda was leaving for good, and the rejection was too much for him.

•　•　•　•

After dropping off Chris at the prison, Beth went to Travel America, a truck stop across the highway. She was four months pregnant and did not feel like running after a toddler, so she and Christian sat in the truck and waited. Beth spent a difficult two hours worrying about Chris. She felt excited and anxious—excited that the meeting might be a breakthrough for Chris, but worried that it might also make things harder for him.

BETH: When I picked up Chris, he seemed different to me. He seemed softer and there was a sense of peace about him. He got in the truck and started talking about the visit. We were both crying. It was more than we ever expected. We didn't expect it to be anything good. Fred was so happy to see Chris. He doted on him and asked him a million questions. Instead of the big, mean man he had remembered him as being, Fred was really a little old man. He was sober and had found God. He told Chris that he loved him. He also told Chris a lot about his childhood— he helped fill in some blanks for him.

•　•　•　•

Unbeknownst to Chris, when he was adopted by Dr. Kellett, Felicia added him to their father's visitor list under his new name. Felicia had always held out hope that someday her brother would want to see their father. Felicia's foresight was fortunate, because had Chris not been on the approved visitors' list he would not have been able to see Fred that day.

It was several weeks before Chris told Felicia about the visit.

FELICIA: I had no idea that Chris had visited Dad. We went to Chris and Beth's over the Christmas holiday, and Chris told me he had been to see our father and had seen him every weekend for both days for three or four weeks. I was shocked, but thrilled. I always felt that a lot of Chris's problems stemmed from his hatred of our father. I didn't want my dad to die before they made peace.

Fred Gilreath (left), Felicia Floyd, and Chris Kellett.
Provided with permission of the family.

Soon after, Chris and Felicia went to visit Fred together for the first time in twenty-two years.

•　　•　　•　　•

Macon, Georgia, is an hour's drive south of Jackson, and for the next several months the Zogg-Kellett family made the trip to death row nearly every weekend, sometimes both days. At first only Chris visited, but after filling out extensive paperwork, Beth and Christian got permission to visit, too. In February 2001, the family went together for the first time.

BETH: I had never been to a prison before. I had never thought that I would ever go to a prison, but I was excited to meet this man—my father-in-law, the grandfather of my son. I was pregnant at the time. I wasn't afraid of meeting Fred, but nervous in a kind of excited way. He had told Chris that he loved him. He had made my husband happy, so I liked him.

I had an image of what the prison was like from Chris. Chris is really good at describing things and he had told me about it. Until Chris went to see Fred over Thanksgiving, I did not have a good impression of him. It just goes to show you that you can't always judge a person by his past.

In Georgia, the prisons permit contact visits with the inmates. Everybody from the same housing block visited together in a large, open room. There were seven or eight inmates and their visitors all in a large room. Kids were running around and playing with each other.

I was impressed at how good Fred looked. He was slim and fit. He had a gentle quality that I have never seen in anybody else before. Seeing him look at Christian made me weep. It was the first grandchild he had ever seen. And like any grandfather, he wanted to spoil him. He bought him candy and soda out of the machines and played with him. Someone looking at us from the outside might have thought that we were giving Fred something, but really he gave us something so much more.

Christian loved to go visit Fred. He talked about him all the time, asking when we could go see Poppy. My parents live in Muscatine, Iowa, so he didn't get to see grandparents very often, and seeing Fred regularly was a treat.

Besides playing with Fred, Christian also played with the children of the other people on death row. I have never felt as safe as I did spending time with all those men on death row. I trusted them. They were very kind to Christian and Chris and me. They asked us questions about our lives and always remembered the details. We got to be friends with some of them.

We got very close to Fred. He was gentle, forgiving, and humble. He always conducted himself with dignity and poise. He never complained about his circumstances or the difficulty of living in a small cell. He accepted his situation. Fred was an inspiration because he had such a strong faith in God. He had the strongest faith of anybody I had ever met. Fred's faith would have been inspirational even to Billy Graham.

He gave Chris a lot in the way of memories. He talked to Chris about his mother. Told him stories about how they met and how they got engaged. Fred also told us some about his childhood. It helped Chris understand why Fred was the way he was. Fred had had a really horrible upbringing. It put what Fred did in a different light. It made Chris think that maybe he would have been capable of the same thing. Everything about our time together was healing.

FELICIA: After Chris reconnected with our father, he spent a lot of time with him and got to be quite close. I was worried about Chris. He was making up for lost time; for all the years he didn't have a father. I feared it would be very hard for him if Fred was executed.

I just continued the same relationship I had always had with Fred. I kept my distance. I was fragile when it came to him. Even when I was an adult I still felt like he was trying to control me to some degree. Over the years our relationship had been fairly casual, and I wanted to keep it there. I know I had the upper hand in the situation because he was on death row and was so desperate for attention that he accepted the relationship on my terms. I just could not allow myself to get that close to him. I got just close enough to let him know that somebody loved and cared about him.

• • • • •

During the year that Chris spent getting reacquainted with his father, the State of Georgia was having a temporary suspension of executions. The constitutionality of the use of the electric chair was being challenged, and Georgia was transitioning into using lethal injections. The last execution had been that of David Cordele in June 1998. Everyone knew that the suspension would eventually be lifted, and Fred was one of the next people in line to be executed.

The family received news that the date had been chosen—November 13, 2001. Felicia and Chris complained that that date fell on their mother's birthday. Linda would have been forty-five years old. Out of respect for Felicia and Chris, the State of Georgia changed their father's execution date to the fourteenth. The parole hearing would be held the day before.

Fred's attorneys were quite optimistic about the chances of winning clemency for their client. After twenty-two years, he had become a model prisoner and a loving father and grandfather. Working with Fred's attorneys, Chris and Felicia vigorously pursued clemency for their father. Felicia took on the role of contacting her mother's family to make sure that none of them would be pushing for Fred's execution. They all agreed not to oppose Felicia and Chris's efforts at obtaining clemency. Their aunt Betty Jane even offered to come to the hearing and speak on Fred's behalf.

Ironically, only eighteen months earlier Chris had been calling the prosecution asking why it was taking so long for his father's execution; now he was spending most of his time trying to stop it.

the board's ruling, Cobb County District Attorney Pat Head, who was not in office when Fred was prosecuted, met with the four members of the Board of Pardons and Paroles and encouraged them to deny clemency. "I believe this was an appropriate case for the death penalty. We are a society of laws, and if we allow emotions to dictate decisions . . . we put society at risk," he said.[16]

CHRIS: The DA went out of his way to go talk to the parole board. They hadn't asked his opinion, he went unsolicited. It was that important to him to make sure our dad was executed.

At around 4:00 P.M., reporters called with the news that Fred's clemency request had been denied. The media informed the lawyers of the decision before the board did.

FELICIA: We were all hanging out at the truck stop, some of us inside and some outside smoking or pacing. It was hard to stand still. I was outside in the parking lot with Chris. David Russell was so anxious he and his wife, Jeannie, were driving around in the parking lot.

I saw a friend, Randy Loney, coming out of the truck stop. He said to us, "We didn't make it." The board denied him completely without making any other remarks.

I grabbed Chris, and we stayed in the parking lot by ourselves for about fifteen minutes watching the sunset. I was surprised. Chris was very somber. He kept saying, "What do these people need to hear?"

We went back inside, and the lawyers were already in the process of plotting their next move. The federal defender was suing the Board of Pardons and Paroles because its members had various conflicts of interest. In Georgia the attorney general oversees the Pardons and Paroles Board, and at that time at least three of the board members were under investigation by the attorney general. Two of them were involved with unethical behavior: fraud and sexual harassment. The female member had recused herself, and the other member hadn't even shown up for the hearing, he was in Las Vegas. It wasn't exactly a stellar process. You would expect a bit more from people who got paid six-figure salaries.

The federal court issued a stay until 3:00 P.M. on November 15.[17] However, the next day it decided not to hold a hearing on the suit against the pa-

Fred Gilreath with his grandchildren. Provided with permission of the family.

role board. The lawyers appealed to the Supreme Court, but the petition was denied.[18]

> FELICIA: While all this is going on we kept going back and forth to the prison to see our father, each time saying good-bye as though we would never see each other again. It looked like that execution was going to be scheduled for 7:00 P.M. on the fifteenth. I hadn't seen my kids in days, so I sent my husband home to get them. Plus, my mother-in-law was very upset; she was sick about the whole thing. Craig left at midnight, planning on meeting us at the prison at noon the following day.

November 15, 2001, was a beautiful Indian summer day. The sky was clear and the sun warm. Felicia's day began early with a phone call from the prison telling her that the execution had been moved up from 7:00 P.M. to 3:30. Instead of being able to visit with Fred until 3:00 P.M. as had been originally planned, the family would only be allowed to stay from 9:00 A.M. until noon. Felicia feared Craig and the kids would not make it back in time.

> FELICIA: The prison officials didn't tell us why they had changed the execution time. We thought it might be because there would be fewer people

at the prison to protest if they did it before people got out of work. We went to the prison, and there was a large media crew waiting for us. Chris had been doing the media interviews, but he got irritated when a reporter asked him how he felt about the decision, so I agreed to do the interview instead of Chris. It was my first one. I called the Board of Pardons and Paroles a Mickey Mouse court and said they had turned our lives into a three-ring circus.

The system is severely flawed. Going back and forth to the prison was so cruel. Every time you leave you never know if it will be your last visit or not. Changing the execution time was cruel, too. Craig and the girls never made it back for the last visit.

After we left the prison for the last time, we stood outside the gate and watched while the guards brought Fred through the gate. He was smiling. We had this expression that we used with each other, "Ye," which meant I love you. We were screaming "Ye" at each other. The guards were crying.

We walked away knowing that we weren't going to see him again unless something drastic happened. I was still hopeful, but as we walked out I looked at Beth and said, "Is that the last time we are going to see him?" and she said, "Yes."

CHRIS: I never wanted to let go of hope. I kept thinking that something could happen. I felt deep down that his death would hurt me more than it would hurt anyone else. It would have been very easy for me to go off the deep end and go crazy. But on the execution day I was trying to be there for my family. My wife had gotten close to my father. Our children and my sister's children had gotten to know him. The day of the execution I was thinking more in terms of protecting the things I had some control over. I wanted to honor my father's wishes. He had told me not to lash out, especially at the prison officials carrying out the execution, and not to live my life angry.

My dad had accepted death. I knew he'd have the least problem with it of anyone. He had a very strong faith. But that made me feel much worse for him. I wanted to fight for him because he wasn't fighting himself.

BETH: After spending a year getting to know Fred it was pretty hard to believe all this was happening. We were sure Fred would get clemency. He was finally in a position to give something back to his children. Why would the state kill him now? What possible good could it serve?

Felicia had long assumed that she would witness her father's execution when the day came. Chris also wanted to be there for his dad. But as time drew near, Felicia shied away from that decision. Chris still wanted to be present, but Fred didn't want his children's last memory to be his execution, and the lawyers advised against it, too. Ultimately, the warden exercised his prerogative and forbade Chris to be a witness.

Some of their reluctance might have come from the fact that the state had just begun using lethal injection as its method of execution and had not yet worked out all the kinks. During the previous execution, that of Ron Spivey, the executioner was unable to get the IV in through the normal process, so he ended up cutting Spivey's neck open and inserting a central line directly into an artery. The hospital that had been providing the doctors to perform the lethal injections refused to continue.

Sometime around 3:00 P.M. on November 15, Fred Gilreath's grandchildren were playing baseball in the warm Georgia sun outside death row in Jackson, Georgia. His children, their spouses, and about a dozen supporters held a solemn vigil: sharing memories of Fred, holding candles, and sometimes singing. A crew of media reporters waited. Word came to the group that the execution had begun. Fred's last words were "My God has forgiven me for all my sins. I have forgiven the people who have done me wrong. I want to thank the men in blue [prison guards] for treating me so well."[19] At 3:53 P.M., Fred was pronounced dead.[20]

Acting as a spokesperson for the family, Renny Cushing made a statement: "The State of Georgia made orphans of Felicia Floyd and Chris Kellett . . . despite their pleas to the State of Georgia that their families not be traumatized. Another body is in the coffin."[21]

Later, Chris told a reporter:

I had always been an advocate of the death penalty. But if this is how it is carried out . . . I saw things that were horrible and incredible. I can't believe there isn't a higher power to stop this. . . .

I thought the death penalty was supposed to be for premeditated murder. Yet, when we went before the board, the first question they asked was about premeditation. They obviously hadn't taken the time to read the reams of information my father's attorneys had given them. They had addressed that point at length. What my father did was not premeditated. But what the state did to him was the epitome of premeditation. They plotted his murder for more than twenty years.[22]

•   •   •   •

More than a year after the execution, Chris and Felicia are still grieving their father's death.

BETH: Chris and Felicia are both amazing people. They have been through so much, but have gone on to accomplish a lot with their lives. A lot of people who have had a lot more have accomplished a lot less. I am very inspired by Chris and his ability to forgive his father. There are not very many wives who can say that their husbands have inspired them. I know how hard it was for him to go see his dad. Our family definitely has been blessed because Chris was willing to do that.

It has been so hard for him since the execution. He has been pretty withdrawn. He doesn't like to talk about it. He has been almost protective of it. It is hard. I am glad we got through the first year. I'm hoping we continue to heal. It took him twenty years to finally forgive his dad, and now he has to start with the grieving all over again.

There are still people on death row that we know and care about. I write to some of Fred's friends. We tried to get on their lists to go visit them, but the prison won't let us. I don't think they know what to make of us.

Everybody thought that Fred would get clemency. It has been very demoralizing for the other prisoners, who assumed if Fred couldn't get clemency then nobody could. That is part of what is so frustrating about the death penalty. It is so random. It is a whim who they chose and when they do it. It is the icing on the cake of how corrupt the whole system is. Right from the time of the murder to the time of the execution it is all so subjective.

Christian still asks about his Poppy sometimes. We tell him that he is in heaven with a dog of ours that died. He is too young to understand death.

Going through an execution is surreal. It was bizarre because it was a beautiful, sunny afternoon and at that moment they were killing somebody that we loved. They made it clean and sterile and pretty to make it seem like they weren't murdering somebody, but they were. Someone remarked how at least Fred hadn't been electrocuted, but that doesn't really matter; in the end it is the same result. He is not part of our lives anymore. It is a void. We still feel bad. Chris only had him for one year, really. If he had his dad around it would be so much better for him. It has been a tough year for Chris and Felicia. I think it will take us all a long time to have peace about Fred's loss.

I used to support the death penalty, but it wasn't a very well thought-out support. I grew up in Iowa, which doesn't have the death penalty, so it was not a real issue in our lives. I guess I supported it because I was afraid that a murderer might get out of prison and hurt somebody that I know. Really, though, it was just revenge—an eye for an eye. I think my support for the death penalty showed a lack of faith. If you trust God to take care of you, then you don't worry about somebody breaking out of a maximum security prison and hurting you. Now, every time we hear of an execution we relive the horrible memories of the day we lost Fred and know that another family is going through that, too. It is such a helpless feeling.

I am a Baptist, a conservative Christian. So many Christians are for the death penalty. How can you look at the crucifixion of Jesus and still be for the death penalty? I think if people knew what we went through they would not support it. They just haven't thought about it in terms of what if it was somebody they knew.

I used to think that only really bad people committed murder, but now I believe that anybody is capable of murder. It is but for the grace of God that we aren't in their shoes. I have heard a lot of the bios of the other inmates in prison, and I look at my four-year-old son and think if he got put in some foster home or was sexually and physically abused you couldn't expect him to grow up and be productive.

I never would have imagined that I would associate with a murderer, but if they had let Fred out of prison I would have had him into my home, and I wouldn't have been afraid of him with my children. He was very mellow and mild, calm and kind.

People need to remember that the people on death row are still human beings. Somebody did love them in the past and will in the future. When Fred went to prison his grandchildren hadn't even been born. The death penalty is hurting people that are innocent and need that person, even if he is in a prison cell. Our life would be a lot fuller if Fred was still alive, even if we only saw him a few times a month. Getting rid of the death row inmate doesn't bring back the victim, it just victimizes other people.

FELICIA: The year after the execution has been hard. The weeks leading up to the execution, it was on my mind a lot. By the time of the anniversary

I was starting to get active. I had spoken at a couple of colleges and churches and I was involved with vigils and the moratorium campaign in Georgia and talking regularly to people. I am on the board of directors for Georgians for Alternatives to the Death Penalty. Georgia is still executing people, although there were six people in a row that ended up getting clemency, and none of them had cases as compelling as ours.

It is important for me to be involved in these activities, but all the people who are protestors and activists are very different people from me. It is hard sometimes to connect with them, and I'm not sure what my role is. Also, I have a family and a life, so I can only do so much. But when I have spoken at different places the response I have gotten has been profound. People have told me that after they heard my story they changed their minds about the death penalty.

So I guess my contribution is that I have a story to tell. I think that if more people could hear the story, they would change their minds. I would love to see some high-profile show like *60 Minutes* or *20/20* do a whole story on this case. I'm not going to go call *60 Minutes* and try to get on the show, but if it is meant to be, it will happen. What I would really like to do is sue the Board of Pardons and Paroles for wrongful death. But then, you know, you can't talk out of both sides of your mouth and be vengeful on one side and forgiving on the other. It is so senseless. It did not have to happen, and it did not serve anyone.

CHRIS: I'm doing okay. I have worked diligently to fulfill my father's wish of not being angry. I'm not as willing to put it in a religious context as he was about turning our cheek to people who are trying to hurt us. I am certainly not Christ-like in that respect, but I am not angry. However, anyone who gets that close to a situation like that is lying to you if they tell you they are not disgusted.

But there have been people who have been tremendously supportive. Randy Loney has been a good friend and is someone who I can talk to about this. I also really appreciated Renny Cushing coming to help us when we really needed it.

So I am not angry, but I miss him. I hate the fact that the memory of him is fading with my children. I hear my son say things and I know he vaguely remembers him, and it becomes more and more vague, and that is tough. It has been hard on Beth, too. She got as close to him in that year as Felicia and I did during our entire lives.

I spent all of my life hating him so much, and then when I was finally able to forgive him and put down that guard, it's scary how intense the feelings can be. I learned early on to hate as a way of dealing with hurt, and then it got to be a pattern in my life. If I hate him he can't hurt me. It can't hurt me if he suffers or lives in a six-by-nine-foot cell or if he dies. For me the real turning point came when I realized it is a lot harder to forgive someone than to hate someone.

CHAPTER 5

Too Young to Die

Eileen Stanford is an attractive, petite fifty-seven year-old with wavy blond hair that frames an open, smiling face; she looks at least a decade younger than she is. Eileen lives in the rural town of Eddyville, Kentucky, about two hundred miles from Louisville. The largest town of any size in the area is Paducah, thirty miles north. She lives in a comfortable home on the shores of lovely Lake Barkley, which she shares with three cats. She has a grown son and two grandchildren who live in California, and she visits them several times a year. She is friendly and well liked in her neighborhood and has several close friends. Eileen shares many attributes of white middle-class American women, with one exception—her husband is on death row.

Eileen's journey to Eddyville began in the fall of 1980, when she flew from her home in San Jose, California, to Louisville, Kentucky, to spend a week with a girlfriend, Marie, with whom she had worked at the telephone company as a switch operator. Even though she had been married to Robert Cano for nearly twenty years, the two vacationed separately. Eileen had never been to the South, so when Marie moved to Kentucky, she thought it would be a good opportunity to go.

EILEEN: When I landed in Louisville, Marie wasn't at the airport to meet me as we had planned. I had no idea how to get around the city. I had reserved a room at a hotel in Louisville because Marie lived in a small studio apartment. The plan was for Marie to drive me there.

It had been a long flight from California, and I hate to fly, so I had had a few drinks on the plane to help me relax. I arrived slightly tipsy, having no idea where to go. I called her house but got no answer, so I sat down to wait for her.

A friendly young man came up and started talking to me—asking me questions about where I was from and what I was doing. We talked for a while, and then he asked me out to dinner. I had never gone out with a black man before and I had never been picked up by a stranger, but there was something about Kevin that made me feel comfortable right away.

He was small—five feet five and skinny. He probably weighed 135 pounds. He had a kind face. He was young; he told me he was twenty-two. I was thirty-five but looked much younger, and I told him I was twenty-six.

Not knowing what else to do, I agreed to go to the restaurant with him. I called my friend and told her to page me at the restaurant, but she never did.

After dinner, Kevin took me to my hotel and ended up spending the night.

I sensed in Kevin deep pain and neediness. He wanted so much to be liked. He was a great listener and very curious, wanting to know all about me. I was also in a lot of pain. I had been gang-raped the year before and was in bad emotional shape. I had been drinking a lot to deal with the pain. The first time we made love I cried, and he held me all night long. He wasn't afraid of my pain.

Kevin and I connected in a way that I never had with anyone else. This was such a change for me. I had been married for almost twenty years to Bob, who was a kind man, but we never talked about anything, not even the rape. I worked evenings and he worked days so that someone was always at home to care for our son, Tim. Tim had just turned eighteen and left home.

Kevin and I spent a whirlwind week together, and by the end I was in love, or at least deeply infatuated. We made plans to write, and I said I would visit again on my next vacation.

Eileen returned home and resumed her life working at the phone company and living with her husband. She did make one change: She rented a post office box so that she could correspond with Kevin without her husband finding out. They wrote letters frequently for several months, and then Eileen got a letter from prison.

EILEEN: Kevin sent me a letter from prison telling me that he had been charged with rape and murder. He didn't go into much detail. Also,

then tied his hands to the bedpost to keep him from running. She then beat him with an extension cord, leaving long welt marks on his back, legs and ribs.

The abuse by Beverly lasted for a year, and she would turn out to be just the first in a long line of people responsible for caring for him who hurt him. Maybe it was his small size and desire to be loved that made him particularly vulnerable, or the fact that most of the time Kevin did not receive adequate adult supervision.

In 1971, when Kevin was eight, two neighborhood teenagers assaulted him, forcing him to have anal sex in an abandoned car. Later, two older neighborhood boys forced him into a doghouse where they made him perform oral sex on them.

An older neighborhood teenage girl, who was nice to Kevin, initiated a sexual relationship with him that lasted for several months. Although she did not abuse him like the others, Kevin was too emotionally and physically immature to handle a sexual relationship.

During this time, Barbara was attending night school studying respiratory therapy and Kevin's primary babysitter was a nephew of his stepfather, Thomas Harris. Over the next four to five years, Thomas abused Kevin repeatedly. One of the most horrendous incidents occurred after Thomas anally penetrated Kevin while Kevin kneeled on all fours. After Thomas ejaculated, he brought over the family dog to lick Kevin's anal area. Then Thomas placed the dog on Kevin and the dog anally penetrated Kevin. Kevin's primary memory of the incident was the dog scratching his rib cage. Kevin did not protest because he believed that "anything goes" when it came to sexual contact. Thomas also had sexual intercourse with his girlfriend in front of Kevin and his cousins.

In fact, the only time in Kevin's life that he was free from abuse was when he stayed with his grandmother, Minnie Stanford, who kept a watchful eye on him.

In 1976, when Kevin was thirteen, Barbara told the authorities that she didn't want him, and he went to live with his stepfather, George Boller, who by then was divorced from Barbara. When living with George didn't work out, Kevin tried living with his mother again. By now, she was living with a new boyfriend, Julius Cushenberry, who did not welcome Kevin, drank daily, and regularly had sexual affairs with Barbara's friends while Kevin was in the house. When the two could not get along, Kevin moved back into his mother's home and lived there alone. His mother called to check on him and left money for food, but Kevin was largely unsupervised. His use of alcohol and drugs continued, and he was unable to function without the relief they provided.

In fact, Kevin endured so much abuse that it affected his intellectual development. At age seven, he scored 116 on IQ tests; by age fifteen, he tested 70 — borderline mentally retarded.[1] Although he started off with above average intelligence, his future seemed doomed, even to Kevin.[2] When he was eight years old, a teacher asked him what he wanted to be when he grew up. He said that all the men in his family went to jail.

At age ten, Kevin began shoplifting because he wanted to be placed in a juvenile home. That began his life in and out of detention at the Jefferson County Youth Center (JCYC). Kevin preferred detention to the family life he had known because he was given three meals a day and a room to himself and was not sexually abused. Although this structure provided for Kevin's basic needs, it did not address the severe emotional damage he had suffered from the sexual and physical abuse, nor did it deal with his addictions. While in detention, Kevin used inhalants such as aerosols and glues to get high. In an eerily foreshadowing memo, Jack Engler, a social services employee who evaluated Kevin in 1978, predicted "Kevin is likely to pose problems for the community in the future if he does not resolve this conflict and come to accept a sense of self-responsibility."[3]

Soon after he was released from JCYC, Kevin's crimes began to grow more serious. By the time he was sixteen, the State of Kentucky had sent him to Green River Boys Camp, where he spent thirteen months in "confrontational therapy," designed to be emotionally abusive and to induce fear and compliance. Punishment could come either from the staff or from other boys. Kevin was small, and often bore the brunt of abuse by boys, including being called racial epithets.

Among his many horrific experiences, Kevin remembered being slapped by a nurse, having a big ashtray thrown at him, having large boys throw him on the ground and beat him while the staff watched, and being forced to do demeaning physical labor like carrying heavy logs a long distance in the summer while wearing heavy clothing, and digging a hole to plant a tree with a teaspoon. Although family members were permitted to visit on weekends, Barbara never visited.

Kevin described Green River as the "worst year of his life." Eventually a U.S. Department of Justice investigation and lawsuit ended the program.[4] The decision by the State of Kentucky to place Kevin at Green River was particularly disturbing given that Jack Engler had specifically stated that "Kevin would be a poor candidate for any type of confrontation therapy."[5]

In 1980, Kevin went to the Rice Audubon Program, a transitional prerelease program, where he met a girl. Although staff reported that he did well in the program, he impregnated his girlfriend, adding yet another stressor to his life.

When Kevin wasn't in the custody of the State of Kentucky, he was prostituting himself in the gay community for drugs and alcohol, spending the night in strangers' homes, on the floor of video arcade halls, and sometimes with relatives. Adult criminals used Kevin to assist in armed robberies in exchange for the drugs to feed his habit.

KAREN: On January 7, 1981, there was a going-away party for Victor, who was leaving for the service. Barbara was drinking a lot. Kevin was upset because Auntie was showing a lot of emotion for Victor—even crying—and was ignoring Kevin, as she usually did. Kevin was very down. He was moping around and Auntie just tuned him out. I gave him some acid that day. I will never forgive myself for giving him acid.

I didn't know then how much Kevin had been running with David Buchanan and that crowd. David was crazy—literally—he had only just been released from a mental hospital. He had gone there because he tried to kill his grandmother.

Later that day, Kevin Stanford's life changed forever. He was a boy-man who had lived experiences well beyond his years, but he had never had a birthday party, and his mother had never read to him or helped him with his homework, hugged him or held him on her lap. The only touching he knew was inappropriate sexual conduct from people who were supposed to be taking care of him.

•   •   •   •

Although Eileen had stopped contacting Kevin, she hadn't stopped thinking about him. She continued with her job as a switch operator and in 1984, after twenty years of service, took early retirement.

EILEEN: It had always been my dream to live in the country, so after I retired, Bob and I bought a house in Northern California, about two hundred miles from San Jose. I moved to the country, and Bob lived with his mother in the city and came out on weekends.

It was wonderful living in the country. I bought a 3,600-square-foot home. I went to college. I wanted to become a social worker. When I had started working at the phone company it was because I needed the money. Now I had a chance to do something I wanted to do.

I bought a lawn tractor and plowed the five acres of land. I had never been really domestic. I didn't know anything about gardening, but I planted a garden and flowers.

I still thought about Kevin a lot. I probably thought about him every week. I knew he was on death row because my girlfriend told me, but I understood nothing about the death penalty. I assumed he would be executed soon.

Then in 1991, I took out a subscription to *Mother Jones* magazine. In the back section they had an ad about writing to people on death row, and I saw Kevin's name. It was such a random coincidence, because I had just subscribed to the magazine, and the times when I had read it before, I had never paid any attention to the ads. It was the only time that Kevin had his name in the magazine. Had I subscribed a month later I would have never seen it.

I thought about writing for a long time before I did. Even when I finally did write, I told myself I would not get too involved because he would be dead soon.

The first few times I wrote to him, I didn't use my real name because I wanted to see where his head was. After a few letters, I told him who I was, and it was like we had never stopped communicating. We wrote to each other every day, pouring out our hearts. Kevin didn't really have anyone else in his life. At the time of his arrest, his mother had told him that she was "washing her hands" of him. He had no support.

We wrote to each other every day for a year, and in June of 1992 I decided to visit. I flew down to Louisville and rented a car. I did not really know where Eddyville was. The plane didn't arrive until midnight, and it is a two-hundred-mile drive on back roads with no lights. I didn't get to Eddyville until almost four in the morning. I had to check in at the prison between 7:00 and 7:30 A.M. I was very nervous. The person in charge of the visiting room was very nasty. She said, "You're a minute late—you'll have to wait until next week." I wasn't late and I wasn't going to wait another week to see him, so I asked to speak with the warden and then she backed down and said that she'd make an exception just this time.

When I got to the visiting area, I wasn't sure who Kevin was. At that time he was housed in administrative segregation, which meant he couldn't have any contact visits. I sat on a steel seat with a Plexiglas wall between us. You have to lean way forward to put your ear next to the hole, and there is no place to put your arms. Normally you are only allowed a two-hour visit, but since I had come so far they gave us four hours. Seeing him was like we had never been apart. We talked constantly for four hours. During the first visit, we really didn't talk about his case.

I stayed in Kentucky two weeks and saw him twice. The rest of the time I went to the mall or drove around. I didn't know anybody and there wasn't a lot to do.

I returned to California, and we continued to write. He started asking me to move down to Kentucky. I talked about it, but I didn't really think I would do it. I had a house. I was married. The next time I went to Kentucky, I stayed for a month, but I still only got to see him once a week. During our third visit, I started asking him about the case. I told him, "Whatever you have done, I will forgive you, but I won't forgive you lying to me. I won't move down here if you don't tell me the truth." He admitted that he had been involved in the crime, but he said that he did not realize until he heard the shots that she was going to be killed. He admitted that he had raped her. You can imagine how I felt about that. I yelled at him, "How could you do that?" I frequently brought up the issue. He just listened with tears streaming down his face. I identified a lot with the victim, but the more I started to learn about the case, it was clear that the jury had not gotten the whole picture of what had happened.

During one of my husband's weekend visits, he found letters from Kevin. He confronted me, and I told him I wanted a divorce and that I wanted to move to Kentucky. He begged me not to go. It was very hard. We had been married for thirty-three years. I loved him. With my husband it was more the way you would love a friend. He was kind and gentle, but the main reason we never got close is because we didn't communicate.

In September of 1993, I rented an eighteen-foot truck, packed up all my possessions, and moved across the country. Bob and I were officially divorced the following year. Soon after our divorce was final, Bob was diagnosed with multiple myeloma, likely caused by working in Silicon Valley with semiconductors at Fairchild and with plastics at IBM. There was no cure.

When I found out he was sick I wanted to go back and take care of him, but he didn't want me to. He accused me of never having loved him. He was really hurt. He called me periodically, but if I tried to reach out to him like by sending him a card or something, he got very angry and told me to stop. By the time he died, we had a civil relationship. I didn't go to the service. He was cremated, so he didn't actually have a funeral. I was going to go, but his family was so extremely bitter towards me. I felt like I couldn't take it but afterwards I felt bad that I hadn't gone, because I regretted not being there for my son.

After Bob died, and even now every few weeks, I have a dream that he is alive and he is happy and I feel happy. But then I wake up and it is not true. We lived separate lives, but I cared about him a lot.

Eileen started to build a life for herself in Kentucky. At first she did not tell people about her relationship with Kevin, believing that if she did, they would not be willing to get to know her.

Her life settled into a routine. Every Friday and Saturday she visited Kevin for five hours. He called once a day, and they spoke for as long as Kevin could have access to the phone. The calls cost $1.25. They also wrote to each other every day.

When she wasn't busy with Kevin, she spent time getting to know her neighborhood and the surrounding area. She took a part-time job taking care of an elderly lady.

Eileen also took a position as the Kentucky director of Citizens United for the Rehabilitation of Errants (CURE), a prison reform organization. She worked on issues affecting the inmates in Kentucky's prisons. Prisoners wrote to her with complaints and she followed up with investigation and appropriate action.

EILEEN: I was very busy in the beginning, between looking into Kevin's case and getting CURE organized in Kentucky. Everyone would come to me with their problems. I wrote letters to the Department of Correc-

Eileen and Kevin Stanford.
Provided with permission of Eileen Stanford.

tions. It is a hard place to organize because the prison is in such a remote area. Most of the families are living at least two hundred miles away from Eddyville. There are a few living in Paducah, but not many.

But Eileen spent most of her energy learning everything she could about Kevin's case. She pored over the trial transcripts, learning the "official" version, and was deeply distressed to learn how much of "the truth" the jury had never heard.

•   •   •   •

On January 7, 1981, eighteen-year-old David Buchanan called Kevin, who was then seventeen, and asked him to help him rob the Checker Oil Company station at 4501 Cane Run Road in Louisville with David's uncle Calvin Buchanan. Kevin agreed, because he owed Calvin and Earl Buchanan, money. The two brothers had a pattern of enticing juveniles to get involved with drugs, then, when the kids owed them money, demanding payback in the form of helping with armed robberies. Calvin was on parole for sexual assault at the time.

Troy Johnson, who the state claimed was fifteen, joined the two boys and brought along a gun. Before the robbery they drank whiskey, smoked marijuana, and consumed mescaline.

At the station, Kevin and David went inside to do the robbery, and Troy and Calvin waited outside. Kevin looked for money while David went to tie up the attendant, Baerbel Poore. Instead of tying her up, though, he took her into the station bathroom and sexually assaulted her. Kevin went looking for David and found him in the bathroom. David encouraged Kevin to rape Baerbel, which he did.

Calvin entered the station to find out what was taking them so long and found them in the bathroom. He was furious that the two had gotten distracted from the robbery. He assumed Kevin had instigated the rape and threatened to kill him.

Taking Baerbel with them, the four assailants drove to a nearby field away from the residential area. Calvin drove Baerbel in her mother's 1973 Chevy Impala. Troy, accompanied by David and Kevin, drove the car that he had driven to the robbery.

When they arrived at the field, Baerbel, evidently believing the worst was over, lit up a cigarette. David got out of Troy's car and joined his uncle. According to David, while Baerbel was smoking, Calvin shot her twice in the head.

Calvin and David left Baerbel in her mother's car and joined the others. Two women, Kerise Ison and Amona Dorsey, drove by. They later picked Calvin out of a lineup as one of the two men they had seen. They did not identify Kevin, who had also been in a lineup.[6]

The four returned to the station, where they stole two gallons of gas, $143, three hundred cartoons of cigarettes, and some lighters.[7] Six days later, the three youths were arrested and charged with capital murder, first-degree robbery, first-degree sodomy, and receipt of stolen property valued at more than $100. (Calvin was never arrested or charged.)

While in custody, Kevin was brutally beaten. A police officer thrust a gun into his mouth and threatened to kill him if he did not give a statement. Kevin told the police that Calvin was the main perpetrator, but David gave a statement exonerating Calvin. David admitted his part in the rape, sodomy, and robbery but claimed that Kevin was the triggerman.[8] This statement was not only self-serving but lacked credibility: The gun did not belong to Kevin, he had not brought it to the scene, and he had not known that it was loaded.

The crime triggered public fury not only because of its brutality but because the three attackers were black and the victim was white. The police decided early on that Kevin and David were the most culpable. So even though it was his gun and his car that were used to perpetrate the crime, Troy was offered a plea agreement with the prosecution and served nine months in juvenile detention.

Both Kevin and David were transferred to adult court. Before being transferred to adult court, a hearing was held to determine whether the boys were amenable for rehabilitation. Judge Richard J. Fitzgerald specifically found that Kevin was amenable to treatment, but that there were no appropriate facilities available to him:

> Kevin has a low internalization of the values and morals of society and lacks social skills. . . . He does possess an institutionalized personality and has, in effect, because of his chaotic family life and lack of treatment become socialized in delinquent behavior. . . . He is emotionally immature and could be amenable to treatment if properly done on a long-term basis of psycho-therapeutic intervention and reality-based therapy for socialization and drug therapy in a residential facility. . . . His progress [in various facilities] has been marginal based in part on the failure of the county and the state to provide meaningful therapy for the child or aftercare intervention when he was returned, after a relatively short time in each placement, to the streets of Jefferson County. His progress was basically that he learned how to behave enough to meet the minimum criteria for release each time, approximately or roughly 6 months after placement, then cut loose to the same chaos and streets that he was not able to deal with, still without social skills, still delinquent, and still uneducated.[9]

But there were no treatment facilities locally. Kevin would have had to go to Ohio at a cost of $20,000, which neither the state nor his mother would pay. Instead, Kevin was transferred to adult court in October 1981 to stand trial for capital murder.

Kevin spent a year and a half awaiting trial at a juvenile detention center. He was extremely depressed. He made two suicide attempts and "huffed" Ping-Pong balls and cleaning supplies to get high. One counselor, Dana Mattison, recalled that "Kevin evinced acquiescence in his own death."[10]

Kevin was "treated" with high doses of Thorazine[11], a drug that is prescribed for someone who is highly agitated or psychotic, not depressed. Kevin remembers being told that the only way to get out of isolation was to take the drugs, which he continued to take even during the trial.

During this time, Kevin's two court-appointed attorneys were missing in action. Frank Jewell went to see Kevin once, and James Shake never met Kevin until the day of trial.

Trial began in August 1982 before Jefferson Circuit Judge Charles M. Liebson, with an all-white jury in a community that had been saturated by negative publicity. The prosecutor collected petitions in favor of the death penalty and presented them to the court as the trial began.[12] Kevin and David were tried together.

Troy testified that Kevin was the shooter. However, the gun belonged to Troy and there were no fingerprints or physical evidence linking it to Kevin. The state also entered into evidence David's confession that named Kevin as the shooter, but since David did not testify, Kevin had no opportunity to cross-examine him. The appellate court later ruled that this violated Kevin's Sixth Amendment right to confrontation. However, the courts found that the error was "harmless" and would not have changed the outcome of the trial.[13]

Probably the most damaging testimony against Kevin came from two employees at the detention center where Kevin stayed waiting for his trial. Neither one had been interviewed by Kevin's attorneys beforehand.

Michael Nalley, a corrections officer, testified that Kevin had told him that he "had to shoot the bitch because she lived next door to me and would recognize me."[14] Kevin did not live next door to Baerbel, a fact that was easily verifiable, but Kevin's lawyers failed to make this point for the jury. Nalley claimed that Kevin made this statement within earshot of seven other juveniles. Kevin had begged his lawyers to interview these witnesses, who would have severely challenged Nalley's credibility, but they never did.[15]

Later, appellate attorneys obtained affidavits from ten employees at the JCYC and two prisoners who had been there while Kevin was. They all said that Kevin was quiet and kept to himself. None of them ever heard Kevin brag about the crime. One social worker, Louise Pennix, said that Kevin cried a lot and talked about the pending birth of his daughter. Louise also said that she had never heard of Michael Nalley and was surprised to learn that he had testified against Kevin at his trial.

Betty Shipp, who was in charge of the detention center, also signed an affidavit. She said that the statements Nalley claimed Kevin made would have been completely out of character. She stated that Kevin was extremely withdrawn during that year and a half in custody and never spoke with anyone about his case. She also pointed out that Kevin was familiar with the juvenile justice system from his other stints in it and was unlikely to be so foolish as to make the statement Nalley claimed he made to an officer. Kevin was also very small and so did not go around instigating fights. Had his lawyers done a little investigating, they would have learned that Michael Nalley had put in for a better-paying job and was transferred after testifying against Kevin.

The crowning insult of the state's case was that prosecutor Ernest Jasmin remarked in his closing statement that Kevin did not show any emotion to the jury, which proved that he lacked remorse for what he had done. Neither the prosecutor nor Kevin's lawyers told the jury that Kevin was practically comatose from the extremely powerful drugs the state was giving him.

The jury found both boys guilty. Since the state had taken the position that David was not the shooter, it did not seek a death sentence against him. Judge Liebson sentenced David to life for murder and sixty-five years for rape, sodomy, and robbery.

This meant that if the jury was going to impose a death sentence against anyone, it had to be Kevin.

Frank Jewell called eight witnesses at Kevin's mitigation hearing, including his stepfather, George Boller. However, some of these witnesses were unaware of the abuse that Kevin had suffered, and others had not been properly prepared for trial. For example, Kevin's stepfather had only been married to and living with Kevin's mother for about two years. He saw the results of the abuse in the way that Kevin acted out but was not aware of his history of sexual and physical abuse at the hands of his mother and many of her boyfriends. Another witness was George's sister, who knew nothing about what had happened to Kevin and had not seen him for years.

Frank did not even meet most of the witnesses until right before the sentencing trial. He did not explain to them the purpose of a mitigation hearing, which was to provide information about Kevin's life so the jurors could understand the forces that led Kevin to take the actions he took. The state painted Kevin as a cold-blooded rapist and murderer. Had his lawyers properly represented Kevin, they would have painted the picture of a confused, isolated, drug-addicted young man who grew up horribly abused and had gotten himself involved with drug dealers he owed money to and agreed to take part in a robbery that ended in a terrible death. While this was tragic, and Kevin bore responsibility for his part of the crime, he did not deserve death. In fact, had his lawyers really done their job, they might have been able to convince the jury that Kevin had not shot Baerbel and had not even known that anyone planned on shooting her. Had his lawyers described the extreme neglect and abuse that Kevin suffered as a child, it would have helped the jury understand that Kevin had such distorted ideas about sex that he did not know what was proper and improper.

But the jury did not learn the full extent of the abuse and neglect that Kevin suffered. Not surprisingly, the jury recommended death, and Judge Liebson imposed the death penalty for the murder and forty-five years' imprisonment for robbery, sodomy, and receipt of stolen property.[16]

KAREN: My whole family watched the news on TV when Kevin was sentenced to death. I just couldn't believe it. I thought about all the problems he had in his life and all the things that had never been addressed. But that was too much for me, so whenever I thought about it too much I just kept drinking to blot it out.

·　·　·　·

After the trial, the public defender agency took over representing Kevin, and the lead public defender, Vince Aprile, became Kevin's lawyer. Kevin's conviction and sentence were upheld on appeal. In fact, Kevin's case became the seminal U.S. Supreme Court case establishing the protocol for executing juveniles.[17] Given all the information that never got into the trial record, it is too bad that this case has been the primary precedent guiding juvenile death cases.

Eileen made her first trip to meet with Vince in 1992, driving nearly 250 miles to Frankfort to see him. She was extremely frustrated to learn that Vince had not read the trial transcript. Eileen shared with Vince what she had learned from her research, but he seemed uninterested. Most of the men on death row had two lawyers, but Kevin only had Vince, and Vince had a heavy caseload. Eileen learned that Vince was good friends with one of Kevin's trial lawyers and wondered if that kept him from working hard on Kevin's case.

However, in 1994, a young, newly graduated lawyer named Stephanie McArdle joined the agency and started working with Vince on Kevin's case. Stephanie took an interest in the case like none of the previous lawyers had.

She went to great lengths, pursuing leads that should have been investigated before. She did a lot of extra research and found out things about the case that the jury never heard, and mitigation information about Kevin's childhood that might have kept him from getting a death sentence.

EILEEN: Stephanie told me a lot of information that was never brought out at trial. For starters, Troy, who the state said was fifteen and the youngest and least culpable, was actually a month older than Kevin. The jury didn't know that David's uncle Calvin, who Kevin had told the police took part in the crime, had been convicted of aggravated rape and had three armed robberies pending at the time of the crime. He was given something like ten years for that, but never tried for his part in this case.

She found out other things, too, like the fact that some of the police officers that beat Kevin belonged to a white supremacist organization. She went to the detention center and interviewed people who had been there when Kevin was. Stephanie learned that Kevin had been in really bad emotional shape when he went into detention. His mother had said that she washed her hands of him and he had no family support. She was the one that learned about Michael Nalley's transfer to a highly desirable position at a federal facility after he testified against Kevin.

Stephanie hired a mitigation specialist who conducted an extensive personal history of Kevin. She interviewed people who had known Kevin as a child—family, people in the neighborhood, teachers—and documented the years of physical and sexual abuse he had experienced. Stephanie was disturbed to learn that Vince had known about this mitigation evidence but had not brought it forward. She asked him why he had not used the information and he made some kind of excuse that Kevin hadn't trusted him enough to bring it up, but that was simply not true.

Stephanie was in a bind because in order to adequately represent Kevin she had to file a claim that Vince had been ineffective, but that was hard for her to do because Vince was her boss. However, she sought the advice of several experienced capital attorneys who told her that she needed to get Vince off the case.

Stephanie filed a four-hundred-page habeas corpus petition claiming forty-two constitutional violations, but the court ruled that all of the issues had been waived because they had not been raised at trial or on appeal.

EILEEN: These issues had all been defaulted because Vince didn't do the investigation. Whenever Kevin and I would speak to him about the issues—lack of mitigating evidence at trial, the fact that trial counsel didn't call witnesses to impeach the juvenile officers, the fact that the state got Troy's age wrong, the fact that Kevin was never able to cross-examine David's statement—Vince just led us to believe that once the case got to federal court it would get sent back to state court, where these issues would get heard. But when the case finally got into federal court, the court didn't even rule on whether the issues were legitimate—it simply said that because Mr. Stanford had not brought them up when he was still in state court they would be defaulted.

And then when we finally had a chance for a hearing in the Sixth Circuit, Judge Robert Cole asked Vince if Kevin had made the bragging statements attributed to him by Mike Nalley, and instead of saying, "No," Vince said, "They were just quick statements." We had been telling Vince for years that Kevin hadn't made the statements.

Another issue was that David Smith, the assistant attorney general, had said that Kevin had never been in a lineup, which was untrue.

I knew right then and there that our chances of getting a reversal were over. When I got back home I tried to call Vince, but he didn't return my calls. We asked him to supplement the record, but he didn't do that, either.

The court ruled against Kevin right away. In the judge's opinion he cited the fact that Kevin's lawyers admitted that he made those statements and that he had confessed. I truly believe that if Vince had brought up these issues it might have made a difference.

·　　·　　·　　·

In her continuing quest to learn everything she could about the case, Eileen visited David Buchanan at the Luther Luckett Correctional Facility. Luckett was only a medium security facility, and normally a person serving a life sentence would not be housed there, but Luckett had a mental health facility, and David had a history of mental illness. In fact, Baerbel's family considered suing the facility where he had been institutionalized shortly before the crime for prematurely releasing him back into the community.

EILEEN: It was very weird to meet David. He is so slow—borderline retarded. His uncles had totally shaped his life. Kevin had been told by everybody not to hang around with David because his family was bad news. But Kevin was a drug addict and Earl was his dealer.

David admitted to me that Kevin had not shot Baerbel but said that he was not willing to go to court to say that. At trial, the police got on the stand to testify as to what David told him, but Kevin had no opportunity to cross-examine David's self-serving version. David had changed his testimony several times, and these discrepancies never came out at trial. David has said he would give Kevin an affidavit, as long as Calvin approved. It probably wouldn't do any good because David doesn't have any credibility.

•   •   •   •

Besides helping Kevin with his legal case, Eileen got to know his family, particularly his daughter, Lakiesha. In 1993, she took Lakiesha to Eddyville to visit her dad for Christmas. It was the first time the two had spent Christmas together.

EILEEN: Lakiesha was twelve years old when I first met her. She had a lot of problems. She was very angry. She had grown up sheltered and kind of spoiled. When she was first born, she lived with her mother, who was very young and had a lot of problems. Lakiesha developed juvenile diabetes and when she was seven went into a coma. It was obvious Lakiesha's mother couldn't take care of her, so Kevin begged his mother to let Lakiesha live with her. She reluctantly agreed.

I realized that her acting out was a result of her troubled childhood, the lack of knowing what was important, in many ways doing what her father had done, looking at material things as a sign that someone cared about them. Kevin, too, had been given material things, but not love, direction, and guidance that a child needs so much more than material things. His mother had given Lakiesha material things, a roof over her head, but she was also trying to correct some of the mistakes she made with Kevin.

Kevin's mother really never learned how to parent. Her own childhood was filled with abuse and pain, and she ended up parenting the same way she learned. As a result of her pain, she retreated into herself and found it too painful to build a relationship with either men or her children. She used drugs and alcohol to alter her mood and avoid feeling pain.

Because Kevin's mother rarely went to see him, Eileen took Lakiesha for visits. This was a difficult undertaking because it involved about eight hundred miles of driving—two hundred to get Lakiesha, two hundred to drive her to the prison, two hundred to drive Lakiesha home, and two hundred to drive back home again. Besides taking her to prison to see her dad, she tried to spend other time with her. Once she took her to California.

LAKIESHA: It didn't seem weird to be going to jail to visit my dad. My dad has been on death row my whole life, so I have never known anything different. I thought of my dad being in prison like I thought of myself being a girl. I never questioned the fact because I couldn't change it.

I think I was about seven years old the first time I remember going to prison to see him. I didn't feel scared to be in jail, but I felt real funny. It was a contact visit. It was the first time that I remember touching my dad.

I went with my grandmother. My mother had never been to visit my dad. They broke up after he went to jail. That was around the time I moved from living with my mother to living with my grandmother, and I was a bit confused about all the changes going on. We lived in the same neighborhood, only about ten minutes away.

We didn't go visit my dad very often because it was a long way away from Louisville and my grandmother didn't like to go. I spoke with my dad on the phone about once a week, and as I got older I wrote letters, too.

I remember from an early age deciding that I would not do anything to end up in jail. I knew I wanted to do something with my life—go to college and get an education and make something of my life. I only have one year left at Northern Kentucky University. I am majoring in psychology and want to be a child therapist.

KAREN: It was hard for Lakiesha growing up. She was picked on and talked about by kids at school. It was hard for her not being able to do anything about her situation. Back then she was getting into a lot of trouble—she wasn't really being herself. Her mom was on drugs and her dad was getting ready to be electrocuted. She wouldn't take her medicine and had more diabetic episodes. She had a really bad attitude. She is now totally turned around.

Kevin's mother has improved, too. She took in Lakiesha, but only reluctantly, after Kevin begged her to. She always reminded Lakiesha of her situation. It pissed her off to have to get medicine, to take time off from work. Lakiesha could tell she wasn't really wanted. Basically the rest of the family told Auntie that if she didn't take care of Lakiesha she could forget about ever having anything to do with the family.

But over time Auntie started admitting her shortcomings. She recognized that she doesn't have a lot of natural talent for mothering. She has eased into taking care of her. And Lakiesha has turned out amazing. If you think about all that child has gone through, between having a father on death row and a drug-addict mother in prison and a grandmother who didn't really want to care for her, what she has accomplished is nothing short of a miracle.

Kevin has asked me to forgive Auntie, but it is hard because she is the reason Kevin is on death row. Even Auntie admits that now. Auntie is just starting to accept her responsibility for her role in Kevin's life.

•   •   •   •

Less than a year after Eileen moved to Kentucky, Governor Brereton Jones signed a death warrant for Kevin to be executed on August 12, 1994. In response to that news, the *Courier Journal* ran a story on Lakiesha about what it was like to have a father on death row. The story pointed out Lakiesha's many accomplishments in spite of the fact that her father was on death row and her mother in prison serving time on a forgery charge: certificates won for perfect attendance and spelling bees, a Young Author's Award from Duke University, an academic letter for outstanding grades, and accomplishments in sports. The article told of how Lakiesha wanted to do something to help her father. She had recorded her thoughts daily in a diary and her aunt suggested she send them to the governor. So Lakiesha wrote a registered letter to Governor Jones in which she asked the governor, "What will you prove of yourself if you kill my father? Why not give him a life sentence or even another trial." Lakiesha's letter also asked the governor why he had switched his position on the death penalty. "During election time you were opposed and against the death penalty. What made you for it?"[18] The article ended with the reporter's observations:

Lakiesha talked serenely Friday about the reality of her father's execution while Boller [Kevin's mother] sat across from her with tears streaming. "He's handling it real well," Lakiesha said. "I'll just have to face it and deal with it."[19]

As it turned out, Kevin was not executed that year. On July 27, sixteen days before his scheduled execution date, U.S. District Judge Edward H. Johnstone stayed the execution until Kevin's lawyers could file briefs raising constitutional violations.[20]

·   ·   ·   ·

After Eileen had lived in Kentucky for two years, fifteen years after they first met, Kevin and Eileen decided to marry on March 20, 1995. They wrote their own vows and found a local Methodist minister to conduct a small ceremony at the prison with Vince and Stephanie serving as witnesses. The warden had promised the couple a special visit but then changed his mind. Eileen brought in a cake and a camera. For a wedding gift, Kevin made Eileen a hand-carved wooden clock decorated with cats and their middle names—Nigel and Mae—carved into the wood.

> EILEEN: I didn't take out the license until the day we got married because I was hoping to avoid publicity. But someone at the prison notified the *Lexington Herald,* a conservative newspaper in Kentucky. They put it on the front page. Someone at the prison even gave a reporter private information about me, including my Social Security number, that I had had to provide the prison before I could visit. The reporter didn't use the information, but I didn't like the fact that he had it.

All the major Kentucky newspapers covered the wedding.[21] One reporter interviewed Baerbel Poore's father, Bob, who said that he didn't think Kevin should be allowed to marry:

> No, I don't think he should have any rights at all. He's a damned maggot, and he ought to be treated like a maggot. He's done it and I want him to pay for it, and I want to watch him pay for it. I want to see him die.[22]

After the article appeared, people she didn't know contacted Eileen to share their feelings about her marriage. One woman sent a particularly vicious e-mail that concluded with "People see you as a woman so desperate for a man that you'd have to marry one on death row just to get one. And they wonder what exactly is wrong with you upstairs, so to speak. No normal woman would do what you have done with intent. (Normal implies to the majority)."

EILEEN: I was not prepared for some of the racial hostility that I encountered when it was first known that I had married a black man on death row. I got several threatening phone calls telling me that Nicole got what she deserved for marrying a nigger and I should get the same. But something I did find, and I believe that this is always true, was that there were many people in this neighborhood who continued to be my friends, who made an attempt to understand my decision to marry Kevin, and have since become stronger advocates for Kevin receiving clemency.

I believe that people are the same the world over basically. While there are people that use racism often to cover their own feelings of inadequacy, many people will be fair given half a chance. I even believe that if the jury of all-white citizens who sat on Kevin's trial had heard the true facts of the case and all of those involved had been tried, Kevin would not have received the death penalty and would have been paroled by now.

I did hate Kentucky when I first moved here. The pace of life, everything was so different from California and what I was used to. But I have learned to love it. I felt people were too slow and backward, but that was not true. So many lies and misconceptions about Kevin and the case came about from the reporting that took place early on and have continued to be perpetuated. It wasn't until Stephanie came on the case that we had a lawyer who really took on the media and tried to get some of the falsehoods corrected. Our system basically doesn't listen to the defendant or his family, only the lawyers. So if your lawyer doesn't present your story in a timely fashion, those facts don't get heard.

KAREN: I think Eileen is wonderful. I think Kevin needed an angel and God sent Eileen to him. She is very strong in her convictions, and she is a good lady. I must admit I thought it was strange at first when they said they were going to get married. I asked Eileen why she would marry somebody on death row. Talking to her I realized she did something that a lot of people wouldn't do—she gave him a chance. She has gotten to know him better than anyone. There is a side of Kevin that nobody sees unless you really sit down to talk to him. He is probably one of the people that I most admire right now.

I feel that way about Eileen, too. There is a strength about Eileen that you don't grasp until you meet her. She stands for so much; she really does. It is the strength of the love that she has for Kevin that impresses me so much. The two of them are like kindred spirits. Eileen is welcome at any family event. Lakiesha adores her, too.

Kevin's life has settled into a pattern. He spends most of his time locked up. He gets to go outside once a week for an hour. He is allowed out of his cell to make a phone call, take a shower, or clean up, at most only a couple of hours a day. He spends his time reading and studying. He completed his GED and associate's degrees in business management and liberal arts. He is only a few credits short of a degree in sociology. The only reason he does not have the degree is that most educational programs in prisons in Kentucky, as in other states, have been eliminated. He taught himself music and plays the guitar and keyboard. Prison rules required him to choose only one instrument; he kept the guitar so that he could play music at the chapel.

He also takes part in a program in which he meets with young juvenile offenders, sharing his experiences of being on death row in hopes of helping them avoid a life of crime.

Somehow, Kevin and Eileen manage to keep their love growing. He still writes her frequent letters, sometimes including poetry.

Love
I love you not only for what you are, but for what I am when I am with you.
I love you, not only for what you have made of yourself, but for what you
    are making me;
I love you for the part of me that you bring out; I love you for putting your
    hand into my heaped up heart and passing over all the foolish, weak
    things that you can't help dimly seeing there, and for drawing out into
    the light all of the beautiful belongings that no one else had looked quite
    far enough to find. . . .
I love you, and feel deeply moved inside by so many factors I fall short of
    expressively releasing the true inner words of loving you. There are times
    when I am so distant from external topic because I know how precious
    life is each day and I patiently wait for the divine inspiration to speak to

governor doesn't give him clemency, my dad will probably be killed this year. I know it could happen soon. I have written letters to the governor asking for clemency and was in a video that his lawyer put together. If I think about the fact that my dad might be executed, it seems weird. I guess I keep it out of my mind unless something comes up about his case.

It doesn't seem like my dad got a fair trial. The jury was kind of one-sided. They basically just went along with what the prosecutors said. I think all three should have gotten the same sentence, or at least the jury should have been able to decide whether they deserved the same sentence instead of deciding that only my dad could get the death penalty.

I think capital punishment is a pretty heinous way to receive punishment. I think my dad should serve a lengthy sentence and definitely get some form of counseling. He has been in prison for twenty-two years—he has probably served enough time. I think he is a different person now. I think he could make it on the outside.

I visited my dad the first week in January of 2003. I took my daughter to see him. Her name is Nia Mykayla Carter, and she was born in November. It was the first time he had seen her. The visit went well. We visited for about six or seven hours. It was a contact visit, and he had a chance to hold the baby. He pretty much held her the whole visit.

Over the years it has been difficult to maintain a father/daughter relationship with him being so far away. It is hard to make it down for visits, but he is a very important person in my life. If he is executed, it will be pretty shocking. I'll feel sad and depressed. It's not something I look forward to.

I haven't had the chance to get to most of my dad's court appearances, but his lawyers keep me informed. Sometimes his case is in the news. That can be hard, but it depends on the story. Some are better than others. Some of them I get really frustrated about. It is hard for the families—the Poore family and my family, too. The reporters don't seem to think about how the stories affect us.

When I was about twelve, the Louisville newspaper called me and asked me if I wanted to meet Baerbel Poore's daughter. It was the first time my dad's death warrant had been signed, and they wanted to do a story on us because we are around the same age. I think her name is

Stephanie. Around that time I read a story in the paper where she was quoted as saying something like "I believe he deserves to pay for whatever he has done." I guess she was willing to meet me, but I decided not to meet her. I didn't think it would do any good. Their family wants my dad to die, and I can understand why they feel that way.

If there is one thing that I would like to tell people it is that my father is a loving, caring person and he trusts and believes in God. I do believe that whatever happens is meant to happen and there is not much that I can do to control the outcome. I have done what I can. Now the rest is up to the governor.

KAREN: So much has happened over the last twenty years. I have been sober now for seven years, and I have changed a lot. What is so unreal about this situation is that Kevin was a child when it happened. He has been in there over twenty years. Basically society is saying that there is no way a person can change. You can't tell me that a seventeen-year-old boy can't change after twenty-two years. I'll never be able to understand it. I don't know what I would possibly say to him if he is actually executed. It makes me feel so empty and so useless. But Kevin has asked me to be all right. He has told me that he wants to live, but if he has to die he accepts that. He doesn't want anyone to fall apart. He asked me to promise him that I would never take a drink. God willing, I am going to honor that promise. I am going to be here for his daughter and granddaughter. She is a monkey-face gorgeous thing. She is such a good baby. I plan to do a lot of babysitting. Whatever I can do for Lakiesha, I will do it.

I have done what I can to save Kevin. I have written to the governor, I did a personal video, I signed petitions, I have circulated petitions, sent e-mails, anything and everything I can do I have done. I will always be active. Even though it is hard for me, I speak openly about the abuse. Helping Kevin has been part of my healing process whether he knows it or not.

I don't believe that Kevin shot Baerbel, but even if he did, he was a child at the time. It is so unfair because they were all three treated differently. One walked, one got life, and one is waiting to fry. A lot of people are out there hollering about fair justice right now, demanding Kevin's execution. I wonder how they would feel if it was somebody in their family. How can you say one child is destined to change and another child is not? Or one child deserves to live and the other does not?

I feel for that family, but I want the right thing to be done. I don't know how I would feel about my child's death, but twenty-two years later if you told me that a child did something wrong, I don't think I would believe that that person was beyond redemption. I don't want to ever think like that.

I think the way Kevin is preparing for his possible execution is by helping other people get ready. Kevin reads people pretty well. I think the one thing that he doesn't want to look down on when he does go is to look back and see all the people that he took down with him. He knows that I am a walking disaster that could explode. He knows that his mom is just starting to feel a lot of guilt. He knows that his daughter has a long way to walk. I think what he wants the most is for everybody to hang together.

The one thing I would ask people is just to get to know the whole story. It is so hard because people only ever saw the worst of Kevin. They didn't see the best of him, and they didn't understand all that had been done to him. The worst part of it now is that so many people don't know and are just thinking the worst.

·   ·   ·   ·

In 2002, Kevin lost his final appeals, and the only avenue remaining for him was clemency. Eileen found herself becoming extremely distraught, not knowing if Kevin would be executed or not.

EILEEN: When we learned that Kevin had lost his last appeal, I was so upset. I was crying all the time. I cried throughout all of our visits. It was so scary because you can't do anything and you don't know when he is going to be executed.

Paul Stevens, a volunteer chaplain at the prison whose daughter had been murdered many years ago, was a great source of comfort to Kevin and me, as was Sister Chris Beckett, another volunteer, who came in with Paul every Thursday. They both provided tremendous comfort to us during this time.

But then Kevin talked to me about it and told me that it was pointless to worry about things before they happened. He said that if we only had a few months left, we should spend our time loving each other and not crying. I reached a point of acceptance. If he was going to be executed, I wanted my face to be the last one he saw before leaving this life.

·   ·   ·   ·

As it turned out, Eileen will not have to witness Kevin's execution. In June 2003, Governor Paul Patton announced that he would not sign a death warrant during his term. He further announced that he would make a final decision about Kevin's sentence before leaving office. In announcing his decision, the governor stated that he did not believe in the death penalty for juveniles but that age alone was not the only factor playing a part in his decision. He believed that Kevin did not get a fair trial. This meant that Governor Patton would not pass the decision about Kevin's case on to the next governor, who Eileen and Kevin feared might have decided to sign a death warrant.

EILEEN: There was a lot of negative reaction to the governor's decision. The victim's family called him a pervert [referring to his involvement in an extramarital affair that was made public]. Some believed that the governor made the decision because the affair destroyed his political career and he no longer had anything to lose.

We are hoping [in September 2003] for a sentence of thirty years, which would make him eligible for parole in a few years. We were very concerned that his case would be left for the next governor and were very thankful that Governor Patton reviewed all the materials about the case. He realized that Kevin's trial was a travesty of justice and that the judges and jury never heard most of the evidence.

I have gotten some negative feedback, some nasty e-mails, but mostly people have been very supportive. The guards at the prison were congratulating Kevin; they did not want him to be executed. Even the warden shook his hand and congratulated him personally, which I thought was very nice.

It's a relief knowing that Kevin will not be executed. It's like there was a big something on the back of my mind that was always there when I woke up but now the dread has gone away.

We had found a certain amount of peace anyway, which makes me believe that when you find peace within yourself things become more positive, because you look at it in a more positive way. We had already de-

Larry said that he didn't need anything, which Lois found strange since Larry had been unemployed and had very few possessions. He did, however, request a German chocolate cake. When Lois got off the phone, she told Ken that Larry sounded really low, and they decided, once again, to renew their efforts to find him help.

Unbeknown to anyone, Larry had been experiencing increased hallucinations. He heard voices that told him to kill. He purchased a .22 caliber pistol. The voices grew stronger, commanding him to kill in order to save the souls of the people he cared about. On August 10, 1982, Larry succumbed to the voices. He shot and killed Ricky. He then severed Ricky's head with a kitchen knife and placed it in Ricky's arms. He mutilated his body, including removing the testicles and eating them. Next, he went next door and killed his neighbor Georgia Reed and her son and mother. After the four murders, Larry waited for a revelation of what to do next. When none came, he contemplated suicide. Bruce Gardner came to the house to pick Georgia up for a date and Larry killed him, too.

Larry drove to Wichita in Bruce Gardner's yellow Pinto station wagon. He was on his way to see his family but stopped in a church parking lot for a nap when a Wichita policewoman approached the car and saw the revolver. She arrested Larry for unlawful possession of a handgun, and while at the station Larry confessed to the murders. He agreed to be extradited to Texas.

In the afternoon of August 11, Ken left work to meet Lois for an appointment at a counseling center on behalf of Larry. He had gone to work that day and talked with his coworkers about the grisly multiple murders, and Ken wondered what kind of person would commit such a crime. Lois was driving to the counseling center and listening to the car radio when she heard the announcer say that Larry Keith Robison was being extradited from Kansas for the murder of five people. She thought it was strange that another person had the same name as Larry.

> LOIS: When I got to the counseling center I told Ken about what I heard on the radio and we wondered if it could be our Larry. We called our house, and our daughter Vickie answered and was very upset. She said that the phone had been ringing off the hook all day, and we realized it was our Larry.
>
> At that moment, our lives changed forever. We were no longer Ken and Lois, the teachers who taught Sunday school and volunteered in our

community. We were now the parents of a mass murderer. Larry Robison had finally done something violent.

Junette Bryant found the decapitated and mutilated body of her son, Ricky. She called the police, who looked next door and found the bodies of Georgia Reed, her eleven-year-old son, Scott, Georgia's mother, Earline Barker, and Georgia's boyfriend, Bruce Gardiner. Each of the victims had been shot in the head and had his or her throat slit. Georgia's body was mutilated by stab wounds.

· · · ·

Lois was mortified that her gentle son had committed such brutal crimes. However, she felt certain that now he would finally get the psychiatric care he needed. But instead of being taken to a hospital, Larry was taken to the county jail. Lois contacted Assistant District Attorney Steve Chaney to tell him that Larry was schizophrenic and needed medical help. He told her that the insanity plea in Texas was "a joke" and said, "Your lawyer, of course will find a doctor who says he is insane. But we have one who will say he is not." Proving someone mentally ill would turn into a battle of the experts, and in the end, the state would win. In the meantime, Larry would have to stay in jail. Chaney advised Lois not to hire a lawyer; the kind Larry would need would start at a hundred thousand dollars, he told her, and the state would appoint Larry a good lawyer anyway.

Initially Steve Chaney said that Larry's case did not qualify as a capital case under Texas law,[6] so Lois believed Larry would not face execution. Chaney was overruled by the district attorney, Tim Curry, who charged Larry with felony murder, a capital crime. Curry alleged that Larry murdered Bruce Gardiner in the course of stealing his car to use as a getaway vehicle. (In Texas, prosecutors typically charge defendants in multiple murder cases with only one count, so if the defendant is acquitted, the state can prosecute him or her again on a different count.) Larry pled not guilty by reason of insanity, which meant that he admitted committing the crimes but claimed that he did so because of his mental illness.

LOIS: It took several days to track down Larry's court-appointed attorney, Charles Roach, who was assisted by J. R. Molina. Charles Roach was fresh off of being in the district attorney's office himself, and he definitely gave me the impression that he thought Larry was guilty.

During those days the prosecutor asked Judy Smith, the woman who had introduced Larry to Ricky Bryant, to tape-record conversations with Larry when he called from the jail. Judy agreed, but she also told me that she was doing this. I called Larry's lawyer to tell him, but he wouldn't return my calls. Finally, I told his secretary I would contact the media if he didn't return my calls, and then he came to the phone.

When we finally got an appointment with this guy, I was upset and frustrated about not being able to reach him sooner. He yelled at me and said, "I do not have time to work on your son's case right now. I will work on his case when it comes to trial and not before. If you have a message for me, leave it with my secretary, and if I have an answer I'll tell her to call you back. Most people think your son has committed the most horrible crime and think he deserves to die for it. If we win this case, the best we will do is a life sentence."

Soon after Larry's arrest, people from the National Alliance for the Mentally Ill (NAMI) contacted Ken and Lois and invited them to a meeting. The group, all family members of mentally ill people, met regularly to share their experiences. Members of NAMI were particularly sympathetic with the Robisons because this was around the time that John Hinckley had tried to assassinate President Ronald Reagan, bringing a great deal of attention to the issue of mentally ill people committing murder. Families of mentally ill people feared repercussions to their loved ones because of the anger and fear generated by the assassination attempt.

During the intervening year before Larry's trial, he attempted suicide twice in the Tarrant County Jail in Fort Worth, once by slitting his wrist and the inside of his elbow, and the other time by saving up tranquilizers that he was given and taking an overdose. He was found unconscious in his cell. Because of his precarious mental condition, Larry was kept in solitary confinement. Ken and Lois and his siblings visited Larry, but it was difficult. They had to stand outside a steel cell that had only a small porthole with a grid underneath for speaking through, which meant they could not see each other while they talked. Contact visits were not permitted.

LOIS: It was a really hard year for our family. We got a lot of support but not everybody was sympathetic. Our daughter Sharon was so upset she couldn't work. One time at her office right after the crime happened some people were talking about what they would do to Larry, how they would string him up by his toes and cut his guts out. She said to them, "Don't be so quick to kill him, he's my brother." Another time our daughter-in-law was in a restaurant eating and she heard someone in the next booth talking about what they would do to Larry. She went over to them and said, "You don't know what you are talking about. He's my brother-in-law and I love him."

But some people were very supportive. Shortly after it happened I called my hairdresser to make an appointment, and she closed the shop and let me come in to have my hair done in private. Then she came to our house to be with us and help. Friends would come by and do things like answer the door and phone and fend off reporters, or bring food or wash the dishes.

I started getting requests to go on television. I wanted to talk about Larry's case and let people know that he was mentally ill, but I didn't want to get in trouble with the school board. I called my principal, who called the superintendent, who said I could go on television, but he didn't know if parents would want their kids in my class when school started. My principal told him that 80 percent of the parents whose children I had taught in second grade the year before had already requested that their children be in my third-grade class. At least one requested it after Larry was arrested. The principal assigned all my former students to my third grade class, which was very helpful.

Years later another principal told me that every year at least one parent had complained and asked to have their child placed with another teacher. He refused to change and told them to call back at midterm if they were dissatisfied. He told me that every one of those parents called back and apologized. Most of my colleagues were kind and understanding, but some had their noses up in the air.

· · · ·

Even though several doctors had already diagnosed Larry as schizophrenic, the defense was having a difficult time preparing to prove that at trial. Dr. Randolph, the family doctor who had first admitted Larry to the hospital, had just moved to California and couldn't be located; Dr. Arauso went to Europe for the summer and didn't want to be involved; the doctor from John Peter Smith County Hospital was available to come to court, but he didn't really remember Larry, who had been a patient four years earlier. Charles Roach had retained another expert, Dr. C. D. Buckholtz, who interviewed Larry. However, before trial he concluded that Larry had not been mentally ill at the time of the offense.

> **LOIS:** I didn't hear from Larry's attorneys again until the week before trial, when Molina called me up and asked me to run a bunch of errands for them like picking up a witness at the airport and delivering papers to different places. I delivered some legal papers to the doctor from John Peter Smith before the trial started, and I insisted on talking to him before I left his office. He told me that some psychiatrists thought that people like Larry should be executed. I thought, *If this guy is on our side we are in trouble.* I didn't feel any better when I saw Molina drinking the night before the trial started while he was going over the case with me.

The trial began in June 1983. Jury selection took six weeks because the jurors had to be questioned extensively about their knowledge of the case and whether they had already formed an opinion. As in all capital cases, jurors had to be "death qualified," meaning that anyone who opposes the death penalty on principle is excused from jury service. And because it was a case with an insanity defense, jurors had to be questioned as to whether they could decide the issue of sanity, and whether they understood that the defendant had the burden of proving insanity. During jury selection, the *Fort Worth Star Telegram* put out a big story about Larry. Jurors were seen passing the paper from one to the other, but the judge continued with jury selection nonetheless.

Most of the family was there for the trial. Steve quit his job and came home from California. Sharon couldn't concentrate at work but couldn't afford to take off, so Ken gave her the equivalent of her salary so she could leave her job and attend the trial. Vickie and Allen were both there. Carol was only twelve, so she stayed with people from church. Only Kathi and David did not attend, because they lived too far away and because of other responsibilities. Also, Larry's partner, Belinda, attended.

> **LOIS:** We went to the courthouse every day during jury selection, but then Ken's mother had a stroke. She was paralyzed and in the hospital. I decided that Ken needed me more at that time than Larry, so I went to

Wichita with him. We stayed a few days and then came back home. Less than a week later his mother died, so we went back up for her funeral and to get her house sold. This all happened while the jury was still being selected.

Nobody who was going to testify could actually watch the trial. Ken and my mother sat through the whole thing, but the rest of us had to sit in the hall for a week. The victims' families sat right across the hall from us; that was strange. We nodded at each other going back and forth. I wanted so much to tell them how sorry I was, but we weren't allowed to talk to each other.

I was the last witness to testify. Testifying was horrible. Neither the DA nor Larry's lawyer would let me fully answer a question. If I answered anything more than a yes or no, the DA jumped up and objected. I didn't understand a lot of what he said. They didn't want me to explain in any way, shape, form, or fashion.

Larry's lawyer told me not to mention about him being in the halfway house or he'd get the death penalty. They told me not to mention that he had ever been to jail. I just wanted to tell the truth.

Then the DA started hounding me to answer, and when I did he'd accuse me of lying. I just wanted people to know how hard we had tried to find help for Larry.

Although the jury selection process had taken six weeks, the actual trial took only one. Larry's plea of not guilty by reason of insanity was an admission on his part that he committed the murders, so the state was not required to prove that Larry committed the crimes. Instead, Larry's attorneys had to prove that he was mentally ill.

Larry himself had wanted to testify, but Charles Roach advised him not to. Larry had written a thirty-one-page autobiographical statement called "The Making of a Schizophrenic," which Charles wanted to introduce, but the state said no, not unless Larry testified, so the jury never learned of it.

Under Texas law, the jury is not allowed to know the consequences of a verdict of not guilty by reason of insanity. Even if jurors believe that the defendant is mentally ill, they may be reluctant to render a verdict of not guilty by reason of insanity for fear that the defendant will be walking the streets the next day. Jurors are not told that if found not guilty by reason of insanity a person is subjected to an involuntary commitment procedure and is hospitalized indefinitely.

During closing argument, prosecutor Larry Moore tore apart Larry's claim of mental illness. He argued that Larry was a drug addict, not mentally ill. Larry's past behavior, he claimed, could be explained by drug abuse. Moore went so far as to blame Lois for Larry's behavior, claiming that she had "enabled" him by always coming to his rescue. He even insinuated that Lois was lying about Larry being mentally ill in order to protect her son.

LOIS: When I heard the DA's speech, I knew what was going to happen and who the jurors were going to believe. After the jury went into deliberations, we all went out to eat. I was sitting in the cafeteria and I couldn't eat. I started crying and got hysterical. My family took me to the infirmary where the doctors gave me a shot. I insisted on going back into the courtroom to hear the verdict, so they took me back in a wheelchair. They sat me down on a bench and I started getting sick to my stomach. I got up to go to the restroom and I collapsed. My two strong boys caught me, but even they couldn't hold me up. They called the paramedics. I was lying on the floor when the paramedics arrived. I remember a paramedic saying, "I can't get a pulse." They carried me to the ambulance. A cameraman tried to go with me, but my son held him at bay. I remember on the ride in to the hospital I kept saying, "They are going to kill my son, they are going to kill my son."

Lois was taken to Huguley Hospital, the same hospital where Larry was first diagnosed as a paranoid schizophrenic. On Wednesday, July 20, 1983, the jury convicted Larry of first-degree murder, and the next day sentenced him to die. After the trial was over, the family gathered at Vickie's home and Larry called from the prison and talked to all of them. He thanked them for their love and support.

Lois learned of the verdict and sentence from her hospital bed. After four days, Lois returned home, where she stayed in bed a few more days. Lois and Ken knew that they could either let the verdict destroy them or they could fight to save their son's life. They chose the latter.

•   •   •   •

Lois learned of an organization called Open Incorporated that provided support to families of prisoners. She called the number and was told that a member of the group named Margie Powell had a son, David, on death row in Huntsville, where Larry was.

LOIS: After a few days, Margie called me. She talked to me for a long time, which was tremendously helpful. She explained the process to me—what to expect. A few days later she called me back to tell me about a CURE convention. I had never heard of CURE and didn't know anything about it except that it was a prison reform group and it was having a convention in Huntsville.

I called Ken at school and said, "Can we go to this? I think it is important." He said, "I'll have to grade papers if we go." And I said, "I have to grade papers, too." So we took turns driving and grading papers.

The couple set out on the 175-mile drive to Huntsville. Before the conference, they visited Larry on death row.

LOIS: The visiting area is a large room with glass and wire around it. There is a ledge on the outside of the glass with chairs for the visitors, and a ledge and chairs for the guys inside. You can't touch each other, but it is better than the jail because there is a grid on the bottom of the glass so you can carry on a normal conversation; you don't have to use phones or anything. The closest you can get to touching is like the movies—you each put your hands on the glass.

Larry was very upbeat. He didn't complain about anything; he was just really happy to see us. We chatted a little with the other prisoners and their families. Ken said, "If it hadn't been for the uniforms I would have thought the prisoners were the guards and the guards were the prisoners," because they were so much nicer than the guards. We felt a lot better after seeing Larry. He seemed to be doing okay.

We got to the CURE meeting, and I didn't know anybody except Margie Powell from our phone call. We tracked her down and she introduced us to Charlie Sullivan, executive director of CURE. He invited us to go to a meeting of families of death row inmates that was one of the convention workshops. At that meeting, I made the statement that I would go anywhere to talk to anybody about Larry's story if it would help keep this from happening to other families. Charlie heard me say that and recruited Ken and me to lead up a CURE chapter for death row family members.

I met Rick Halperin, a professor at Southern Methodist University who was on the national board of Amnesty International and the NCADP. Rick made a speech that I will never forget. He said that things were bad now and they were going to get worse, but in the end we would win because we were right. I have lived on that speech ever since.

•　　•　　•　　•

Larry continued to adjust to prison life, although his schizophrenia was untreated. He did not request treatment because he did not like the side effects of taking Haldol and Thorazine, the strong drugs prescribed for schizophrenia in the prison. There were newer, better drugs, but they were more expensive.

Larry continued having hallucinations, which he claimed were spiritual insights. An inmate introduced him to the Sant Mat, a derivative of the Sikh tradition. He corresponded with members of this faith and established a relationship with one of its Masters, Sant Ajaib Singh Ji. Larry described his religion in a letter:

> In fact, there has only been one good thing that I ever did. That one thing was that I met Sant Ajaib Singh Ji, a living Master, a perfect Saint who is God's representative on earth, who I recognized and received the Holy Initiation of Naam from. And it has been that thing which has made all the difference. Without it, all the good deeds in the world would have been for naught. Because of it, despite my countless transgressions, my life has been crowned with success. Yet I cannot claim the credit for even that one thing for it was all a gift by the grace of God. Through it God used me to touch the lives of everyone who has ever come into contact with me. I can never hope to repay this incredible gift. I can only be amazed and grateful that this is how the infinite power of God manifests itself; through unconditional love, mercy and forgiveness. Of course, He is the Supreme Giver and we are merely the receptacles; for such we were created. Yet here is a wonderful secret: Even as receptacles we are given the opportunity to become co-givers and co-creators with the One—through transforming our desire to receive for the self alone to the desire to receive for the sake of sharing with others. This is our true purpose—to become channels

for the Infinite Light and Love and discover the magic of selfless service. If we do not choose to be servants of the Divine Will it is we who will be the losers.[7]

Family members observed that Larry continued to suffer from delusions. Against the advice of his lawyer, he wrote a fourteen-page letter to his friend Judy Smith, who had testified against him at trial. The letter tried to explain to Judy his feelings about the murder.

God works in mysterious ways. Because he has chosen to shower His Grace on me by allowing me to come into contact with a Perfect Saint and because of my concern for their (the victims) spiritual welfare they will be taken under the protection of the Master Power and obtain liberation soon in a subsequent life. I think what saved me was that my motives (for the murder) were pure, if you understand what I mean by that. For although I acted on a faulty premise, it was not out of anger or greed that I caused their physical deaths. It was out of a sense of universal love and brotherhood.[8]

LOIS: Larry became a follower of Sant Mat—who was a lot like Gandhi, all peace and love and justice and reincarnation and karma. Someone at the prison introduced him to it. It really helped him a lot. He considered himself a Christian, but he did a lot of meditation, which helped him cope with his illness and with being in prison. Larry said he could leave the prison every day through meditation. At one point he got to talk to Sant Ajaib Singh Ji when he came to Texas for a visit. Larry made arrangements to talk to him by phone.

Larry's doctors told us that the religion fit his illness. One reason it helped him was he believed that the people he killed would come back to life. The realization that he killed someone was very traumatic for him, and he tried to kill himself twice when he was at the Tarrant County Jail.

Larry was suicidal when he went to death row. He had a razor hidden in his shoe. He was planning on attempting suicide again. Joining the religion was good for him because it is against their religion to take your life. So he didn't try to commit suicide anymore—although when he had been on death row a few months he wrote a letter to the court of criminal appeals and told them to stop his appeals and set the date. I went and talked to him and encouraged him to hang in there. I believed that he would get a new trial.

In the spring of 1986, the Court of Criminal Appeals for the State of Texas reversed Larry's conviction on the grounds that the jury selection process had been unfair.[9] Larry's case was scheduled for retrial in 1987. As before, he pleaded not guilty by reason of insanity. The Robisons were feeling more hopeful about the second trial than they had at the first. The new lawyers, David Bays and Sherry Hill, communicated with the family and included them in the case preparation. The judge who had presided over the first trial died of a heart attack, so a new judge was assigned. Judge Earl E. Bates seemed to be more sympathetic toward the Robisons.

Another important factor was that Lois had uncovered more evidence of mental illness in the family. Between Larry's death sentence and his new trial, his sister Carol was diagnosed as bipolar with schizoaffective disorder, a milder form of schizophrenia. This time, they were successful at finding someplace for their child to go—they found a psychiatric halfway house, staffed twenty-four hours a day, where Carol could live in safety.

Carol's diagnosis convinced Lois that there must be a genetic predisposition to schizophrenia in the family. She tracked down her first husband's relatives and pressed them for information. She learned that Larry's great-grandfather had been hospitalized in a state sanatorium at Fort Supply, Oklahoma, and his natural father's brother had been hospitalized in the Pavilion at Amarillo, Texas, and in the Vernon State Hospital with a diagnosis of paranoid schizophrenia. Lois also found out that several cousins and an uncle on her side of the family had been mentally ill.[10]

In the course of her investigation, the former wife of the mentally ill uncle agreed to testify at Larry's trial. Lois believed that the new information about the history of mental illness in the family would enable the defense to establish Larry's mental illness and hopefully lead to treatment for him. Another positive development was that Larry's lawyers had attended a conference on mental illness where they met Dr. Randall Price, who became interested in Larry's case and was willing to examine him.

In November 1987, the second trial began. The state made all the arguments it made at the first trial that Larry was not mentally ill. Unfortunately for Larry, the jury did not hear all the new evidence of mental illness in his family.

Larry's aunt arrived at court, but when the defense called her to testify, prosecutors Greg Pipes and Stan Hatcher objected on the grounds that the defense did not have the medical records of the family members she was testifying about. The judge listened to the witness testify outside the presence of the jury but ultimately agreed with the state that she could not testify without also introducing the medical records to back up her testimony. This was particularly frustrating for Lois; she had asked the lawyers if they needed to track down the family medical records—a task that would have been daunting—but David Bays had assured her that that was unnecessary.

Next, the defense called Dr. Price. He testified that Larry's thought process at the time of the murders indicated chronic paranoid schizophrenia.

> He believed that . . . after he killed the first person, that the clock in the—it was the bathroom, I believe, a digital clock, he said that it flipped over to where it was zeros, and then it started acting like a stop clock, and he thought that was a message that he was supposed to start trying to free other souls.
>
> I said to Larry . . . , "Well, but, you know clocks don't do that." And he said, "Well, this one really did that." And I said, "Well, don't you think that was something that you thought it did?" And he said, "No, that's what it did."[11]

Unfortunately, Dr. Price was impeached during cross-examination when the prosecutor asked him what information he had relied upon to form his opinion as to Larry's mental illness. Dr. Price had to reply that he had read a report from Dr. Buckholtz, the doctor the defense hired at the first trial, who had concluded that Larry was not mentally ill at the time of the crime. When the prosecutor asked Dr. Price for Dr. Buckholtz's opinion, Dr. Price had to disclose that the other doctor did not think Larry was mentally ill. Instead of hearing evidence about a lengthy family history of mental illness and the favorable testimony of one doctor, the jury heard only the opinion of one doctor, who was discredited by the opinion of another doctor who had been hired by the defense.

On November 10, 1987, Lois once again testified.

> **LOIS:** It was so frustrating. We had researched all the family history and the DA listened to it but then stood up in front of the jury and said, "He's not mentally ill, he's just mean."

Once again, Larry's attorneys advised him not to testify, and once again, Larry's manifesto, "The Making of a Schizophrenic," was never shown to the jury. Once again, a jury found Larry guilty and sentenced him to death. The jury returned with the guilty verdict, and the sentencing hearing began right away. By the end of the day, the jury had sentenced Larry to death. In learning of the sentence, Larry said, "It seems to be God's will. I accept it."[12]

LOIS: The lawyers made some mistakes, but they tried real hard and spent a lot of time with us. They really went out of their way for Larry. Both of them went to a seminar in Dallas about mental illness so they could learn more about schizophrenia. I bought a book from PBS about a show they did on the brain and gave it to David, and Sherry told me that he read it cover to cover. He tried real hard, but he was just very inexperienced. He had never done a death case before. You have to learn the hard way.

After the death sentence was returned, Lois walked out of the courtroom trying to comfort Judy, who was crying and telling Lois how sorry she was.

LOIS: I walked out of the courtroom with Judy, who was crying her heart out. Ricky's family was outside, and I said, "We just want you to know how sorry our family is about what happened, and if there is anything we could have done to prevent it, we would have." I had been wanting to say something to them since the murders, but we were told not to contact them in any way. After the second trial I made up my mind that after the verdict was in they couldn't accuse me of trying to tamper with witnesses. One of the women said, "I've been waiting five years to hear you say that," and I said, "I've been wanting to say it for five years, but the lawyers wouldn't let me." One of Bruce Gardner's brothers walked into the scene and said he didn't want Larry to get the death penalty, he just didn't want him to hurt anyone again. They had been told that if Larry was found insane he'd be out in thirty days and do it again. The district attorneys had told all of the victims' families that if Larry did not get the death penalty he would be out in thirty days, which was a lie.

Judy told me that the investigating officer from the DA's office had told her that Larry was planning on killing her and her kids because he was seen at a 7-Eleven near her house buying ammunition. She learned later that the 7-Eleven where he went was all the way across town. We went down the elevator together and talked about how we could prevent this kind of crime by getting better mental health care. I felt a lot better after that.

· · · ·

After the second conviction and death sentence, what little faith Lois and Ken had had in the criminal justice system was gone. Instead, they redoubled their efforts to take Larry's case to the court of public opinion. On March 29, 1988, Lois made her debut on *Geraldo,* hosted by Geraldo Rivera.

LOIS: Geraldo's producer called me when I was at school teaching, and I said no, I didn't want to be on his show because it was going to be about murder victims' families and we were supposed to balance the ticket. I told him I didn't want to go against murder victims' families.

They wouldn't give up. His producer, Cee Cee, kept calling me. She promised solemnly that there wouldn't be any fighting. Finally we agreed. They interviewed us for hours on the phone before we went on the show.

Wearing a pink vest over a floral patterned blouse, with gray curly hair and wide pink glasses, Lois shared the stage with several others—murder victims' family members who supported and opposed the death penalty and family members of people who had been executed. Ken and Carol sat in the audience.

Lois solemnly answered Geraldo's probing questions and made her plea that mentally ill people get the treatment they need in order to prevent future tragedies. When asked if she thought her son deserved to die, Lois responded, "I think the world will be just as safe if he spends the rest of his life in a mental hospital."

LOIS: When I went on the show, my heart was pounding so hard you could see it. I had been listening to a relaxation tape, and it advised to put your thumb and finger together. I sat there with my thumbs and fingers from both hands pressed together. They kept to their word and didn't turn the show into a big argument. It was a good experience. The audience was kind of hostile, but the crew was very nice. One time

Geraldo asked me a question and I couldn't answer because my mouth was so dry, but he went to a commercial to give me a chance to get a drink.

After the show, I asked Geraldo if we could have our picture taken with him, and he first insisted on having a picture taken just with Carol. She had a huge crush on him, so that made her day. The show paid for our hotel for a couple of extra days so we could go sightseeing, and Geraldo paid for us to eat at a really nice restaurant.

Three weeks later, Geraldo called again, asking Lois to be on another show he was doing in Fort Worth about a victims' rally. Lois agreed, but when she showed up on site technical difficulties prevented the taping. Lois appeared on the show twice more, one time with Ken. One show was taped after Geraldo had spent a night on death row.

LOIS: Geraldo was talking about what it had been like to be on death row, and finally someone in the audience asked his position on the death penalty, and he said, "I think that except for the most horrible murders we probably don't need the death penalty." After he said that he looked at me and asked me if I was disappointed. I said, "The ones that commit the most horrible murders are the ones who are mentally ill." That seemed to make him think.

Eventually, by the time his show went off the air, he had changed his mind and opposed the death penalty. As much as I didn't want to go on the show, I ended up having a soft spot for him. He cares about people. He did some controversial stuff but I think he did it because he was trying to make a difference.

On May 4, 1989, Lois and Ken were on *The Oprah Winfrey Show* on a program about families of mass murderers. Lois wore a blue floral patterned dress; Ken, a dark gray suit. They answered Oprah's questions about being the parents of a mass murderer with their soft-spoken Texas accents. Also appearing on the show were the mother and sister of mass murderer Leonard Lake and a psychologist who wrote a book called *Serial Killers*. The show paid for their accommodations in a deluxe hotel suite and paid an extra day for them to sightsee in Chicago. Lois said, "What I liked about Oprah was she will really give you time to talk and tell your story."

•   •   •   •

Invitations to speak about their situation poured in from around the country. In 1990, they had their first opportunity to travel abroad when Amnesty
International invited them to the Philippines to speak in favor of abolishing
the death penalty there.

LOIS: Amnesty invited me to go to the Philippines, but I told them I
wouldn't go unless Ken went, too. They agreed that I could use my per
diem to pay for Ken's plane trip, and Amnesty paid for the hotel. Neither
of us had ever been out of the country before. It was a very long trip—
a seventeen-hour flight. We got to meet a lot of wonderful people—
Bill Pelke, George White, SueZann Bosler, and Anne Coleman—from
MVFR. They treated us like family. Every morning somebody picked us
up and took us to schools and community groups. We spoke to three or
four groups a day. The people were very friendly. They fed us well and
treated us like royalty. We stayed ten days.

We were appalled by the poverty we saw most places. There was
sewage running in the gutters, and people lived in cardboard shacks. We
got to go and visit the prisons. The physical plants were not as nice as
they are in Texas, but the way they treated the prisoners was far above
the way we treat people here. The women prisoners lived in dormitories
with furniture and curtains. They did their own washing and helped in
the kitchen and made crafts. They let one of the prisoners sell us a purse
and keep the money. They let young children live with their mothers.
We saw everything from nursing babies to kids that were four or five
years old.

In the men's prison we got to visit some of the guys from death row.
We met in groups of three people with a translator. The guards stayed
out in the hall and let us talk to them—that was so different from Texas.
The prisoners can have visits anytime. When the wife visits, the other
prisoners leave the area so they can have conjugal visits.

There was a Catholic church on the grounds of a convent, and we
stayed there. Some of the families of the prisoners lived there. One
woman's husband was a political prisoner who had been in prison
eleven years, and they had an eight-year-old girl. We were quite impressed with that.

velop. Larry, dying to get off death row rather than being found mentally incompetent or living indefinitely among the condemned in torturous prison conditions, then agreed with Harris to drop his appeals and the court battle in exchange for working with the prosecutor to set Larry's execution date of choice.

Along with the petition was an affidavit from Dr. Anthony G. Hempel that stated:

Based upon my examination of Larry Keith Robison, which took place over eight hours as detailed in my report, I think there is cause for serious concern that Larry Keith Robison is not competent to be executed. I believe this because there is enough information about his belief system to suggest that he is not competent because of his magical beliefs about death. His thoughts and understanding of the concept of death are integral to his psychotic thought process. In fact, Larry had suggested that he cannot die. Accordingly, I believe there is a serious issue concerning whether he understands the nature of the punishment of death.[14]

In his full report to the court, Dr. Hempel laid out thirty-six factors that indicated Larry had killed during a psychotic episode that was a result of his paranoid schizophrenia. Among the more disturbing factors were these:

While in Wichita before the killings, Larry purchased a machete, lured a dog into the garage, killed it, strained the blood and drank it;

Larry's consistent reports of command hallucinations telling him to kill, together with a tremendous urge to "kill people";

His victims were friends who he had no logical or rational motive to want to hurt;

The severing of his friend's head, severing of the victim's penis and testicles and the consumption of these testicles by Larry Robison;

Larry's use of a kitchen knife versus a more efficient tool such as a large hunting knife or saw. One commonly sees the psychotic perpetrator pick up whatever weapon is close by and convenient as opposed to a pre-planned killing where a person uses a more efficient weapon;

Larry's several hour delay from the time of his killings to his departure, this delay could increase the odds of him leaving more evidence and getting caught on the premises of the murder;

After the murders driving a prolonged distance in daytime hours and ending up in a church parking lot which would make his detection easy.[15]

Although some in the family had been reluctant to file a competency petition, they seriously questioned whether Larry did really understand all of what was happening to him and filed supplemental affidavits to accompany the competency petition. One of his sisters signed an affidavit that said:

Larry told me that he has knowledge that the government, including the CIA, knows about his powers but refuses to make this information available to the public; Larry told me that the people he killed years ago were the same people who killed him in a prior life; Larry told me that he first knew about his past life when he was age twelve and specifically remembered encountering five aborigines with spears; Larry recently told me that he has already died, and so the state cannot kill him and he cannot die again.[16]

Larry told his brother Allen that he had recently visited a friend in California via his meditations at night and that his life was an instant in time and he couldn't be killed because he had already died three or four times over.[17] He told his cousin that he had the ability to communicate with God via a "tenth" hole in his body, which was located slightly above and behind his eyes. He stated that we all use this hole subconsciously but that he had learned to use it beyond the capability of others.[18]

Meanwhile, the prison made preparations for Larry's execution. Larry filled out a questionnaire in which he answered questions like who did he wish to witness his execution, who did he want as his spiritual advisor, what did he want for his last meal, what did he want to wear to his execution, and what did he want to have happen with his body and his possessions after he was killed.

Larry considered asking his family to witness the execution but ultimately decided to ask members of his faith community instead, in part because they did not get as upset as his family. He told his mother that the last gift he wanted to give his family was to spare them from having to watch his execution. Kim

Robison, a former sister-in-law who had maintained a friendship with Larry, agreed to serve as Larry's spiritual advisor, because she was also in Sant Mat.

Larry declined a last meal, as he had decided to fast before his execution, which he began doing fourteen days before the scheduled date. He decided to be cremated and to give some of the ashes to his mother and some to members of his religious community to scatter in India.

In the days leading up to the execution, Larry lost fifteen pounds and did not sleep for five straight nights. Larry said that during this time he felt "different" than normal, closer to God, and experienced a sensation of power, euphoria, and serenity of "metaphysical proportions."[19]

His parents and siblings, Melodee, members of his religious community, and his daughter all visited with Larry on his last day. Larry's daughter observed that while the family was upset, Larry seemed to be happy that he was going. He talked about his religion and about going to meet his Master and getting rid of his worldly possessions. Larry did not say good-bye to anyone but instead stared intently at each of them, without blinking, for up to ten minutes. He told his lawyers and family members that the state had no power to kill him, and in his mind, the real reason for the execution was karma and destiny. While Larry's family thought that his staring and comments were strange, members of his religious sect looked at one another and smiled, not needing to speak because they could read each other's thoughts.[20]

Before Lois left, Larry told her, "It's okay, Mom. Don't worry about it. It's in God's hands. If God's ready for me to go, I'm ready to go and get out of this life, because that's the only way I'll ever get out of it. If God wants me to live and help other people, that's okay, too, even if it means spending the rest of my natural life on death row."

After the visit, Steve Earle, a well-known musician and a friend of the family, offered to take everybody out for a steak dinner in the afternoon before returning to the prison to stand vigil for the 6:00 p.m. execution. Lois asked the camera crew from *48 Hours* not to come to the restaurant because the family needed a break. The reporters had kept taking pictures of Larry's daughter when the family had asked them not to. They had made Sharon so angry that she lost her temper, which the cameramen eagerly recorded.

LOIS: We were outside the restaurant around 1:30 p.m. waiting to be seated when we heard this scream and Melodee came running out yelling, "We got a stay! We got a stay!" We could hardly believe it and were very excited. I felt kind of bad because the crew from *48 Hours* was not there to photograph that critical moment, but Micki Dickoff [an independent filmmaker and family friend] was, and she ended up selling them the pictures for a lot of money.

The day turned into a celebration. After the meal, we headed over to the Methodist church and had a victory celebration—instead of a memorial service, we had a thank-you service.

Melodee and I went to visit Larry the next day. A friend of his, Joe Mario Trevino, was scheduled to be executed that day. Joe was also mentally ill and had not had a visitor in twenty years. After our visit was finished I went over and talked to him. I told him I would tell his story to the media and our family would be praying for him. When I was getting ready to leave, a guard came rushing down and said, "He's not your son. You're not on his list. Get out of here." As I walked out I started chanting, "You're all our sons. You're all our sons. You're all our sons. We will never give up. We will never give up. We will never give up." One by one the men said, "'Bye, Mom. 'Bye, Mom. 'Bye, Mom."

I was so exhausted after we visited Larry, my family put me to bed. I told them to make sure to wake me up before the vigil for Joe. They didn't wake me up. I fell into a sound sleep but woke up at 6:20 with a start, which was the time they pronounced Joe dead. I guess he came to visit me.

·   ·   ·   ·

Now that the Texas Court of Criminal Appeals had agreed to stay Larry's execution in order to consider the issue of his competency, his lawyers had to prove that he was incompetent. When they requested a court hearing, the district attorney said that in Texas competency decisions were normally made without hearings, to which Melodee suggested that maybe Texas should "follow the constitution."

The court scheduled a competency hearing for November 8, 1999. Four experts had interviewed Larry—two appointed by the court and one each by the defense and prosecution. All had found that Larry met the legal definition of competence: He understood that he was to be executed, he understood that his execution was imminent, and he understood the reasons for his execution.[21] Of the two court-appointed experts, Debra M. Osterman, M.D., found Larry competent, and Mark Cunningham, Ph.D., opined that Larry was schizophrenic but declined to give a professional opinion as to his com-

quantity sufficient to cause the death of Larry Keith Robison, and until Larry Keith Robison is dead, such procedure to be determined and supervised by the Director of the Institutional Division of the Texas Department of Criminal Justice.[31]

On December 16, 1999, Larry signed an affidavit authorizing Melodee Smith to file a clemency petition on his behalf.[32]

On December 28, 1999, Lois and Ken wrote a letter to Governor Bush and the Texas Board of Pardons and Paroles outlining Larry's history of mental illness and their efforts to get him treatment. They ended the letter:

Our whole family, including my husband and me, our other seven children, fifteen grandchildren, aunts, uncles, nieces, and nephews, are suffering terrible grief. We are concerned that our youngest daughter, Carol, who is in a residential mental health facility in Alto, Texas, may have another breakdown because she identifies so much with Larry.

Larry's daughter, who because of his illness and his incarceration has been denied the presence of her father from early childhood, is now struggling with the prospect of losing him completely because the State of Texas plans to execute him. She wants him to be alive when she graduates from college, and when she marries. She wants him to be able to see his grandchildren some day, even if it is in the visiting room of a prison.

Reading the death warrant sent chills down our spines. It seems so incredible to us that our own state of Texas, after refusing Larry treatment for years, plans to strap him down on that gurney and pump poison into his body until he is dead. We don't know how we will survive this final trauma.[33]

After losing the competency hearing, the last possible means for saving Larry's life was through executive clemency. By this point, Bill Harris had decided not to pursue any further legal means to save Larry. Melodee was left with the arduous task of producing a several-hundred-page bound document. Lois and Ken had collected thousands of signatures during their travels around the world requesting that Larry's life be spared, and hundreds had written letters on his behalf. Lois and Ken made thirty copies of the petition and supplemental materials and delivered them to the appropriate authorities.

LOIS: We personally delivered the papers to the governor, petitions and letters and all of his medical records. We did it twice, once before the first execution date and then again after the competency hearing. I had tried to meet with Governor Bush twice. One time I went and he refused to see me and I got escorted out by capitol police. The next time I went, he was out campaigning for president saying he was a "compassionate conservative." His compassion didn't seem to extend to the mother of a mentally ill death row inmate.

Melodee met with Governor Bush's staff twice, begging them to spare Larry's life. One Bush staff aid and legal counsel, who had just lost a good friend in a traffic accident, cried while Melodee pled Larry's case.

·　　·　　·　　·

On January 13, 2000, *48 Hours* broadcast the Robisons' story. The show focused on the family conflict but otherwise gave a fairly accurate portrayal of their story.

Family and friends prepared to gather once again for the execution. This time Molly decided not to come. All the media attention had been very difficult for her, and she didn't think she could handle the emotional strain of being present at her father's execution. Instead, she visited her dad the week before.

LOIS: This time we didn't have much hope of getting a stay. We made plans to go to Huntsville again. We reserved the University Hotel's banquet room for a memorial service for Larry, and we booked a hotel room to stay there for the last days.

A photographer for the *Dallas Morning News* that I had come to trust was taking pictures for a story about me. I told him that I had grown up in Huntsville, and the day before Larry's execution date we asked him if he wanted to come on a tour of Huntsville with us. We went to the house where I had grown up and were standing there taking pictures when this man came out. I told him that I used to live there, and he told us we could look at the back. Walking around in the backyard I started to cry,

Larry Robison. Provided with permission of the family.

thinking about my mother. Then the woman of the house came home from work and thought something terrible had happened. When she found out that I used to live there, she invited us inside to tour the house and told us to come back sometime for dinner.

By now Larry was really ready to go. I didn't want him to die, but there was nothing more I could do. The whole family visited Larry and left around noon. My last words to Larry were "I will work for the rest of my lift to help the mentally ill and prisoners," and then as I was leaving, I said, "Larry, you are finally getting off death row."

During these last days I hardly had time to think because so many reporters wanted to interview me. There were people from public radio, CNN, NBC, ABC, CBS, all the morning shows. One reporter from Baltimore interviewed me for three hours on my cell phone—that really added up.

We started gathering at the prison at around 4:00 P.M. There were about a hundred people there—our family, friends, supporters, and members from our church in Fort Worth. We held candles and sang songs. Our CURE official photographer, Alan Pogue, came and gave me a picture of Larry that he had taken in prison a few days before. He had blown it up to life size on poster board. I stood there holding it and crying and trying to sing. Sometime after 6:00 P.M., prison officials came outside and told us that Larry was dead.

Larry's execution was on Friday, and Billy Hughes was executed on Monday. We had gotten to know Billy well over the years of visiting Larry. His mother lived in Alabama, and his father died while he was on death row. We visited him a lot, and he helped us with our prisoner art projects. We went to visit him the day after Larry died. We also went to see him on Monday morning and told him good-bye. I was so tired that I went back to the hotel to take a nap in the afternoon. Then we got up around 4:00 P.M. and went back to the prison for Billy's vigil. Charlie Sullivan from CURE had promised Billy he would witness the execution.

Melodee Smith presided over the memorial services of Larry Robison on Friday night and Billy Hughes on Monday night at the Sam Houston Hotel. Many activists were there: people from the Journey of Hope, the ACLU, MVFR, and the Texas Coalition to Abolish the Death Penalty. Steve Earle sang Lois's favorite song, "Ellis One," at Larry's memorial.

•   •   •   •

Larry's body was cremated, and the family decided to bury his ashes at a small cemetery in Huntsville where Lois's parents were buried. It took the family nearly two years before they could find a date when everyone could get together. In November 2001, they all met in Huntsville.

LOIS: Larry had made a Christmas card for CURE that we sold or gave away to people. On it, he drew two doves with the caption "Peace on earth." When we were picking out a headstone, I told the headstone carver that I wanted him to make a headstone that had two doves holding a banner that said "Free at last." He designed it and it was beautiful. Our daughter Sharon got a wind chime that says "Free at last," and we hung that up on a tree next to the headstone.

•   •   •   •

Lois and Ken are still active with CURE. Their most recent project has been raising money to buy fans for Texas prisoners. The cells in Texas prisons are not air-conditioned, and in the summer the sweltering heat takes its toll, especially on the sick and elderly. Lois sent out an announcement to all the prisoners and got five thousand requests the first year. They bought fans for 638 inmates in 2002 and 1,143 in 2003 and are raising money to buy more. "They are so grateful," says Lois. "They write us the nicest letters. One man sent a letter saying, 'You don't know what you have done. You are saving lives in here.' We are just keeping the promise we made to Larry."

CHAPTER 7

A Regular Guy

Christmastime of 1989 started out fairly normally for Esther Herman, a successful businesswoman who lived in Arlington, Texas. She owned two nail salons that also provided facials and massages and had plans for opening a retail clothing store. Besides running her businesses, she took care of her aging mother, who had recently moved in with her after breaking her hip and being confined to a wheelchair. She also cared for her brother, Bob, who was dying of cancer and lived in a house across the street with her father.

Esther's two grown children, twenty-nine-year-old Kathy and thirty-two-year-old David (whom everyone called "Dave") lived nearby. Dave was a tall—six feet, five inches—mild-mannered man, with short dark hair who occasionally sported a mustache. He had gentle eyes. He and his wife, Patti, had a sweet two-year-old daughter named Jennifer. Dave was artistically inclined but had never studied art. Instead, he had become a stockbroker and established David Herman Investments in the 1300 block of South University Drive in Fort Worth.

Esther was worried about Dave. Money had been tight for him since Jennifer was born and Patti quit her job to stay at home with Jennifer. It was especially hard this time of year with all the pressure to provide nice things for Christmas. Unfortunately, there had been a huge economic downturn in Texas. A lot of people had lost their jobs, and Dave didn't have much business. He had been forced to move out of their house in Arlington to a rental in Kennedale, an outlying suburb. At one point, he had even taken a job at a topless nightclub, Lace, to make ends meet.

Esther thought everything would work out okay for Dave sooner or later. He was smart and talented, and a good guy. Whenever she asked how things were going Dave always said everything "was fine," "was great." He was not a complainer. Dave spent a lot of time with his grandmother and uncle helping Esther with their care. Each week, he took little Jennifer to visit her ailing relatives.

Esther thought Dave had seemed particularly anxious on Christmas day when the family got together, but she attributed that to the stress of Christmas and having his mother-in-law, Jean, visiting from Idaho.

At four o'clock in the morning on December 30, Esther got a call from her ex-husband, Lee. "You better come to the police station," he said. "Dave's been arrested for murder." In disbelief, Esther quickly dressed and within a half an hour was at the station, certain there had been some horrible mistake. Dave had never been arrested, or been in any trouble with the law.

ESTHER: My first thought was that it was impossible. I had heard he was charged with murder, and I thought, *No way is it him.* Lee and Patti and I sat at the station for several hours waiting for somebody to come out and talk to us. Eventually they did, and at that point they came and got Patti to see him. When she came back out from her visit with him she said, "He did it, he confessed." They wouldn't let me see him or anyone else other than her. I knew he must be suffering deeply, so I called the Methodist church Mother and I attended to see if someone could go visit him and spoke with Reverend Grubb, who was on call. He said he would go right over. Eventually, they transported Dave from the city jail to Tarrant County Jail, and at that point he was able to call me. He was distraught.

·   ·   ·   ·

Things had been much worse for Dave than Esther had realized. Dave was frantic to make some money. Patti wanted to return to Idaho with her mother for a visit, and he was humiliated that he couldn't afford to send her. He couldn't pay rent on either his home or office, and he was ashamed and embarrassed—and desperate.

On December 20, at 9:30 A.M., Dave had forced his way into the Lace nightclub dressed in camouflage and carrying a .357 magnum. According to Dave, the club owed him some money. Not expecting anyone to be there so early, he was surprised when he encountered Clay Griffin, the manager. Dave ordered him at gunpoint into the office, where there were two other employees, Jennifer Burns and Sally Fogle. Dave demanded that twenty-one-year-old Jennifer give him all the cash. She put $11,200 into a canvas bag. David ordered Clay to the floor and bound him and Sally with a wire coat hanger.

He then turned to Jennifer and said, "This is where it gets good." He ordered her to undress. He touched her breasts and tried to rape her but was unable to. He became enraged. He shot Jennifer in the head, shoulder, and arm. He placed the gun at the back of Sally's head, but she turned before he fired, so she was hit in the jaw. He shot Clay in the upper arm and head. All three were taken to Arlington Memorial Hospital. Clay was treated and released, Sally was admitted for treatment, and Jennifer died at the hospital.[1]

A crime-stoppers tip led police to Dave, and both survivors easily identified him from a photograph. Ten days later, on a Saturday night, a SWAT team stormed his home and ransacked it, looking for evidence of the crime. They found $2,700 in cash, and the car in his driveway matched the description of a vehicle seen at the club on the day of the crime. The police arrested Dave and took him in for questioning, where he immediately confessed. On Sunday, Dave led the police to the gun, which he had hidden.[2]

ESTHER: I was shocked, of course. I couldn't believe it. Dave had been acting very serious over the holidays. He was always a very upbeat person, but he hadn't been acting that way. He was clearly troubled. I regretted that I hadn't focused on him more. I was very stretched; I had two very active businesses at the holidays, and health issues, and overseeing the care of people, and I was pretty much overburdened. My mother, my dad, and my brother had just moved here from New Mexico. Mother and my brother were in very bad health. Mother lived with me, Dad and my brother lived across the street, and I had a lady that helped with the meals and health care. They shuttled between two houses. Dave knew it was an extremely difficult time. He was always a very kind person. He didn't want to overload me.

·   ·   ·   ·

The Reverend Larry Grubb was on call the night Esther called his church. He had visited other people at the Tarrant County Jail, so he already had the necessary credentials in place that permitted him to visit.

REVEREND GRUBB: I would guess it was about 9:00 P.M. when I got the call from Esther. I immediately agreed to go, and I was familiar with the jail

• • • •

Early on, the state gave notice of its intention to seek the death penalty. Tarrant County already had a reputation for seeking the death penalty, and this was a high-profile case. The district attorney, Tim Curry, was also running for office. Tarrant County had just built a brand-new courthouse, and Dave's was going to be the first high profile trial held there. A new judge, Elbert Young, was to preside.

The court appointed David Bays to represent Dave, but Esther, believing he would be better off with private counsel, set out to find a lawyer to take on the case. She contacted several local defense lawyers, but most refused the case or charged more money than Esther could afford. Finally she located Judy Bridges, a Dallas lawyer who agreed to take the case and seemed to know what she was doing. Esther paid her a $35,000 retainer. Judy said that she did not have a lot of experience in criminal cases, but reassured Esther by saying that lawyers from a large Dallas firm where she had interned had volunteered to help with the case.

• • • •

The business of keeping the family together—besides running her two businesses and caring for her aging relatives—fell to Esther. Her daughter became very depressed. Both she and Esther started taking antidepressants and going to therapy.

Esther also was Dave's primary support person. Patti visited Dave several times during the first two months after his arrest, but the visits did not go well. Understandably, she was very angry, and her anger kept her from being able to support him. She soon divorced Dave and moved out of state with their daughter. She did not tell Jennifer what had happened to her father, and she refused to keep in touch with Dave or anyone in the Herman family except Lee, Dave's father.

Esther tried to protect her mother from knowing the full extent of Dave's crime. She told her Dave had been arrested for robbery but did not tell her about the murder. Before the trial, Bob died; Esther asked the reporters covering the story not to mention his death in connection with the crime, and they respected her wishes.

Esther also had to contend with her ex-husband, Lee, who supported the death penalty and refused to have any contact with Dave.

ESTHER: It never occurred to me to give up. This was my son. I loved him and I believed in him. He had never even had a traffic ticket before. I have a lot of faith, and I didn't believe in the death penalty. I had to try to save Dave's life.

Not everybody in my family opposed the death penalty. My daughter, sister, father, and ex-husband all supported the death penalty. However, none of them openly opposed me. My attitude was, You are either with me or against me, and if you are against me, then get the hell out of the way.

• • • •

Dave persevered by developing his faith under the guidance of Reverend Grubb, who visited at least once a week. The two also corresponded. Reverend Grubb gave Dave an annotated Bible, and he began studying in earnest. Dave wrote this letter on March 3, 1990, about three months after the crime.

Dear Rev. Grubb,

I hope this letter finds you, your family, and congregations in good health and good spirits. I hope the Lord has been blessing you all at least as much as he has been blessing me.

My Christian walk is progressing—it's not a smooth stroll in the park, but the highs and lows are both getting higher. It is due in large part to putting that magnificent study Bible you helped procure to good use. Another reason is a major project I'm working on, which we'll talk about on your next visit.

I'm aware of the difficulties you've encountered getting in to see me. I enjoy our visits, and know you will come by at every opportunity— and with all "procedures" lined up!

I hope you enjoy this envelope. In conjunction with another Christian man in this cell block, I am making envelopes with the crucifixion, Jesus giving a blessing, and various flowers. (Mom and Kathy have examples of the flowers.) I put verses and proverbs under the drawings, and the other guy distributes them to inmates at gym. (I'm still on "solo" gym.) He takes that opportunity to witness to them. It gives us both a real good feeling to be reaching out with God's word.

I want to thank you for the help you've given me, and especially for the help and counsel you've given my family. May God bless you!

Sincerely,

Dave Herman[4]

•   •   •   •

On the anniversary of the murder, the *Fort Worth Star-Telegram* ran a story on Jennifer Burns's family and the nightclub. Judi Freeman, owner of the club, reported that the murder had not hurt business. Clay Griffin had returned to work, but Sally Fogle had not. Shannon had given birth to a baby daughter on Thanksgiving of 1990, and she named the girl after her sister. Jennifer's mother, Paula Foster, who worked at the nightclub with Jennifer, had returned to work but struggled with grieving her loss. The article was accompanied by a photograph of Paula and Shannon holding the new baby, with a larger-than-life picture of Jennifer in the background. The reporter wrote:

> The pain has been constant for Foster, who remembers her daughter every time she looks at the green teddy bear that was given to Jennifer by her sorority and at numerous pictures of her that adorn tables and shelves.
>
> Foster also has some special mementos, like her daughter's rings and an algebra test on which Jennifer scored 97. . . .
>
> Foster went through five months of counseling after her daughter's death but still grapples with loneliness and depression. But she is determined to get on with her life.
>
> "Jennifer was a very happy person," she said. "Jennifer would not have wanted her world to collapse."

The article concluded:

> [Foster] said she has no compassion for the pain the Hermans have encountered because her own is so great.
>
> "The thing that scares me more than anything else is that David Lee Herman will not get the death penalty," she said. "I want David Lee Herman put to sleep, basically. I want him gone."[5]

· · · ·

As the trial drew near, Esther became increasingly concerned that Judy was not able to handle Dave's case. The help in the form of an additional attorney never came through, and the court ended up appointing David Bays, the original lawyer, to assist Judy. Unfortunately, the two lawyers did not get along well and seemed to Esther to spend more time fighting than working on Dave's case. Esther paid additional money—over $15,000—to hire a psychologist, Cliff Kary, and an investigator.

Dave had wanted to plead guilty and avoid going to trial. He was prepared to spend the rest of his life in prison and, ideally, if the state had offered him a chance to plead guilty in exchange for a life sentence—thus sparing the state and the victims a trial—he would have jumped at the chance. According to Judy Bridges, prosecutor Greg Pipes never made such an offer, and Judy did not ask for it, either. So in May 1991, Dave's trial began at the new Tarrant County Courthouse.

The trial was very short. Prosecutor Pipes called Sally Fogle and Clay Griffin, who provided emotional testimony about their ordeal. Then the state presented Dave's full confession to the crime.

Judy did not put on much of a case, but in her defense, there wasn't much of a case to be offered. She called Cliff Kary, but his testimony was not compelling. He later told Esther that Judy didn't "ask him the right questions." Esther later learned that he was not a forensic psychologist but a child psychologist. Like Judy, he was inexperienced and unqualified for a death penalty trial.

Esther attended every day of the trial with her friend Sue Steiber. Because she was going to be a witness, Esther could not watch any of the other witnesses testify; she waited outside. Sue watched most of the trial, keeping Esther up to date. Others—Tami, and her husband, John, and Kathy—attended when they could.

ESTHER: I didn't feel like Judy knew what she was doing. The district attorney kept stressing the fact that Dave used to hunt with his dad and had knowledge of guns as proof that he was violent and likely to kill again. Having guns is hardly news in Texas. Dave had never done anything violent in his life, yet the jury was left with the impression that he was likely to kill again.

pleted. The *Fort Worth Star-Telegram* wrote a story about the stay, accompanied by another photograph of Paula, Shannon, and Jennifer. This time, Jennifer was four. In the background were dozens of family photographs with Jennifer. The story quoted the victims' families. " 'It's still moving along,' said Foster. . . . 'I'm thrilled every time his appeal is rejected, rejected, rejected.' 'I believe that what comes around goes around, and he'll have to answer for what he's done,' said DeShay. . . . 'Whether it's in our justice system or God's.'"8

Tami's husband, John, had started an online campaign soliciting people to sign petitions in support of clemency for Dave. Paula Foster contacted John by e-mail and told him that he shouldn't be involved in trying to save Dave's life because he didn't understand the pain of losing a child. He sent her a reply telling her about the tragic car accident that took his two children. Paula never wrote back.

On October 10, 1996, Dave lost his final appeal. The court opinion was less than four pages long.9 Dave's case went from crime to final appeal in less than seven years, several years earlier than most death penalty cases at that time. Execution was set for April 2, 1997.

•   •   •   •

Dave spent his last few months wrapping up loose ends, writing letters to family, finishing art projects, and working on his Bible stories. Although he had had no contact with his daughter for over six years, he wrote his daughter a letter:

My daughter, Jennifer,

When you were born, I was there holding your mother's hand. I cut the umbilical cord. Then, with both of you in a rolling bed, I pushed you out to an alcove next to the waiting room, and said to our families, "I want you all to wish a Happy Birthday to Jennifer Michelle." I cried tears of pure joy.

I was there when you were born, I was there during the first few years of your life, but I have not been there since, and I want you to know how I feel. I have loved you every day of my life. Not being with you and your mother is the price I've paid for the terrible wrongs I've done. If I could undo those wrongs, I would. Instead, I have spent the years wondering what you were like now, dreaming of helping you grow up, and wishing. . . .

I'm crying again—tears of joy, remembering our brief time together, and tears of sadness, mourning the loss of the rest of our lives together. I hope I make it to heaven, so I can look down on my little girl. Jennifer, I love you!

Your Daddy[10]

He also wrote letters to Reverend Grubb and to his mother.

Dear Larry,

You are a wonderful man, and it has been an honor to call you friend. A large part of my peace with all this is knowing you will be there for my family. Thank you.

Please share hugs with everyone from me. When you hug them, and especially when you hold my mom, please tell them I said, "Keep the faith."

I'm going to include a sheet of paper in this envelope giving a statement to the victims and their families. Please show it to them, if there is ever an opportunity. I trust you to hold it until the right time, if ever.

I feel peaceful. In the fullness of time, we will see each other again. Sincerely your friend,

Dave[11]

To the victims of my crimes and their families:

I have taken so much from you all. If my death helps with your healing process, then I embrace my mortality. If it would have undone any part of the loss, I would have taken my own life years ago.

I won't add to your pain by asking forgiveness. God will decide how to punish me for my sins. What I do ask is that you all not allow the evil I've done to close your hearts to compassion, love, and faith.

Dave Herman[12]

Mom,

I LOVE YOU!

You kept the faith. Let my love in your heart give you strength to keep the faith with all the others who love and care for and need you.

I'm coming home.

Your loving son,

Dave[13]

and gave him a long hug. Everyone said the Lord's Prayer together. It was very respectful.

REVEREND GRUBB: Esther was very composed about it and appeared to be at real peace. I think she had really done her homework and accepted it. From my perspective she appeared to have handled it very well. I could have envisioned other families being uncontrollable with grief and rage and pain. Esther had gotten a lot of good support from a lot of sources. She was okay.

Dave had added a codicil to his will in which he expressed his wishes regarding the handling of his body after his death.

After my death, whenever and whatever the circumstances may be, I would *not* like for there to be a traditional memorial service in a chapel for me. Instead, I would like an Irish wake. I leave the option to my family and friends as to whether my body attends the party. If there is a conflict on that point, then it is my wish that my body *not* attend, and instead a large photograph of me is placed on a table. I want the wake to be an upbeat gathering, with food and drink, celebrating the good times in my life. I would like my father . . . [or] whomever else may be hosting the wake in my father's absence, to end the evening by raising a toast to the good times I have shared with them all. I cannot ask that there be no crying, but I do ask that there be smiles when they do. I would like those not attending the wake to raise a toast whenever they are able.

When my body is interred, I would like a short Christian ceremony, open to whomever wishes to attend. I harbor no hatred for anyone, and do not want anyone barred from watching my body buried, for whatever reason they may have for attending. I would like a simple headstone with a cross in the upper left corner, an angel in the upper right corner, my name, dates of birth and death, and an inscription below that reads, "His soul now dances with the skies."[17]

•   •   •   •

Two weeks later, sixty or so people gathered at Esther's house to honor his request. Dave had written a letter that he had asked his mother to read at the event.

Esther Herman next to a picture of Dave and an urn containing ashes of his remains. Provided with permission of Esther Herman.

My Wonderful family,

I must say good-bye in one sense, but it is not good-bye. I am simply changing perspectives—I'll be watching you all with new eyes. And I will be alive forever in your hearts.

I wish I could say a great many things to each of you, but that is not to be. I feel you all will know how much you mean to me.

I look forward to being at the wake. I'll be home. I'll be with the ones I love. It's the time to put the dark thoughts behind, and begin the healing that joyous memories and laughter bring. Give each other lots of hugs.

You all have kept the faith. I am a lucky man.

With all my love,

Dave[18]

·　·　·　·

The tragedy of December 1989 continues for Esther. Openly grieving the loss of her son has not been socially acceptable. She still suffers the effects of the execution. Mary and Esther live together in Arlington, and Tami and John now live in Dallas and visit frequently. Kathy still lives nearby. Esther's businesses continue to thrive. There has been a rapprochement between Esther and Patti, who has agreed to let Esther see her granddaughter. Jennifer still does not know the whole story about what happened to her father. Esther has been collecting letters and mementos written by friends and family that she will give to Jennifer one day.

ESTHER: Grief is a day-by-day thing. Some days are good, and some days it sneaks up behind you and bites you in the butt. It is always there, but the "sneak up behind you and get you days" are the worst.

The crime was front-page news and by the time of his execution international news. He will forever be memorialized as a criminal, but with the exception of that one horrible moment, he was a good man. I cannot openly sing his praises as other mothers do remembering their deceased children. I miss his smile, his hugs, his "Hi, Ma," his jokes—all of him. He will always be my son, whom I love dearly, and I will always feel the loss of him in a very sad way.

For methodical, premeditated murder to be legal in our great nation has always seemed so very wrong to me. The biblical "eye for an eye, tooth for a tooth" is what lots of people believe in these cases. I believe in love and forgiveness. I have instructed everyone close to me that if I should meet a violent death I do not want the courts to seek the death penalty.

TAMI: Before Dave's case I had always been for the death penalty, if you take a life you pay with yours, but actually seeing it at work is different. It is not consistent. It is not applied evenly across the board. Not everybody gets the same shot, whether it is due to money or political pressure, it is just not even. Also, it doesn't just punish the killer; it punishes the family, too.

REVEREND GRUBB: I haven't always been against the death penalty. I have only come to oppose it since Dave's ordeal. I think part of it has to do with the fact that the research indicates that we are killing innocent people and it is not a deterrent to crime. Before, I would not have bought into the innocent-people argument, but now I am confident because of DNA testing that can be done. Also, I had no idea before how crooked the legal system is in Texas.

We are going to try to abolish the death penalty in Texas. That is our ultimate goal, but we realize that is not going to happen overnight. We were hoping to pass a resolution at the annual meeting of the Methodist

Church in central Texas, but unfortunately the person who was going to present it decided not to. I anticipate it will come up in the future. It is not going to change the state, but it is one little infinitesimal step. I think the crime lab scandal in Houston[19] is having an impact, but we have a long way to go.

Esther is a strong lady, and I thought she did a wonderful job of supporting her son while he was in prison. She was pretty stoic about it, but the experience was devastating to her. I have been impressed at how soon she became a real advocate for abolishing the death penalty. She speaks to attorney groups and even went to the larger universities and shared her point of view. She turned her grief into trying to create something worthwhile.

Dave was an unusual prisoner. I don't think he would have ever been involved in another crime. He was willing to serve the rest of his life in prison. He did a lot of good things and could have done a lot more.

·　　·　　·　　·

In 2003, Esther and Paula finally spoke, thirteen years after the crime.

ESTHER: I was at Jason's deli picking up lunch on a Saturday and Paula walked up to me. She was very nice. I put my hand on her arm and asked how she was doing. She said, "I am doing good." Her hair was a lot shorter and different than when I remembered her, and I commented on it. I said, "You do look good, and I like what you've done with your hair." It wasn't meant to be a superfluous statement. I am in the beauty business, so I meant it in all sincerity, and I believe she took it that way. It was good to see her.

It was a very short encounter. I told her how sorry we were and she thanked me; no hugs or tears or open emotions. I had always wanted to tell her I was sorry but never knew when the right time would be. It just happened when it happened.

of Rocks Bridge—that was being reported on TV and the newspapers by Friday morning. But the media had been reporting that Tom Cummins, a cousin, had confessed and the police had arrested him. Everyone thought the case was solved. I was really taken by surprise when they came to my house. I was terrified for Reggie and didn't know what to do.

Officers Pappas and Walsh took Reggie to St. Louis Police Department headquarters and put him in interview room number one, an eight-by-ten-foot windowless room with a four-by-six-foot table, four chairs, and an assortment of books.[1] The room was in the middle of the homicide unit, guaranteeing that anyone who tried to leave would be confronted by detectives. Several hours later, police also arrested Marlin Gray, whom he had been with on Thursday evening. Marlin was in interview room number two.

By 10:30 that evening the police had still not returned Reggie home, and Vera, panic-stricken, called Detective Pappas. He was not there, so Vera left a message asking him to call her back. At 11:00 P.M., Chris Pappas called and told Vera that he had "some bad news"—Reggie was being arrested and charged with murder and rape.

VERA: Of course at this point I am terrified, not believing all of this is really happening. I didn't know what to do. I didn't have an attorney that I could just pick up the phone and call. I hadn't had a chance to talk to Reggie—he never called. I was in shock. I cried off and on all night. My children Veronda and Arvon came over along with my sister, and the whole family stayed up all night talking and praying. We were in disbelief, in shock.

As soon as business opened the next day, Vera was on the phone trying to find a lawyer and figure out how she could visit Reggie. When she called the police station, she was told that only family members could visit, and that since she had a different last name from Reggie (Vera had remarried) she could only get in to see him if she could prove she was his mother. Vera didn't know where her marriage license was and didn't know how else to prove she was Reggie's mother. At 1:00 P.M., Vera located an attorney, Michael Kelly, who was willing to go check on Reggie.

On the afternoon of Monday, April 8, at 2:15 P.M., Michael visited Reggie at the station. Reggie told his lawyer that he had not raped or killed anyone, but that he had "confessed" to raping one of the girls because the police beat him, telling him what to say, until he did so. Michael noticed that the right side of Reggie's face was swollen. Reggie opened his shirt, and Michael saw bruising on Reggie's chest.

By Monday evening, Vera had still not been able to visit Reggie herself, so she asked Veronda to visit Reggie. Unlike Vera, Veronda had her marriage license readily available; it showed her maiden name was the same as Reggie's. Veronda visited Reggie between 7:00 and 8:00 P.M. Reggie told her that the police had beaten him during questioning, and Veronda noticed that Reggie's face was swollen.

> **VERA:** It was a day before I could get anyone inside to see Reggie and find out how he was doing. I didn't understand why he hadn't called. I can't describe the helplessness and frustration I felt—and the terror. I couldn't eat. I couldn't sleep. I couldn't concentrate on anything, except trying to figure out how to help Reggie.

Tuesday afternoon, April 9, Reggie was arraigned on the murder and rape charges. Vera attended the proceeding and from across the courtroom could see that the right side of her son's face was swollen. Reverend Thomas, Reggie's brother Derrelyn Thompson, and an aunt and her two children also attended the arraignment and observed Reggie's swollen face. After Judge Michael David saw it, he ordered Reggie transported to the Regional Medical Center emergency room.

After the arraignment, Reggie was transported to the city jail for prisoner processing. A clerk, a caseworker, and a nurse contacted the internal affairs division to report Reggie's facial injuries. An internal affairs officer took photos of his swollen cheek and split lip. Michael Kelly attended the interview with Reggie while he spoke with the internal affairs officers. During that tape-recorded conversation, the officers noted Reggie's injuries. Another prisoner, Michael Kent, saw Reggie on April 9 while he was at the city jail. He also noticed that Reggie's face was swollen.

Next, Reggie was transported to the hospital, where Dr. Stephen Duntly examined him and diagnosed facial trauma, myalgia, mild myositis, and a swollen right cheek. He recommended that Reggie return to the hospital on April 17 for plastic surgery.[2]

Codefendant Marlin Gray also reported being beaten by Officer Pappas and Lieutenant Steve Jacobsmeyer. Michael Kent saw Marlin Gray at the city marked that he was afraid of heights, but agreed to go.[8] He was disappointed that he would not be alone with Julie.[9]

Julie parked the car near the bridge, and the three snuck through an opening in a chain-link fence where a sign warned trespassers to stay away. The night was cold, damp, and foggy. The bridge rose ninety feet above the turbulent, swift-moving water.[10] As they walked onto the bridge, they passed a group of four teenagers. They struck up a conversation, and Julie told the group that she had written a poem that some in the group had seen. They praised her poem, talked some more about art and music, smoked cigarettes, and then parted company. Julie and Robin took Thomas to see the poem. Whether by accident or attack, within an hour the girls' bodies were in the Mississippi River, raising many questions.

Sometime around 1:30 A.M., Thomas was standing on the side of Riverview Drive hailing traffic. Shortly before 2:00 A.M., Eugene Shipley, a truck driver, stopped. Thomas told him that he had been attacked and pushed off the bridge. The driver called for help, and by 2:00 A.M. police and rescue vehicles arrived. Thomas's and the girls' parents were notified, and they went to the bridge sometime around 5:00 A.M.[11]

What happened on the bridge is what is in dispute.

Thomas initially told Detectives Raymond Ghrist and Gary Stittum that he and the girls had been attacked by a group of four males and forced off the bridge. Thomas said that the males started off robbing him—they took money and his Swatch watch. He said that it was too dark for him to see what was going on.[12] When asked if he at any time resisted the attack or did anything to help his cousins, who he believed were being raped, he said that he had not because he was a paramedic and a firefighter and had seen many victims of assaults and did not want to end up like one of them. He believed he would fare best if he was passive.[13]

Thomas said that someone pushed the girls into the river and told him to jump, which he did,[14] and that when he surfaced in the river he initially saw both girls. Soon Robin went under the water and never surfaced again. Julie was a few feet away from him, and Thomas yelled to her to swim. Julie swam to Thomas and grabbed onto him. Fearing that he would drown, Thomas shook her loose. She went under, and Thomas never saw her again.[15]

Thomas, who was a trained lifeguard, swam between thirty and forty-five minutes in ten-mile-per-hour currents until he reached a wooded riverbank on the Missouri side, south of the water treatment plant,[16] near the bridge. He pulled himself up the steep embankment and walked twenty minutes to a set of railroad tracks and followed them until he reached the highway, where it took him between twelve and fifteen minutes to flag down a truck driver.[17]

Thomas showed the detectives a red-painted manhole in the middle of the mile-long bridge where he said they had been. Detectives pointed out a scratch on Thomas's face, his sore midsection, ink marks on his arms, and the fact that he was dry from the waist up. There was a lot of debris on the bridge. The officers took into evidence some items including a used condom, an unused condom, some keys, and a large flashlight.[18] After Thomas talked to the police and showed them where he and the girls had been, the police took him and his father, Gene, to police headquarters to make a formal statement. Gene Cummins was not present in the interview room, but he sat in an adjoining office and Thomas was permitted to consult with him, and he retained an attorney for his son, Frank Fabbri, who came to the police station, where Thomas was able to consult with him.[19]

The police found Thomas's story of jumping from the bridge and swimming ashore unbelievable. According to U.S. Coast Guard Chief Ed Moreland, a person who fell off the bridge would have fallen approximately ninety feet into raging whirlpools. The currents at that location were so strong that it was impossible to drag the river for bodies. The person would have hit the water traveling about eighty miles an hour and, unless he landed in perfect diving form, would most likely have broken bones or at the very least been severely bruised. The police took photographs of Thomas in his underwear, and he had no abrasions, bruising, or swelling.[20] The police also observed that Thomas's hair appeared to be completely dry and neatly combed.[21]

Corporal James McDaniel of the Missouri Water Patrol advised that the water temperature of fifty-four degrees Fahrenheit would cause hypothermia and cause a person to drown. He added that the extremely strong current and a whirlpool to the south of the bridge made it unsafe for searchers to drag the bottom. Also, the current at that location would carry a person to the Illinois side of the river, while Thomas said he had swum to the Missouri side; McDaniel said that to accomplish the feat that Thomas claimed to have done would be extraordinary.[22] Gene Cummins also said he had a hard time believing his son's story.

At 1:30 P.M., Officer Robert Meyer asked Thomas to take a polygraph test, which he agreed to do. Officer Meyer informed Thomas and Gene, that the test results were classified as "deceptive." Gene Cummins stated that he was afraid of that result and added that when Thomas was an adolescent he concocted elaborate stories to justify his shortcomings in school performance and that he was a pathological liar.[23]

When Thomas was confronted with these discrepancies, his story changed. He said that after the trip to Florida he had wished for his relationship with Julie to be more than platonic, and that he had been disappointed that Robin was in the car when Julie came to pick him up. During his interview at the bridge with Detective Ghrist and Detective Sergeant Daniel Nichols, Thomas indicated that he brought a prophylactic to St. Louis and that his girlfriend in Maryland was on birth control. When that discrepancy was pointed out to him, Thomas said, "You never know when you'll get lucky."[24]

Thomas told the detective and his father that he had developed strong feelings for Julie in Florida and that at one point they were close to having sex, but Julie said they were cousins and it would be wrong. The two had spoken on the phone long distance and wrote letters regularly after their Florida visit. During his time in St. Louis, they had spent time together every day visiting various area attractions.[25]

Thomas then stated that the real truth was that Julie had been sitting on the bridge railing and he advanced toward her, wanting to hug her. She became startled, lost her balance, and fell into the river. He became hysterical and blacked out, at which time Robin must have jumped into the water to save her. Thomas began crying and said, "That's the truth, believe me."[26]

Thomas was taken in for prisoner processing. Before he left, Gene Cummins made a circular motion with his right index finger at the side of his head and said, "That thing he said about jumping off of that bridge; check into that. That can't be right. I'm of the same opinion as you guys. Thomas isn't telling the truth, but I don't know why."[27]

Rescue attempts were made but proved futile. In fact, it wasn't until April 26 that a body the state identified as that of Julie Kerry was discovered by a fisherman in Caruthersville, Missouri, 180 miles south of St. Louis.[28] Robin's body has never been found.

·   ·   ·   ·

Reggie Clemons went to the Chain of Rocks Bridge on the night of April 4, 1991. He had spent the evening hanging out at the house of a friend, Michael Shaffner, with Marlin Gray, Antonio "Tony" Richardson, and Daniel Winfrey. After watching a hockey game on television, the four left in two separate cars and drove to the Chain of Rocks Bridge. Reggie took with him a large police-issue flashlight that he had gotten from a friend of a friend whose father was a police officer. He kept the flashlight in his car to use for delivering pizzas.

The four walked to a giant peace sign and hung out talking for a while and exploring the bridge. As they were leaving the bridge they encountered a young white man and two young white women.

Thomas described this encounter to the police, as set forth in the police report:

> They [Thomas, Julie, and Robin] walked just short of halfway to a point just west of the bend in the bridge, and while approaching the Illinois side, they saw four figures approaching from the east. When the four got closer, he saw that the group consisted of one white male and three black males.
>
> The two groups momentarily exchanged greetings. One of the black males mentioned that he was from Wentzville, Missouri. The reason Thomas Cummins remembered same was because his family had visited a relative in Wentzville on Wednesday and in that vein, he was somewhat familiar with its location in relation to St. Louis.
>
> During that time, first names were exchanged, and he recalled the names of Robby and Adrian. [Neither the police nor defense ever looked into the names of Robby and Adrian.] He mentioned that he was visiting from Maryland. One of the guys said they were looking for a black flashlight they had misplaced on the bridge and if Thomas Cummins and the girls found same, it was his. The four males commented that they were leaving and continued walking toward the Missouri side.
>
> He and the girls then continued to walk toward the east end of the bridge.[29]

Through the flashlight found on the bridge, police tracked down Reggie. The state decided to believe Thomas's version about the rape and robbery because by April 7, 1991, Reggie, Marlin, Daniel, and Tony had all been arrested. In a police report, Captain Robert Bauman, commander of the crimes against persons division, explained the state's official position:

> As reflected per CN #91-65574, subject Thomas C. was arrested and booked for the murder of Julie and Robin Kerry on 4-5-91. Warrant application conducted on 4-6-91 resulted in warrants in this matter being taken under advisement.

gan. It is impossible to contradict the state's evidence if you don't know what it is. The attorneys had done hardly any investigation, so I decided I needed to hire an investigator to figure out who we needed for witnesses. They did a good job, especially considering that I had limited funds to pay them.

Once Vera started learning about the criminal justice system and what her son was up against, she started to become an activist. She held benefit fundraisers for Reggie's case. She hosted gospel music concerts and breakfasts at the church. She even organized a gala event at a hotel. She traveled around to public events and set up a table or booth where she gave away helium balloons and potato chips in exchange for donations to Reggie's case. She also passed out a flyer about the criminal justice system explaining what families were up against. She raised a few thousand dollars, which helped pay for the investigator.

·   ·   ·   ·

Because of his willingness to cooperate with the state, and probably also because of his age and race, Daniel Winfrey agreed, under the threat of the death penalty, to testify against the other three defendants in exchange for a ten-year sentence, of which he would likely only serve between six and eight years.[31] Having made the deal with the state, Daniel made a written statement about the case with the assistance of his lawyers after reviewing police reports.[32]

Because of his deal, Daniel Winfrey's case did not go to trial. Marlin went to trial first, in October 1992. Judge Thomas Mermot presided over the case. Marlin was convicted and sentenced to death on October 21, 1992. Reggie's case was scheduled to begin in January, and Tony's was to follow.

VERA: There was a lot of publicity around Marlin's case. The prosecutor used Marlin Gray's case to poison the public against Reggie. The prosecutor kept bringing Reggie's name up during the trial, so it was in the newspaper morning, noon, and night. How could Reggie get a fair trial?

Meanwhile, we were getting closer to Reggie's trial date and were still not ready. Reggie had not had a chance to see all of the videos or police reports that he was entitled to see. I called Robert, and he told me to call Jeanene. I had a hard time reaching Jeanene because she was in California. Worse yet, the prosecutor didn't even give all the evidence to the lawyers, so they couldn't give it to Reggie. How could he be prepared for trial if he didn't know what the state's case was?

By the time I realized that they were not doing a good job representing Reggie, it was too late to hire anyone else. I didn't have any money, and they would not have given me back the money that I had already paid them.

The state severed the rape charges from the murder charges and proceeded to trial on the murder charges. Reggie's trial began on January 25, 1993, before Judge Edward M. Peek. From the beginning, things did not go well for Reggie. His lawyers moved to suppress Reggie's statements on the grounds that they had been forced and the police had violated his *Miranda* rights. Nobody disputed that Reggie had been injured while in police custody. Moss argued that even so, there was no testimony that anything Reggie said as a result of his treatment by the police was false. He summarized his argument, "The State merely needs to show by a preponderance of the evidence that he was not coerced into these statements, and repeatedly advised of his rights. And the affirmative testimony, a lack of beating on their part [the police], I believe that the credibility is with them [the police] as opposed to with the defendant and his witnesses."[33] Judge Peek ruled for the state, finding that "the statement as a preponderance of the credible evidence proves that the confession made by the defendant was not involuntary.[34]

Then the prosecutor struck three out of five African Americans from the total jury pool of thirty possible jurors, leaving only two. Reggie's lawyers struck one of the others, leaving only one black person to serve on the jury.[35]

Daniel Winfrey and Thomas Cummins were the main prosecution witnesses. Throughout the course of the investigation, both had given conflicting versions of the evening's events. During trial, Reggie's attorneys brought out the fact that Moss had flown to Maryland and met with Thomas for at least ten hours.[36]

There was no physical evidence linking Reggie to the crime. In fact, the coroner's examination revealed no indication of the rape that allegedly served as the motive for the crime.[37]

At trial, Thomas testified that one of the four robbed him. He had told the police that he could hear the rapes but didn't do anything to stop them, and then someone pushed the girls off the bridge.[38] Thomas explained that the other version of his story, where Julie had accidentally fallen from the bridge after he made a sexual advance, was suggested to him by the police, and he had only agreed with the officer's version of what happened because Detective Jacobsmeyer had beat him.[39] Thomas also claimed that he changed his story because his father told him that he did not believe him.[40] Although Thomas picked Reggie out of a lineup as one of the people he saw that evening, that lineup did not occur until May 8, more than a month after the crime. By that time, Reggie's face had been on television and in the newspapers repeatedly. Thomas could not say who among the defendants had actually raped the girls or pushed them from the bridge.[41]

As part of his deal, Daniel Winfrey testified against Reggie and the co-defendants. Daniel testified that Reggie had instigated the robbery. Daniel also testified that he witnessed the rapes but did not actually see anybody get pushed off the bridge, because he was looking for Marlin. However, in his initial statement given at the police station (before he met with his lawyer and reviewed the police reports) he wrote, "I pushed them." He then crossed out the "I" and wrote in "we."[42] Additionally, key aspects of Daniel's testimony were contradicted by a letter that he had previously written to his girlfriend in which he implicated another co-defendant as the one who proposed the robbery and did not mention that Reggie had been involved in the rape.[43]

Reggie's attorneys tried to impeach the trial witnesses. The officers denied that Reggie or anyone else had been beaten. However, Detectives John Walsh, Jacobsmeyer, and Pappas all admitted under cross-examination that they had not believed Thomas Cummins when he said that he jumped off the bridge and swam ashore.[44]

The attorneys did not mount a vigorous defense. There was evidence that tended to prove Reggie's innocence which they could have used more effectively to defend their client—for example: Thomas's contradictory statements and the unlikelihood of his surviving the jump; the police brutality that led to coerced confessions; the question of whether the body found was actually that of Julie Kerry; and the inconsistencies in Daniel's statements. (The attorneys did try to bring out Daniel's inconsistencies during cross-examination, but they were not very effective in connecting the pieces for the jury.)

The attorneys themselves had not located or prepared to call any witnesses in Reggie's defense, relying instead on the ones that Vera's investigator had found. Thomas Cummins's testimony was crucial for the state to prove its case; thus Thomas Cummins's credibility was a key issue. Thomas gave the police two totally different versions of the evening's events. In one, Julie fell off the bridge accidentally, Robin jumped in to save her, and then Thomas ran to the bank of the river to look for them. In the other, assailants pushed the girls from the bridge and demanded that Thomas jump. Had defense attorneys called an expert witness to testify about the unlikelihood of Thomas surviving unharmed his jump from the bridge, the jury might have disbelieved Thomas's entire statement regarding the assailants.

The attorneys made no effort to have any DNA testing done on the evidence. None of the internal affairs records, officers, or reports were brought out; nor were X-rays of Reggie's injuries presented. The attorneys did not call several other witnesses whose testimony might have helped Reggie. They did not call Luis Vega, another inmate, who reported that Daniel had told him that "no one is going to believe a bunch of niggers" and that he would "do anything he could to get through this thing."[45] More important than not calling jailhouse witnesses, they did not call Gene Cummins—who had called his son a pathological liar and had told the police while his son was being questioned that he did not believe his son's story about jumping from the bridge—even though he was present in the courthouse.

In their defense, the attorneys were at a disadvantage because Moss had not provided the defense with all the evidence. Right before trial started, the defense was requesting copies of video statements by Tony Richardson, evidence from the body, Thomas's confession, photographs, grand jury testimony, and other things that should have been provided to them months earlier. Moss responded to the requests in a variety of ways: he denied that he had the information, he claimed the defense was not entitled to it, or he said that he did not know where it was.[46]

Besides this unprofessional conduct, Moss repeatedly made prejudicial remarks during the trial. Judge Peek admonished Moss several times and told him that he was in jeopardy of causing a mistrial.[47] After trial, during appeals, a letter from Moss was revealed in which he threatened Reggie's defense counsel.

The jury found Reggie guilty of two counts of first-degree murder on February 13, 1993. Two days later, the sentencing trial began, in which the jury had to decide whether to impose the death penalty.

The strongest point in Reggie's favor was that he had no criminal record and no history of violence. In an attempt to establish that Reggie had a propensity for violence, Moss called a guard who testified that Reggie had instigated a

have taken a toll on the family. Reverend Thomas has suffered from congestive heart failure, and Vera has had high blood pressure.

It is hard for the family members to visit Reggie in jail. Veronda is the closest in age to Reggie and visits more than his other siblings. Avron, the next older son, wants to visit his brother, but it is very painful for him to see him in jail. Vernell has nightmares whenever he goes.

Reggie's days on death row are pretty much the same. He gets up early in the morning and cleans his five-by-ten-foot cell. If it is an exercise day, he'll leave his cell for an hour. Otherwise, he spends his time writing letters to family members or reading. On Wednesdays he is allowed to call his family and attorney. He is only allowed to leave his cell three hours a week for an hour at a time.

REGGIE: Every day that I wake up I feel as though I am on a countdown to an unspecified date in the future. You don't know exactly how much time you have. Other inmates count how many days have passed because they want time to pass. I don't want time to pass, because the more time that passes the closer I am to execution.

When I think about my case and the way it was prosecuted, truthfully I don't think I'll ever get out of here. It feels futile, like there is no sense in fighting. When I feel that way I'll do some yoga and meditation. And whenever I feel like I am going off center I'll work out or think about my family or look out the window or pray or wait until it passes. I just got through a spell like that when I was feeling real down and felt like the inevitable is that I am going to be executed. The best way to prepare for this is to allow myself not to feel.

I don't know how I keep from going crazy. I don't know how I keep a smile on my face. I have seen other death row inmates who have lost their minds and they don't even know it, but you can see it. But sometimes I wonder if I already went crazy. I don't have a way of finding out for sure if I am sane, because I am not in the free world to find out how functional I am.

I have gotten to be friends with other people on death row. I became friends with Michael Owlsey. He was executed on Wednesday, February 6, 2002. It hurt. I lost someone that I could communicate with intellectually and someone who I had a lot of respect and admiration for. Michael Owlsey was a man that lived according to what he believed and said what he meant. He helped me stay grounded. Losing somebody like that is a loss that is hard to bear and sometimes makes you not want to get close to anybody, so you kind of push people away.

The day after an execution you wake up and the person is just not there anymore. Sometimes people aren't executed at the last minute, so you can't be sure if they are dead or not. I'll ask a guard or an inmate or try to catch the news at 6:00 A.M. They don't blink the lights or anything like that. Missouri does executions the first Wednesday of every month at midnight. It is more convenient on Wednesday. Government officials don't have to miss their weekends.

I try to treat people with respect, and I try to be as helpful as I possibly can, but that is different from not speaking out against injustices. I have done some hunger strikes since I've been inside protesting different things. One time the guards wouldn't let us use the law library. Most people in here don't do anything about their cases. These guys have no fight left in them; they are in a zombie state. Have you ever seen someone who is overloaded with too much to bear?

Vera tries to visit Reggie every weekend, but she refuses to drive on the highway because she is so sleep-deprived that she is afraid she'll fall asleep while driving. Usually she gets a ride with another mother who has a son on death row.

Vera is a member of many different organizations working to improve the criminal justice system. She joined the Missouri Eastern Coalition to Abolish the Death Penalty and represents it on the board of directors of the National Coalition to Abolish the Death Penalty. With the statewide Missouri Coalition to Abolish the Death Penalty she has worked in the legislature on campaigns to end the execution of the mentally retarded and juveniles in Missouri. She is working on a committee for a statewide moratorium. She is a board member of Missouri CURE. She is enrolled in a two-year associate criminal justice program at Ashworth College. Vera believes that all of these things are important because they give her tools to help families and to improve the justice system.

She also visits Reggie nearly every week and gives support to other people who have family members on death row. She rarely has time to think or feel, but she fears that if she doesn't keep busy the enormity of the situation will overwhelm and paralyze her emotionally.

VERA: Every day you just go through the motions of living, but you always have this feeling inside that something is missing. It is like a big gap. I'm sure families that have lost loved ones have gone through similar things to death row families. It is hard to explain, having someone on death row. You feel like you are living in an hourglass because you are always conscious of this clock ticking, ticking, and ticking. Every day is a day closer to an execution. You know this when you visit. You know this no matter what you do or no matter where you go. You always know that there is a possibility of an execution. This is how you live, very limited, mentally and physically.

The Missouri Supreme Court upheld Reggie's conviction, but fortunately, in August 2002, U.S. District Court Judge Catherine Perry reversed Reggie's death sentence on the grounds that jurors had been improperly excluded. Judge Perry also found that prosecutor Moss had been "over-aggressive." In her opinion, Judge Perry wrote: "The transcript is replete with admonitions from the trial judge to the prosecutor for improper questions, objections, and comments. . . . The prosecutor was abusive and boorish, and his tactics overall were calculated to intimidate the defense at every turn."[54]

Judge Perry ordered that the state had to conduct a new sentencing hearing or Reggie's sentence would be commuted to life in prison. The state has appealed her ruling to the Eighth Circuit Court of Appeals. Reggie's appeal raised over fifty legal errors, but most were procedurally barred because his attorneys failed to raise them at trial. Reggie waits to see if Judge Perry's ruling will be upheld, and if it is, whether the state will seek another death sentence.

VERA: Of course, we were very happy when Reggie's sentence was reversed, but then the case was in the news again. Every time this happens, I feel for the Kerry family. They have to relive the nightmare all over again.

Reggie tries to hang on to hope. Without his faith he would not be able to survive.

REGGIE: I feel grateful that my sentence was overturned, but now I have to wait to see what happens with the appeals court. If they reverse the judge's ruling, I'll be where I was and nearly out of appeals. If they uphold it, the state will probably seek another death sentence. We are getting to the last stages. Marlin has already run out of appeals, and Tony is nearing the end of his. Unless something drastic happens, they will be executed.

Nobody has turned against me, but I don't have the amount of support that I need. My family believes I am innocent; so do my friends. I don't get to see my family or friends often. As these cases go on, people pull away emotionally. My daughter turned eleven this June. I have never held her. I talk to her on the phone at least once a month and write to her once or twice a week. She writes to me sometimes. I try to do small things to help with her education. Whenever I write her a letter, I always put a math problem in the bottom. That way she'll learn her ABC's and 1-2-3's with each letter. We have a very positive relationship.

She knows I am in jail, but she doesn't understand that I am on death row. I don't want to shock her. It is hard enough to prepare an adult for your impending death, let alone a child, so I just tell her I am locked up and trying hard to come home and I love her very much and want her to do well in school. I know that she knows that I love her. I can't do too much more than that.

VERA: Before this happened I hadn't given a lot of thought to the criminal justice system. I just assumed people got fair trials, and if someone was convicted they must be guilty. You'd hear a hideous description about what someone did and you'd think they were a really horrible person, but I didn't find out until our case that what you see on television or even in court is not always the whole story. Never in my wildest dreams would I have thought I would experience being the mother of a person sentenced to death.

There are regular executions in Missouri, which makes you keep reliving your pain. You see the families that have people scheduled for executions, and you see the hurt and pain they go through. I am lucky because I have had a lot of support from friends and neighbors and people in the community. I know some people who have no support at all, and even some who had to relocate because of threats against them.

All the executions are hard on Reggie because he knows many of these guys. Some have been cellmates at various times. Also, the inmates are often written up for the smallest things and put in the hole [solitary confinement], sometimes for several months, where their privileges are restricted. They are allowed fewer visits and are not allowed contact vis-

CHAPTER 9

Beyond Grief

Katherine Norgard

"Ashes to ashes, dust to dust." It's all part of the creation myth. Grief is born when life itself first appears. Everything has a cycle. I accept that to be true.

The story I am about to tell began on August 29, 1989, at 2:00 A.M. when a telephone call interrupted my husband's and my sleep. That call and the events following it changed the rest of my life, propelling me into a state of chronic grief and despair.

My adopted son, John Eastlack, had been a constant heartache almost from the day we adopted him when he was a year and a half old. We got practically no information about his biological family since his records were sealed. That is how adoptions were conducted in 1969.

John was an affectionate child, athletic and musical, and brought joy into our small family. But he took things that did not belong to him. He did not learn easily at school or from his mistakes. He had trouble telling the truth. We tried every way we knew to help him—individual and family counselors, psychologists, tutors, and summer school. All I ever wanted was for John to grow up and be a happy, good citizen.

Everything we did failed to help. At fifteen, John was in a residential treatment center. Then the juvenile court sent him to a locked correctional facility when he was sixteen, and back again a second time where he stayed until he turned eighteen. Both times, the staff was puzzled as to why he was there. He was a star resident compared to the other boys, who were drowning in disadvantages.

At nineteen, John was put on adult probation. By twenty-one, he was in prison for using someone's credit card.

I held on to the hope that he would eventually lead a responsible life, since everyone who ever met John believed he just made "bad choices." I was worn

270

Katherine Norgard with her son, John Eastlack.
Provided with permission of the family.

out and angry that he was not getting about the business of changing to a responsible lifestyle.

That early morning phone call was from an official at the Department of Corrections. A male voice ordered us to open our front door. Two men from the fugitive division were waiting to talk to us.

They told us John and another young man had climbed the fence at Echo Unit, a minimum security prison on the outskirts of Tucson, between 7:30 and 9:30 P.M. the night before and had fled on foot across the desert toward town. Had we seen John?

Don's thinning sandy hair was messy from sleep, and he swore under his breath before answering. "Last time we saw him was when we visited him at the prison on Saturday."

What next? I was stunned.

John had been transferred that week to Echo Unit from a prison in Florence, Arizona, where he had been in the "hole." He had been sent to Florence as a disciplinary measure for having a romantic relationship with a female guard at the Douglas prison, where he had been incarcerated. John's recent letters were different from his others. He talked nonsense saying that he was not really in prison, but was an FBI drug informant. It was as though he had snapped.

When we visited John that Saturday, he continued the crazy talk. "I have a car outside the fence. I can leave anytime I want," he said. We tried to help

Cindy had saved all the newspaper articles for us. Newspaper stories revealed that John had been walking down a dry wash in Tucson and heard a helicopter overhead. Assuming it was the police looking for him, he knocked at the elderly Sherrills' door and asked if he could use their telephone. Letting him into their house proved to be a fatal mistake. While he was trying to call a cab, his picture flashed on the Sherrills' television screen. One version of John's story is that Mrs. Sherrill recognized him and said she was going to call the police. She threatened him with a fireplace poker. Another version John told reporters was that when Mrs. Sherrill recognized him, he "freaked" and attacked them.

No one will ever know the truth. But I do know that the frail octogenarian couple was no match for John.

Months later, I read the gruesome pathologist's report. Mr. Sherrill had fifty-seven wounds on his body. Mrs. Sherrill, who had asthma, had thirty-seven wounds, including bruises, lacerations, punctures, and a head wound.

Before John left the Sherrills' house, he tried to render aid to Mr. Sherrill by bringing him a wet towel to stop the bleeding. He gave Mrs. Sherrill her asthma inhaler and a towel. He barricaded them into separate rooms, leaving them to die alone, not knowing about the welfare of the other. No one should ever die that way. The Sherrills, good people, deserved to live out their days and die peacefully in their sleep.

I told Ann Nichols, a colleague and friend, that I did not know how I could face my students with all the shame I felt about John. Ann said, "Just hold your head up high and move forward." I needed to tell the students what was going on and urge them to talk to me if they had any qualms about my capacity to be their teacher.

Worse yet, I needed to tell each one of my psychotherapy clients. Our different last names would not shield me forever. The media would eventually make the link public.

One of my clients worked as a guard at the county jail where John was being held. His supervisor told him there was no problem because he had no direct contact with John.

Time was a blur. Closing the door to my psychotherapy office shut out my own reality and allowed me entry to someone else's. I threw myself into my work to the point of becoming a workaholic. Looking back, I see that I was numb, just going through the motions.

A friend had worked at San Quentin as a prison guard. She urged me not

John Eastlack. Provided with permission of the family.

to visit John. She thought John had chosen to commit the crime so he would never again be out of prison.

Two weeks after we came home, I mustered enough courage to visit John. My hesitancy was not about John and his choices. I was petrified that I would encounter a reporter at the jail, because John was regularly giving them interviews. I did not want to be connected with any of the sensationalism. Throughout the whole ordeal, I never granted an interview to the media.

During that first visit, John said, "I really messed up this time, Mom. How could I have done such a terrible thing? There must be something wrong with my brain." I did not know then that the authorities could have been recording our conversation as John recounted details of his time in the Sherrills' house.

For years afterwards, every time I visited, John talked about the crime over and over. He used me as a priest, and I had no power to absolve him. I couldn't even stomach what I heard. He did the same with Don and with Sonda. Listening retraumatized me. It stirred up my own insanity over having failed at the most important job in the world—parenting my child.

Our family, Ann, Claire, a few other friends, and a dozen of my graduate students sat together. I did not have enough emotional energy to even feel grateful for their presence.

John was already in the courtroom. He turned around, giving me the same inappropriate grin he had used all his life. A smile struggled to lift the corner of my mouth. The television camera swung around to focus on me.

Ed questioned John about all the media attention he had gotten at the jail. John said, "I gave them everything they wanted so they would come back and see me again. I was living it up, you know." Ed asked him why he was writing escape plans while he was at the jail. John said it was to get the reporters to come down and interview him. They had gotten tired of his other stories, so he tried to create more news to get their attention.

Ed asked John why he had written a confession to the presiding judge. John explained that his emotions changed constantly, swinging from high to low, while he was in isolation at the jail. John said he "factually accepted that he had murdered the Sherrills," even though he said he would mentally never be able to accept that he did. Ed's last question to John was "Did you kill Mr. and Mrs. Sherrill? Did you cause their deaths?"

John answered, "Yes."

My shoulders touched my ears and my head ached.

Tom Zawada began cross-examining that same afternoon and continued into the next day. Zawada verbally badgered and mocked John.

Ed's only redirect questioning was to ask John if he had ever had a trial before or testified in front of a jury. John said, "No." The judge ended the day telling everyone to have a nice weekend. Court would reconvene the next week on Tuesday for jury instructions and closing arguments.

November 20, Zawada pranced around the courtroom holding the fireplace poker, telling the jury that John had poked, mashed, and bashed the Sherrills to death. He reminded the jury that John had called the Douglas prison to talk to an incarcerated friend there and told him he was having a "good time, the best days of his life."

Ed began his closing statement by saying that John bore responsibility for the deaths of two people, but he did not murder them. He pointed out that John had not planned anything, from the escape to the burning of the house he broke into. "A thinking person would have said, 'Oh well, I better not set this place on fire, because there will be smoke and fire people are going to show up.'"

Ed said that John was not a violent person, but that he went into a rage when he was in the Sherrills' house. "John is a liar. You can tell when John is lying. His lips are moving." He explained that John loved all the media attention because he had always been a nobody and the media made him famous. He said John told the reporters what they wanted to hear so they would keep coming back. "I only ask that the final headline be the truth . . . not what everybody wants to hear," Ed concluded.

The evening newspaper featured a photograph of John laughing in the courtroom. The caption said he smiled throughout his testimony.

Zawada capitalized on the photo the next day, calling John "Joking John Eastlack." He reminded the jury that John bashed, poked, and beat the Sherrills to death. I could not listen.

Judge Scholl had promised the jury they would be done before Thanksgiving. And they were. John waived his right to be present at the verdict since he did not like waiting in the small cage in the courtroom basement. I went to work. Ed said he would call me to come down for the verdict. Instead, a few hours later, Ed called saying the jury had found John guilty of two counts of felony murder and all the other charges of escape, arson, and burglary.

I had not had a full night's sleep for over fourteen months. Now my worst nightmare was official.

The next day was Thanksgiving. That morning's headline read, "Happy Thanksgiving," in red lettering. Underneath, in black print, it said, "Eastlack Guilty: May Get Death Penalty." We spent Thanksgiving alone, in shock.

John Hanna, a lawyer who worked for the Capital Representation Project, an agency that provides resources to capital defense lawyers, called me after the verdict. I had asked Ed to work with them, but Ed did not think it was necessary. Ed said he was setting things up for John's appeal. Hanna told me it is very difficult to overturn a death sentence on appeal. He urged me to hire an attorney to represent John at the sentencing hearing.

I met with several criminal attorneys and finally hired Carla Ryan, who specializes in death penalty cases. "Kathy, you have to do everything you can to prevent a death sentence. And in the process, you've got to press Nesbitt to present every possible mitigating factor so there will be a record when this thing goes to the Supreme Court on appeal," Carla said.

At our first meeting, I had no idea how dependent I, an ultra-independent auditorium-style seats. Carla Ryan, who had come to hear the arguments, explained the "rules." Each side had twenty minutes to sway the majority of the justices to its position.

John was a "paper person" to Colleen French who represented the attorney general's office. She had never even seen him. It was her first time arguing in front of this court, and her mother had come to watch. If Colleen French's mouth had been foaming, it would have matched her rabid appeal to uphold John's death sentence. John's attorneys, Kathleen and Robb, had worked hard and represented him well.

Waiting, hanging in limbo, was now commonplace in my life. Each day, I expected the phone call that eventually came on November 3, 1994. Robb announced that John's death sentence had been vacated and Judge Scholl was ordered to conduct a resentencing hearing.

If I had not insisted on testifying at John's mitigation/aggravation hearing, the machinery of death would have continued to move forward. The justices noted "red flags" about John's psychological make-up. The fifty-six-page document from the Arizona Supreme Court included:

> Defendant's mother, a practicing psychologist, testified she believed her son was psychologically impaired. He had lived in numerous foster homes before being adopted at 16 months of age. She thought he might have brain lesions or neurological problems and was concerned that he did not receive proper bonding and attachment during the early part of his life, which she believes are critical to adult development. She reported that defendant did not cry, even as a baby, in situations when a child would normally cry. He would grin inappropriately when he was disciplined, when he was embarrassed, or when he was caught doing something wrong. Defendant had learning problems, and she had him evaluated by professionals, one of whom characterized defendant as an "enigma in terms of diagnostic assessment." None of the professionals could discover the source of defendant's problems. He stole from other children and from his family, lied, created and lived in his own separate fantasy world, and had a pronounced fear of being alone.

Sonda and Don had no faith Judge Scholl would change his sentence. This ray of hope was my answered prayer. The stark reality was that John's case could bounce around in the courts for years, and we would bounce with it. Life and death sentences seemed no different when I first accepted that John had killed Mr. and Mrs. Sherrill. Either way, he would die in prison. I realized over time that a life sentence is just that—life. A death sentence is murder by another name. After a person has been executed, the cause of death listed on the death certificate is "homicide."

Four days after John's sentence was remanded to the sentencing court, I was in Washington, D.C., at a National Coalition to Abolish the Death Penalty event honoring retired U.S. Supreme Court justice William Brennan for his stand against the death penalty. Rosalyn Carter, Tim Robbins, Susan Sarandon, and other celebrities were there, too. I shook hands with Justice Brennan and told him about John. He said the only words that ever reach that hollow place inside me, "I am so very sorry."

During the next years, I cannot say that I was responding to a spiritual call. I was obsessed. Carla and I were a great match. Like mine, her whole life centered around the death penalty.

Every waking moment, I planned and plotted how to get Carla Ryan to represent John. Accomplishing that through manipulation and sheer good luck, I devoured information about fetal alcohol syndrome, since John's birth mother drank to the point of blacking out while she was carrying John. I explored the issues of genetics, brain functioning, growing up in multiple foster homes, bonding and attachment, the impact of a divorce, and being in a stepfamily. I had ongoing contact with the postadoption social worker at the adoption agency to elicit her help in gaining information about John's past. I could leave no stone unturned to preserve his life.

Don's heart disease was not cured by the open heart surgery he had in 1990. He had problems with his hips and back related to a helicopter crash he had had in Viet Nam. Most disturbing to me was that he was caught in depression's web.

Sonda met and married Kevin Donovan in 1996.

I was only partially present for either Don or Sonda. Although I loved them both, my primary focus was always John. Saving his life was center stage for me.

I remember feeling in a daze, as though I was dissociating, the day Sonda and I went shopping for the most important dress in her life—her wedding dress. Sonda is not an angry or vindictive person, but after her wedding she said to me, "I know I am an adult, Mom. I know that John needs you. I just wish that you could have been really present with me on my special day. Anytime someone mentioned how sad it was that John wasn't there, you launched into talking about the death penalty. I felt like you weren't really there."

many would say, 'Oh well, if we could just change the environment.' Well, the environment was changed." He explained that our family has a lot of strengths, but not enough to overcome the genetics, disruptions in attachment, and John's prenatal exposure to alcohol.

Dr. Thompson told the court that John's pervasive developmental disorder means that his central nervous system is not equipped to process the things necessary to succeed in his various roles in life. He explained that John's tendency to exaggerate and tell lies is common for people with pervasive developmental disorders: "People who can't adapt or fit in begin to become sealed off in their own world and begin to fabricate." Dr. Thompson explained that John cannot mediate between what he feels and what he does, he cannot think before he acts, and he does not learn from experience.

It was no solace to me when Dr. Thompson said that John's normal intelligence score on psychological tests is a contradiction. He looks normal, but he does not learn. He also said that even had we taken John to a psychiatrist, people at that point in time were not diagnosing fetal alcohol syndrome. Sitting there, I kept thinking about my friend, Pam Mayhall, who had known John as a kid, saying, "He has a thinking problem."

Dr. Thompson closed with saying that John had been a model prisoner. Prison is a structured living environment, and "the more structure you have, the less ambiguous and less choices you have to make, the less things you have to deal with, and the less organization you have to bring to the situation."

The second day, walking through security in the morning, I asked whether I could take my tape recorder into court. I did not realize the judge's order prohibiting reporters from recording applied to me. Just before the noon recess, Tom Zawada brought this to the attention of the judge. Fortunately, the judge only confiscated my tape recorder and did not also throw me out of the courtroom.

Carla cleverly asked Dr. Thompson, when she returned him to the stand still another time, whether John could be considered to fit into the category of "antisocial personality disorder." I knew if the prosecutor could brush everything into that diagnosis, it would help him get John back to death row. Thompson seemed surprised at the question and replied that John's symptoms could fit a number of diagnostic categories. He elaborated that we tend to use the term "antisocial personality" or "sociopath" when a person gets into the criminal justice system, but the label has very little to do with the etiology of the problems.

Carla's last question—asking Dr. Thompson to explain what happened when John was in the Sherrills' house—brought a hush to the courtroom. Dr. Thompson said John was under the most stress he had ever experienced in his entire life. He was totally without external structure and was captured by the emotional reaction of the moment. His executive functioning was not sufficient to modify his emotions. Given that John had no history of violence, Dr. Thompson explained, "I think what you have here is an individual whose cognitive system is simply not able to deal with the emergence of the affect that occurred on that day."

Zawada began his rapid-fire cross-examination, jumping from subject to subject, as he did throughout the hearing. When he asked about the escape, Dr. Thompson explained it was still another example of a poorly thought out plan. He said that John is a poor con artist, and when he tries to put on different identities, it is almost ludicrous.

Carla showed two videotapes of interviews of longtime family friends, Joyce Lichtenstein and Sonia Maxwell. Both corroborated John's childhood difficulties, as did Don's, Sonda's, and my testimony.

At the end of every day, our large group of supporters (numbering over fifty) stood in the hallway outside the courtroom waiting for our family. I was overwhelmed with gratitude that so many would take time from their lives and work to be with us. Don and I thanked everyone and asked John Fife, our pastor, who also came every day, to say a short prayer. We all made a large circle next to two uniformed guards at the courtroom door. Every day, we continued the same practice.

The second day, Mr. Zawada came out of the courtroom. When he saw the human circle, he abruptly turned and went back inside. He came out a second time and said, "I need to get through." People opened the circle to give him space. John Fife, who had been praying for the judge said, "And prayers for you, too, Mr. Zawada."

The third day, Carla called seven witnesses, including two young men who had known John in high school. They testified that John used to tell tall tales and tried to buy friends by giving them gifts. Carla played a videotape of James Hamm, a convicted murderer who had been released after seventeen years in prison and was living a productive life. Sister Helen Prejean had made a videotape for John's defense directly addressing Judge Lindberg about the fallacy of the death penalty.

I walked out in the middle of a videotape about the death house. The narrator was explaining that the condemned person is stripped of all his cloth-

and supporters, some even sitting on the floor or standing around the edges of the room. Resuming my breathing, I heard Judge Lindberg list two mitigating factors—John's significant impairment and his age. It was two to two. Lindberg continued and began listing nonstatutory mitigators. First, he cited John's genetic history. Tears ran down my face. The judge was sentencing John to life! He listed six more nonstatutory factors (fetal alcohol syndrome, a limited ability to comprehend cause and effect, impaired judgment, a lack of control over behavioral responses, an ability to function in a structured environment, and a nonviolent history). There was a stir in the courtroom as Judge Lindberg sentenced John to two life sentences. The judge left the courtroom, and people in the audience hugged one another joyously.

Thankfully, I will never have to know how it would be if John were executed. During the year, as I have continued my fight to end the death penalty, I have met people whose loved ones were executed. Looking into their eyes, I have seen the familiar despair and inability to connect with the world around them. We create a new category of victims with the death penalty, the family of the condemned.

NOTES

FOREWORD

1. Elizabeth Beck, Brenda Blackwell, Pamela Leonard, and Michael Mears, "Seeking sanctuary: Interview with family members of capital defendants," 88 *Cornell Law Review* 382 (2003).
2. Post-traumatic stress disorder is a chronic and debilitating condition; people with PTSD experience exaggerated startle responses, sleep disturbances, guilt, memory impairment, trouble concentrating, and phobias. The study refers to symptoms of PTSD rather than PTSD, as a diagnosis of PTSD requires specific gateway criteria involving threat of death to oneself or the violent death of a loved one; these criteria are not met prior to execution, yet symptoms are present.
3. Sarah Eschholz, Mark Reed, Elizabeth Beck, and Pamela Leonard, "Offenders' family members' responses to capital crime: The need for restorative justice," 7 *Homicide Studies: A Interdisciplinary and International Journal* 154 (2003).

INTRODUCTION

1. Rachel King and Katherine Norgard, "What about our families? Using the impact on death row family members as a mitigating factor in death penalty sentencing hearings," 26 *Florida State University Law Review* 1119 (Summer 1999).
2. Steven Bright, "Counsel for the poor: The death penalty not for the worst crime but for the worst lawyer," 103 *Yale Law Journal* 1835 (1994).
3. Death Penalty Information Center at http://www.deathpenaltyinfo.org/article.php?did=412&scid=6.

CHAPTER 1: IT COULD HAPPEN TO ANYONE

1. Memorandum to Dave Stafford, Supervisor, Exhibits and Classified Materials, to Carol Schreiber, Director, Court File Services, June 7, 1994, page 235 of the Appendix to the Special Action, *State v. Krone*.
2. *State v. Krone*, Affidavit by Dr. Homer Campbell, Appendix to Special Action at 96.
3. Ibid. at 242.

4. Ibid. at 261.

5. Ibid. at 161.

6. *State v. Krone*, State's Response to Defendant's Pleadings Re: Removal of Exhibits, August 10, 1994.

7. *State v. Krone*, Order granting state's request to seal trial exhibits, the Honorable Jeffrey A. Hotham, September 15, 1994.

8. Unpublished manuscript of Jim Rix, chapter 6, page 3, used with permission of the author.

9. Ibid.

10. *Arizona v. Krone*, 897 P. 2d 621, 625 (1995).

11. Information about the trial was obtained from notes taken by Jim Rix during the trial.

12. Scott Dodd, "Defense may have been too sure," *York Daily Record*, April 13, 1996.

13. Ibid.

14. Laura Laughlin, "Judge lets Krone live," *York Daily Record*, December 10, 1996.

15. Ibid.

16. Ibid.

17. Scott Dodd, "Krone family, friends continue fight: Supporters have started a petition because they believe the justice system has failed," *York Daily Record*, May 9, 1996.

18. Ibid.

19. Ibid.

20. Hans Sherrer, "Twice wrongfully convicted of murder—Ray Krone is set free after 10 years," *Justice Denied Magazine*, March 3, 2003, at http://www.justicedenied.org/volume 2issue8.htm.

21. Teresa Ann Boeckel, "Long-awaited reunion: There were no tears when members of Ray Krone's family reunited in Arizona Wednesday," *York Daily Record*, April 11, 2002.

22. Teresa Ann Boeckel, "Krone loses a relative: She lived just long enough to learn that he had been released from prison," *York Daily Record*, April 20, 2002.

23. Teresa Ann Boeckel, "Freedom soon for Krone," *York Daily Record*, April 25, 2002.

24. Teresa Ann Boeckel, "Christmas in May: Friends and family celebrate: Making up for a lot of lost holidays, Ray Krone's loved ones held a party for him Saturday," *York Daily Record*, May 6, 2002.

25. O. Ricardo Pimentel, "Pay Ray Krone his $100 million," *Arizona Republic*, May 4, 2003.

CHAPTER 2: A HERO'S LIFE

1. Gerald M. Carbone, "Manny Babbitt's road to death row," *Providence Sunday Journal*, September 27, 1998.

2. Ibid.

3. Ibid.

4. Gerald M. Carbone, "From Wareham to death row," *Southcoast Living*, October 12, 1998.

5. See note 1.

6. Ibid. Bridgewater State Hospital was notorious for its poor conditions and treatment of

inmates. It gained national attention in 1967 as the subject of a documentary film, *Titticut Follies*.

7. Ibid.

8. Julie Chao, "Battle not over for Babbitt's brother," *San Francisco Examiner*, May 5, 1999.

9. Karen Molan, "His last-minute plea for justice," special to *TheReporter.Com*, April 17, 1999.

10. See note 1.

11. In 1980, the American Psychiatric Association added PTSD to the third edition of its *Diagnostic and Statistical Manual of Mental Disorders* (DSM-III) nosologic classification scheme. Although controversial when first introduced, the PTSD diagnosis has filled an important gap in psychiatric theory and practice. From a historical perspective, the significant change ushered in by the PTSD concept was the stipulation that the etiological agent was outside the individual (i.e., a traumatic event) rather than an inherent individual weakness (i.e., a traumatic neurosis). The key to understanding the scientific basis and clinical expression of PTSD is the concept of "trauma." Matthew J. Friedman, M.D., Ph.D., executive director, National Center for Post Traumatic Stress Disorder, "Post-traumatic stress disorder: An overview," at http://www.ncptsd.org/facts/general/fs_overview.html.

12. *People v. Babbitt*, 45 Cal. 3d 660, 669 (Sup. Ct. of Cal. 1988).

13. Ibid. at 699–700.

14. Ibid. at 700.

15. See note 1.

16. Ibid.

17. Ted Bell, "Murderer of elderly woman sentenced to death," *Sacramento Bee*, July 7, 1982.

18. See note 1.

19. Ibid.

20. See note 8.

21. Ibid.

22. Ibid.

23. David Kaczynski, "A message from brother to brother," *Sacramento Bee*, April 8, 1999.

24. Julie Chao, "As execution date nears, killer's fate in Davis' hands," *San Francisco Examiner*, April 23, 1999.

25. See "Manny Babbitt: Vietnam vet does not deserve to die," *Sacramento Bee*, April 25, 1999; "Should Manny Babbitt die?" *San Francisco Chronicle*, April 5, 1999; "Spare Babbitt," *SN&R*, April 28, 1999.

26. Jim Doyle, "Families duel over Babbitt at hearing," *San Francisco Chronicle*, April 27, 1999.

27. Letter written by Cpl. Lynn Warner Dornan to Governor Gray Davis, March 23, 1999, published in "In Loving Memory of Manuel Pina 'Manny' Babbitt," by Manny Babbitt's Legal Defense Team, July 16, 1999.

28. Published ibid.

29. Jim Doyle, "Ex-jurors ask clemency for killer: Death row inmate's Vietnam trauma not fully explained, they say," *San Francisco Chronicle,* April 2, 1999.

30. Ibid.

31. Jim Doyle, "Clemency plea rests on trauma testimony," *San Francisco Chronicle,* April 27, 1999.

32. Julie Chao, "Vietnam veterans ask mercy for killer," *San Francisco Examiner,* April 27, 1999.

33. Jim Doyle, "Prison Board advises against Babbitt clemency," *San Francisco Chronicle,* April 30, 1999.

34. Sam Stanton, "Battle lines drawn at Babbitt clemency hearing," *Sacramento Bee,* April 27, 1999.

35. Ibid.

36. Ibid.

37. Ibid.

38. Ibid.

39. Michelle Locke, "Killer or casualty of war?" Associated Press, ABCnews.com, April 26, 1999.

40. Jim Doyle, "Killer content to leave fate up to governor," *San Francisco Chronicle,* April 23, 1999.

41. Jim Doyle, "Inmate doesn't deny killing, but cannot recall it," *San Francisco Chronicle,* April 23, 1999.

42. Ibid.

43. Decision in the Matter of Clemency for Manuel Pina Babbitt, Governor Gray Davis, April 30, 1999, 10–11.

44. Jim Doyle, "Babbitt's lawyers raise race issue as execution nears," *San Francisco Chronicle,* May 1, 1999.

45. Ibid.

46. Clark Brooks, "War hero's life ends in death chamber," *San Diego Union-Tribune,* May 5, 1999.

47. Sam Stanton and Claire Cooper, "Killer executed as appeals fail," *Sacramento Bee,* May 4, 1999; Emily Bazar, "A cold vigil for death penalty foes," *Sacramento Bee,* May 4, 1999.

48. Marianne Costantinou, "About 700 hold candlelight vigil," *San Francisco Examiner,* May 5, 1999.

49. Larry Hatfield, "Babbitt's last words: I forgive . . . you," *San Francisco Examiner,* May 5, 1999.

50. Ibid.

51. Charles Patterson, "Manny's war," *Cal Law,* June 23, 1999.

52. Wilbur Haines, "Chuck Patterson," *Sacramento Lawyer,* July/August 1999.

53. Jim Doyle, Pamela J. Podger, and Harriet Chiding, "Vietnam vet Babbitt executed," *San Francisco Chronicle,* May 4, 1999.

CHAPTER 3: LIVING WITH DEATH

1. Letter written by Abdullah Hameen to Shakeera Hameen, March 12, 1997, provided with permission of the estate of Abdullah Hameen.

2. Abdullah Hameen, "Delaware Citizens Opposed to the Death Penalty (DCODP) was created because," *Just Say "No" to Death Row,* March/April 1997.

3. Sally Milbury-Steen, "Mercy denied, mercy shown," *Friends Journal,* October 2002.

4. Shakeerah Hameen, "Living with death," in *Frontiers of Justice,* vol. 1, *The Death Penalty,* ed. Claudia Whitman and Julie Zimmerman (Brunswick, ME: Biddle Publishing, 1997).

5. Shakeerah Hameen to Judge William R. Toal Jr., November 8, 1999.

6. *Abdullah Tanzil Hameen v. State of Delaware,* Unpublished Opinion, No. 96-9007, 3d Cir., May 17, 2000.

7. *Abdullah Tanzil Hameen v. State of Delaware,* Order denying petition for rehearing, June 15, 2000.

8. Canadian Coalition to Abolish the Death Penalty, Abdullah Hameen, #715 at http://www.ccadp.org.

9. *State v. Hameen,* Order No. 245, Joseph T. Walsh, May 24, 2001.

10. See note 8.

11. J. L. Miller and Patrick Jackson, "Man executed for drug slaying," *Wilmington News Journal,* May 25, 2001.

12. Statement of Ruth Ann Minner, issued May 25, 2001.

13. See note 11.

14. Ibid.

15. Katherine Nevin, "The Execution Party," 2001, poem published with permission of the author.

16. Katherine Nevin, "After Justice?" 2001, poem published with permission of the author.

CHAPTER 4: FROM REVENGE TO RECONCILIATION

1. *Gilreath v. State,* 279 S.E. 2d 650 (Ga. 1981).

2. Ibid. at 656.

3. Ibid.

4. Ibid.

5. *United States v. Fred Gilreath,* 234 F. 3d 547, 551 (11th Cir. 2000).

6. Affidavit of Dr. Barry Scanlon at 30-31, Application of Fred Marion Gilreath for Commutation of His Sentence of Death.

7. Ibid. at 66–67.

8. Affidavit of Felicia Gilreath, filed in Habeas Corpus No. C87-50A.

9. Letter written by Chaplain Fred W. Hood, Appendix to Application of Fred Marion Gilreath for a Commutation of his Sentence of Death.

10. Ibid.

11. Ibid. at 6.

12. Ibid., Exhibit 13, Affidavit of Dolores Cooper.

13. See note 6 at 26.

14. Fred's behavior in his relationship with Linda is consistent with patterns of domestic violence first identified by Dr. Lenore Walker. Walker interviewed fifteen hundred women and noticed similar patterns in their relationships, which she identified as a cycle of violence. "This cycle begins with positive or close relations that develop into tension caused by anything from a bad day at work to a major life crisis. The second stage of the cycle is when the battering incident occurs, which may or may not include physical contact (it may be verbal abuse). This occurs so that the abuser can gain power and control. The third and final stage of this circular cycle is when the batterer tries to make up with the partner. He may feel guilt, but will minimize the event by claiming that it was the woman's fault that she was hit. Both partners deny the severity of the abuse, and the cycle continues. The couple is convinced that each abusive episode is isolated and that the incidents are unrelated to each other. Without intervention, the violence becomes more serious and eventually the third stage of apology and denial will no longer exist." See "Women's intellectual contributions to the study of mind and society," at http://www.webster.edu/~woolflm/walker.html.

15. Stacey Eidson, "The state made me an orphan," *Spirit Magazine,* March 14–20, 2002.

16. Amnesty International's Web site: Fred Marion Gilreath Jr., #743, http://www.clarkprosecutor.org/html/death/US/gilreath/743.htm.

17. *Fred Gilreath v. State Board of Pardons and Paroles,* 273 F. 3d 932 (November 15, 2001).

18. *Fred Gilreath v. Head,* 122 S. Ct. 585 (November 14, 2001).

19. Rhonda Cook, "Convicted killer Fred Gilreath executed," *Atlanta Constitution,* November 16, 2001.

20. Ibid.

21. Amnesty International Update, "Against the victims' family's wishes, the state killed Fred Gilreath on November 15, 2001," November 16, 2001 at http://geocities.com/gfadp/gilreathnews.html.

22. John Sugg, "A dead issue: where does it say, 'Kill for Jesus?'" *Atlanta Creative Loafing,* November 21, 2001.

CHAPTER 5: TOO YOUNG TO DIE

1. Jefferson County Department for Human Services—Division for Social Services, September 18, 1978, evaluation conducted by Jack Engler, psychological evaluator.

2. Plea for Commutation of Death Sentence of Kevin Stanford, September 2002, at 8.

3. See note 1.

4. See note 2.

5. Ibid.

6. These facts were taken from an interview with Eileen Stanford; she learned them from reading police reports and talking with Kevin and David. Regardless of whether one believes this version, there is independent evidence—namely, the eyewitness identification of Calvin Buchanan and not Kevin Stanford—to raise reasonable doubt that Kevin was

the killer. While he readily admits to being part of the robbery and rape, he denies that he killed Baerbel or had any knowledge that she was going to be killed. Had Kevin's trial lawyers more vigorously defended him, Kevin might not have been convicted of murder and sentenced to death.

7. Andrew Wolfson, "Attorney General Urges Execution of Stanford," *Courier-Journal*, November 22, 2002.

8. *Stanford v. Kentucky*, 734 S.W. 2d 781, 783 (Sup. Ct. Ky. 1987).

9. Transcript from juvenile waiver hearing in case 81CR1218 29, June 29, 1981.

10. *Stanford v. Parker*, Memorandum and Assignment of Constitutional Claims in Support of Petition for writ of habeas corpus from a sentence of death, file no. 94-CV-0453 L(J) at 94.

11. Ibid.

12. See note 2 at 9.

13. *Stanford v. Parker*, 266 F. 3d 442, 456 (6th Cir. Ct. of App. 2001).

14. See note 8 at 788.

15. See affidavits of Adrian Stewart, Major Crane, and Curtis Mayes filed during postconviction proceedings, which would have disputed Michael Nally's testimony.

16. See note 13 at 450.

17. *Stanford v. Kentucky*, 492 U.S. 361 (1989).

18. Nikita Stewart, "Despite the odds: Having dad on death row is no obstacle for girl, 13," *Courier-Journal*, July 31, 1994.

19. Ibid.

20. Ibid.

21. Bill Estep, "Til death do us part: Condemned man in Kentucky marries with flowers, cake but no honeymoon," *Herald-Leader*, April 1, 1995; Associated Press, "Convicted killer married in prison," *Paducah Sun*, April 1, 1995; Associated Press, "Death row inmate weds advocate for prisoners," *Courier-Journal*, April 1, 1995; Associated Press, "Stanford weds while serving on death row," *Louisville Times*, April 1, 1995; Associated Press, "Convicted killer marries in state prison," *Kentucky New Era*, March 31, 1995; Associated Press, "Convicted killer married at Eddyville," *Kentucky Post*, April 1, 1995.

22. Herald Leader Staff Report, "Death row marriage angers victim's father," *Herald Leader*, April 2, 1995.

23. Letter by Kevin Stanford to Eileen Stanford, February 19, 1999, reprinted with permission of the author.

CHAPTER 6: A MOTHER'S LOVE

1. Letter written by Col. Robert Richard, commander, USAF School of Applied Aerospace Sciences, September 24, 1975.

2. Discharge Summary of Larry K. Robison from Huguley Memorial Hospital, November 13, 1978.

3. The doctor inaccurately stated Larry's age.

4. Consultation Sheet for Larry Robison prepared by Annie Baugh, Ed.D., December 12, 1978.

5. The names of Larry's partner and daughter have been changed to protect their privacy.

6. Carl Freund, "Capital murder charge unlikely in FW slayings," *Dallas Morning News*, August 13, 1982.

7. Letter written by Larry Keith Robison at http://www.larryrobison.org/pages/lastletter.htm.

8. Letter written by Larry Robison to Judy Smith on March 6, 1987, obtained from state's files on April 18, 1996, and provided by the family.

9. *Robison v. State*, 720 S.W. 2d 808 (Texas Crim. App. 1986).

10. Clemency Petition for Larry Robison, July 23, 1999, Exhibit 6.

11. *Robison v. Johnson*, 151 F.3d 256, 261 (5th Cir. Ct. of App. 1998).

12. Clara Tuma, "Robison is sentenced to death for the 2nd time," *Fort Worth Star-Telegram*, November 15, 1987.

13. *Robison v. State*, 888 S.W. 2d 472 (Tex. Crim. App. 1994).

14. Affidavit of Anthony G. Hempel, D.O., M.A., August 16, 1999.

15. Evaluation of Anthony G. Hempel, D.O., M.A., at 6–7.

16. Affidavit of Vickie L. Barnett, August 16, 1999.

17. Affidavit of Allen Robison, August 16, 1999.

18. Affidavit of Michael Deen, August 16, 1999.

19. Clemency Petition, Exhibit 3, Evaluation of Henry A. Nasrallah, M.D., October 1, 1999, at 5.

20. Clemency Petition, Exhibit 3, Evaluation of Mark D. Cunningham, Ph.D., October 15, 1999, at 23-23.

21. Ibid. at 88.

22. Ibid. at 15-84.

23. Ibid. at 16-17.

24. Ibid. at 85.

25. Jim Yardley, "Texas court halts a death to determine competency," *New York Times*, August 13, 1999.

26. Clemency Petition, Exhibit 4.

27. Ibid., Exhibit 13.

28. Ibid.

29. Ibid., Exhibit 5.

30. Ibid., Exhibit 7.

31. Ibid.

32. Ibid., Exhibit 8.

33. Ibid., Exhibit 10.

CHAPTER 7: A REGULAR GUY

1. Todd Copilevitz, "Suspect arrested in Arlington shootings: Investment firm owner had managed topless club briefly," *Dallas Morning News*, January 1, 1990.

2. Ibid.

3. Ibid.

4. Letter written by Dave Herman to Reverend Larry Grubbs, March 31, 1990, provided with permission of the estate of Dave Herman.

5. Mary Doclar and Christopher Ave, "Nightclub shooting ended a life and started year of pain," *Fort Worth Star-Telegram,* December 17, 1990.

6. News Digest, "Condemned inmate headed for death chamber," *San Angelo Standard,* April 3, 1997.

7. Details of Dave's life in prison are from the journal of Reverend Larry Grubb and provided with his permission.

8. Mary Doclar, "Stay stirs painful memories for a family eager for justice," *Fort Worth Star-Telegram,* April 4, 1995.

9. *Herman v. Johnson,* 98 F. 3d 171 (1996).

10. Letter written by Dave Herman to Jennifer Herman, provided with permission of the estate of Dave Herman.

11. Letter written by Dave Herman to Reverend Larry Grubb, provided with permission of the estate of Dave Herman.

12. Letter written by Dave Herman to the family of Jennifer Burns, provided with permission of the estate of Dave Herman.

13. Letter written by Dave Herman to Esther Herman, provided with permission of the estate of Dave Herman.

14. Information taken from Reverend Larry Grubb's journal, provided with his permission.

15. Ibid.

16. Last meal and last words published by Star-Telegram.com at http://www.star-telegram .com/specials/98deathrow/herman.htm.

17. Letter written by Dave Herman to Judith Calk Bridges on August 25, 1993, provided with permission of the estate of Dave Herman.

18. Letter written by Dave Herman to his family, provided with permission of the estate of Dave Herman.

19. In the spring of 2003, it was discovered that dozens of DNA tests conducted in serious criminal cases at the Houston crime lab were done improperly. The situation was so extreme that the FBI removed all lab results conducted at that lab from the national DNA database.

CHAPTER 8: A REASONABLE DOUBT

1. *State v. Clemons,* Motion to Suppress Hearing, testimony of Detective Chris Pappas, transcript at 1313 [hereinafter Transcript].

2. Ibid. at 1433.

3. Ibid. at 1390.

4. Police Report Complaint No. 91-65574, synopsis of second interview with Thomas Cummins, April 5, 1991, at 11 [hereinafter TC-2].

5. Transcript at 2452.

6. Associated Press, "Two accused of assaults on bridge—victims were raped, robbed, and pushed into the Mississippi River," *Kansas City Star,* April 9, 1991.

7. Many of the "facts" in this chapter are taken from police reports and are thus the written record of what the officers said that the witnesses told them. They are hearsay and inadmissible in court. I have relied on them to document the facts as they became known before the trial to give the reader an understanding of what the police knew as the case unfolded. For purposes of readability, I have not noted "according to police reports" before every sentence.

8. Police Report Complaint No. 91063187, interview with Thomas Cummins, April 5, 1991, at 15 [hereinafter TC-1].

9. TC-2 at 10.

10. The distance between the bridge and the water was described during this case as ranging from as low as seventy feet to as high as ninety feet. The distance from the concrete pier under the bridge was about twenty feet less. This difference can be accounted for by the fact that the river is constantly rising and falling depending on the time of year and rainfall and the person's exact location on the bridge.

11. TC-1 at 1–2.

12. TC-1 at 9–10.

13. TC-1 at 11.

14. TC-1 at 11.

15. TC-2 at 7.

16. TC-1 at 11.

17. TC-2 at 8.

18. Police Report No. 91067991 at 1-3.

19. TC-2 at 10.

20. TC-2 at 10.

21. TC-1 at 8.

22. TC-2 at 1.

23. TC-2 at 9.

24. TC-2 at 2.

25. TC-2 at 3.

26. TC-2 at 10.

27. TC-2 at 11.

28. At trial, the defense disputed that the body located was actually Julie Kerry's. The dental records of the dead body differed significantly from Julie's. See Testimony of defense expert Dr. Samuel Dedman, transcript at 1650. The body had no injuries in the vaginal area or any other area, such as would be expected in the case of rape. See Cross-Examination of Dr. Michael Graham, forensic pathologist, transcript at 1539.

29. TC-1 at 9.

30. Police Report No. 91068998, April 9, 1991, at 1.

31. The deal with the state was for Daniel to plead to second-degree murder and accessory to rape in exchange for a thirty-year sentence, but because the sentences would run concurrently, the total time to serve would be ten years, and Daniel would likely serve less. Also, Daniel would be guaranteed not to receive the death penalty. However, the final resolution of Daniel's sentence would depend upon the judge, who would take the state's recommendation into account but would not be bound by that recommendation. Transcript at 2128.

32. Ibid. at 2158, 2167.

33. Ibid. at 1439.

34. Ibid. at 1440.

35. Ibid. at 1442.

36. Ibid. at 1796.

37. Petition for Writ of Habeas Corpus, *Reginald Clemons v. Michael Bowersox,* No. 4: 97CV2344 CDP, May 30, 1998, at 10.

38. Transcript at 1800–1888.

39. Ibid. at 1906–1917, 1941.

40. Ibid. at 1919–1920.

41. Police Report No. 91-69259 at 4.

42. Transcript at 2076 and 2145.

43. Police Report No. 91-69259 at 1.

44. Transcript at 2225.

45. Ibid. at 2082.

46. Transcript of pre-trial motions, January 23, 1993, at 2–52.

47. Transcript at 2854.

48. *Clemons v. Missouri,* Hearing for Post-Conviction Relief, P.C.R. Cause No. 3043, September 26, 1995, at 942-947.

49. Editorial, "Evidence, not emotion," *St. Louis Post-Dispatch,* February 20, 1993.

50. See note 37.

51. Ibid. at 3.

52. Ibid. at 10.

53. *In Re: Robert Costantinou,* Missouri Supreme Court, No. 79610, January 27, 1998.

54. *Reginald Clemons v. Allen Luebbers,* 212 F.Supp. 2d 1105, 1123 (U.S. Dist. 2002).

RESOURCES

For additional information about the death penalty, please contact:

Abolitionist Action Committee
c/o CUADP
PMB 297
177 U.S. Highway #1
Tequesta, FL 33469
(800) 973-6548, www.abolition.org

American Bar Association Death Penalty
Representation Project
717 15th Street NW, 9th Floor
Washington, DC 20005
(202) 662-1735, www.abanet.org

The American Civil Liberties Union
Capital Punishment Project
915 15th Street NW, 6th Floor
Washington, DC 20005
(202) 715-0833, www.aclu.org

Amnesty International USA
600 Pennsylvania Avenue SE, 5th Floor
Washington, DC 20003
(202) 544-0200, www.aiusa.org

Death Penalty Information Center
1320 Eighteenth Street NW, 5th Floor

Washington, DC 20036
(202) 293-6970

Equal Justice USA/Quixote Center
P.O. Box 5206
Hyattsville, MD 20782
(301) 699-0042, www.quixote.org/ej

Journey of Hope . . . From Violence to
Healing
P.O. Box 210390
Anchorage, AK 99521-0390
(877) 924-4483, www.journeyofhope.org

Murder Victims' Families
for Reconciliation
2161 Massachusetts Avenue
Cambridge, MA 02140
(617) 868-0007, www.mvfr.org

The National Coalition to Abolish
the Death Penalty
920 Pennsylvania Avenue NW
Washington, DC 20003
(202) 543-9577, www.ncadp.org

For more information about criminal justice reform, please contact:

Centurion Ministries, Inc.
221 Witherspoon Street
Princeton, NJ 08542
(609) 921-0334, cenmin@aol.com

Citizens United for the Rehabilitation
of Errants (CURE)
P.O. Box 2310
Washington, DC 20013
(202) 789-2126, www.curenational.org

The Constitution Project
1120 19th Street, 8th Floor
Washington, DC 20036
(202) 721-5620, www.constitutionproject.org

The Innocence Project
55 Fifth Avenue, 11th Floor
New York, NY 10003
(212) 790-0375, www.innocenceproject.org

The Justice Project
1725 I Street NW, 4th Floor
Washington, DC 20006
(202) 638-5855, www.thejusticeproject.org

Penal Reform International
1120 19th Street, 8th Floor
Washington, DC 20036
(202) 721-5610, www.penalreform.org

The Tariq Khamisa Foundation
2550 Fifth Avenue, Suite 65
San Diego, CA 92103
(619) 525-0062

ABOUT THE AUTHOR AND CONTRIBUTORS

Rachel King is an attorney with the American Civil Liberties Union Capital Punishment Project. She was a founding member of Alaskans Against the Death Penalty and was active in a successful campaign to oppose reinstatement of the death penalty in Alaska. Currently, she lives with her partner, Richard McAlee, and stepdaughter, Julia, in the Takoma Village Cohousing Community in Washington, D.C. Her previous book is *Don't Kill in Our Names: Families of Murder Victims Speak Out Against the Death Penalty* (Rutgers University Press, 2003).

Katherine Norgard, a clinical psychologist and university teacher, received her doctorate from Union Institute. She specializes in working with refugees from around the world who are seeking political asylum in the United States. She founded Sanctity of Life: People Against Executions and helped found Coalition of Arizonans to Abolish the Death Penalty. Currently, Norgard is completing a book, *Property of the State,* about her experience with the death penalty with a focus on fetal alcohol syndrome.

Elizabeth Beck is an associate professor at the Georgia State University School of Social Work. Her work has been in the areas of community practice and forensic social work. She has brought these two areas together by developing ways for defense attorneys in capital cases to explore community effects on clients' lives, and examining restorative justice in a community context. In addition, Beck is involved in a number of community-based and forensic initiatives. She has served as an expert and consultant in state and federal death penalty cases. Currently, she is at work on a book about the effect of capital punishment on the families of the accused that will be published by Oxford University Press.